AN ANGEL in SODOM

HENRY GERBER
AND THE BIRTH OF THE
GAY RIGHTS MOVEMENT

JIM ELLEDGE

Published by Chicago Review Press Incorporated
814 North Franklin Street
Chicago, Illinois 60610
ISBN 978-1-64160-605-9

Library of Congress Control Number: 2022941128

Typesetting: Nord Compo

Printed in the United States of America
5 4 3 2 1

For David

To hell with the do-gooders and filthy hypocrites
trying to tell us how to fuck.
Fuck 'em!

—Henry Gerber

CONTENTS

ACKNOWLEDGMENTS

NO BIOGRAPHER, OR SCHOLAR of any discipline, can conduct research without the support of librarians and archivists. For me, those include the staff of the Chicago History Museum, Chicago; the David M. Rubenstein Rare Book and Manuscript Library, Duke University, Durham, North Carolina; the Gay, Lesbian, Bisexual, and Transgender Historical Society, San Francisco; the Homosexual Information Center, California State University, Northridge; the Illinois State Archives, Springfield; the J. D. Doyle Archives at http://www .jddoylearchives.org; the Kinsey Institute, Indiana University, Bloomington; Manuscripts and Archives Division, New York Public Library, New York; and ONE National Gay & Lesbian Archives, University of Southern California Libraries, Los Angeles. I thank them sincerely for all the work they have done to provide me with information I needed for this book.

But there are more personal acts of support that friends and loved ones perform that also need acknowledgment. To Damon Dorsey, Romayne Rubinas Dorsey, Maggie Mattison, Mike Mattison, and Alison Umminger—who all added to this volume in ways beyond my powers of description—I tip my hat and send my love.

My editors at Chicago Review Press, Jerome Pohlen and Devon Freeny, and copyeditor Alexander Caputo went beyond the call of duty and deserve accolades beyond measure.

Finally, my husband, Aelred B. Dean, can never be repaid for the patience and love he showed me during the process of writing this and previous books. Neither thanks nor expressions of love quite offer what he deserves, but regardless, I send them his way, hoping that they might repay him, at least in a small amount.

An Introductory Note

HENRY'S EPISTLES
TO THE PERVERTS

I FIRST LEARNED ABOUT HENRY GERBER when, in 1976, I bought and devoured Jonathan Ned Katz's *Gay American History: Lesbians and Gay Men in the U.S.A.* This seminal volume in queer studies became a classic the moment copies arrived in bookstores across the nation. A documentary, it provided thousands of letters, photographs, and a variety of historical records to anyone wanting to know about the queer past. Among them, Katz included several pages about Henry Gerber and his Society for Human Rights, which Gerber founded while living in Chicago in 1924. It was the first organization formed in the United States to attempt to work toward reforming the plight of gay men, to publish a journal focused on them, and to be legally incorporated as an organization.

As time passed, I used Katz's volume off and on for many of the projects I eventually undertook. It pointed me to sources for several of my own books, including *Henry Darger, Throwaway Boy* (2013), *Masquerade: Queer Poetry in America to the End of World War II* (2004), and *Gay, Lesbian, Bisexual, and Transgender Myths from the Arapaho to the Zuñi* (2002).

Over the years, scattered mentions of Gerber and his activities popped up here and there during my research in footnotes and paragraphs in articles, but I never came across an actual biography. I assumed that the documents needed to write the story of his life didn't exist. All that changed when, several years ago, I visited ONE National Gay & Lesbian Archives in L.A. to work on a project. The archive, I discovered, holds a treasure trove of Gerber and Gerber-related materials, specifically his, Frank McCourt's, and Manuel boyFrank's exchange of letters, what boyFrank dubbed "Henry's epistles to the perverts."

The dynamics of the three-way correspondence is fascinating. boyFrank and McCourt were members of Contacts, a correspondence (or pen pal) club that Gerber headed in the 1930s. He had moved to New York by then. Correspondence clubs were important to many gay men's lives in the first half of the twentieth century. Through them, men passed information back and forth about all sorts of topics, including hot spots for cruising in specific cities, formed friendships and romantic relationships, and discussed society's various crusades against them. boyFrank instigated the trio's correspondence when, on September 22, 1935, he wrote to Gerber, thanking him for sending him a notice that reminded him his membership in Contacts was about to lapse and to let Gerber know that he had recently begun exchanging letters with three male members of the club. Gerber, an atheist, had made his stand against organized religion known in several of the articles he wrote for a magazine he had published a few years earlier, *Chanticleer*, and boyFrank told him that he was also an atheist and gave his reason: Christianity's teachings against sexual expression. In the process, he also hinted he was gay. At the time, they were subject to extremely punitive laws, and they had to be circumspect in their dealings with other people, especially in their correspondence with strangers, which could be opened legally by postal authorities. He concluded the letter two pages later, one of the shortest letters he would ever write Gerber, with his thanks to Gerber for hearing him out. Their correspondence was sporadic during the rest of the 1930s but picked up in February 1940 and continued, off and on, for approximately twenty years.

McCourt joined in the letter writing on January 30, 1940. Gerber had disbanded Contacts by then, and boyFrank wanted someone to revive it. He even badgered Gerber to resurrect it. boyFrank learned through Contacts about McCourt and his hobby—collecting and taking physique photographs, a euphemism for black-and-whites of naked or near-naked men, usually bodybuilders but also any physically fit male—and sent him a letter. That letter has been lost, but he must have asked about McCourt's collection, if he were willing to take the helm of Contacts, or if not, if he knew someone who might. McCourt wasn't at all interested in stepping into Gerber's shoes, didn't know anyone who would, but supported boyFrank in his quest, especially hoping for a men-only club. He concluded the letter by inviting boyFrank, who lived on Staten Island, to his brownstone on West 140th Street in Manhattan, which he shared with his partner Charles "Chuck" Ufford, for cocktails and to check out his photograph collection. boyFrank and McCourt's letters often focused on physique photographs, including information on the amateur and professional photographers who sold them. McCourt sent many he had taken to boyFrank, and his last letter to boyFrank, which was barely a note, included several of his recent ones.

McCourt and Gerber didn't correspond with one another nearly as often nor as long as boyFrank and Gerber did. Their friendship was strained by religion. Because Gerber, the atheist, realized that Christianity's regulations against homosexuality and its partnership with city, state, and federal legislators created the struggles facing queer people, he didn't completely trust McCourt, the devout Roman Catholic. Gerber believed sex was a natural expression and couldn't understand how any gay man could align himself with those who wanted to punish them for following their natural inclinations.

That changed to a small degree when, after finding himself without a place to live, Gerber moved into McCourt and Ufford's brownstone. Although he was rankled by McCourt's sex parties and his collecting, sharing, and selling physique photographs, Gerber warmed up to him. Not only did he eventually consider McCourt a dear friend, but also Gerber listed McCourt as the person who would always know his whereabouts when he registered for what would be called the Old Man's Draft in 1942. Nevertheless, their correspondence remained mildly adversarial much of the time.

McCourt's religious affiliation wasn't the only stumbling block in his and Gerber's relationship. McCourt wasn't as philosophically inclined as boyFrank and Gerber. Their correspondence is full of theoretical musings and observations about laws criminalizing homosexuals, as well as what would eventually be called gay liberation that, they believed, could only be achieved if they were willing to organize. While Gerber and McCourt's correspondence was often argumentative, Gerber and boyFrank's was, to a large extent, tutorial. From the beginning, boy-Frank gave Gerber, who was nine years older, the role of mentor, although he often ignored his mentor's advice. Nevertheless, as a whole, the trio's letters are fraught with "repetition, a lot of unnerving non-responsiveness, references that get lost, and letters that seem to be missing in the idle of some of the most important parts."

Beginning with the very first one he sent Gerber, boyFrank's letters are full of fantasies about uniting men by creating correspondence clubs or what we might consider communes. He even went so far as to dream up a boarding school for boys in order to give them a sexual outlet with one another and adult men and thereby curb teen pregnancy, a thinly disguised ploy for his pedophiliac leanings. He spent hours envisaging all sorts of get-rich-quick schemes and describing them to Gerber (and McCourt), the principal one of which was a box for filing letters, clippings from newspapers or magazines, and other paper items. For most of his life, he tried to get one manufacturer after another interested in producing and marketing it but failed. In all these and several other schemes, boyFrank sought out Gerber's approval, which he got only occasionally.

Gerber was too realistic to buy into boyFrank's fantasies, and his responses to them were always blunt. Once, when boyFrank complained to Gerber about not being able to get anyone interested in manufacturing the box, Gerber asked, "If it is such a fine invention, why does no one buy it?" boyFrank never responded. At other times, when boyFrank fantasized about banding men together, Gerber warned him against it, citing his own experience as proof of how difficult it was to get them to stop socializing and concentrate on liberating themselves and one another. Gerber was just as blunt to McCourt and virtually anyone else who crossed his path.

Gerber had good reason for distrusting others. He had tried to organize gay men while he lived in Chicago from 1923 to 1925. He was able to persuade nine men into joining the Society for Human Rights but was betrayed by one of them, arrested, tried in court, fired from his job, and lost most of his savings on defense lawyers. He was so deeply hurt by the experience that he couldn't shake it, and it affected him for the rest of his life. Anyone who wanted to become Gerber's friend had to work at it and, as important, had to ignore his cynicism and lack of diplomacy. Gerber said what was on his mind.

The image of Gerber that quickly evolves from the correspondence is the one that most people who have heard of him know. It's not flattering. He was headstrong, unbendable, opinionated, and straight-talking. To a large extent, he appeared to be friendless and miserable, unloved and unlovable, and in virtually all respects, despite a few months of valor in which he created the Society for Human Rights and applied for and received incorporation for it from the Illinois state government, his life was fraught with failures.

In the mid-1940s, for example, he created a second organization to benefit homosexuals and gave it the unwieldy name of Society Scouting Sex Superstition, but it was doomed to failure from the outset because he only invited boyFrank and McCourt to join. boyFrank threw himself behind it wholeheartedly and became a member of its "committee of correspondence," writing letters to editors of newspapers and magazines that ran articles against homosexuality and homosexuals, not to protest them but to educate the publication's readers.

McCourt vigorously approved of the effort but did nothing on its behalf. He and Ufford were suffering from ill health and had fallen into financial straits, so he was too busy trying to keep their heads above water to spend his time and energy on letter writing. Gerber already had a history of writing letters to publications and stepped up his efforts, sending a number of lengthy—and often rambling—diatribes. Of all the letters that the two wrote, only one of Gerber's was published. Technically, the two-member Society Scouting Sex Superstition lasted longer than the Society for Human Rights, but only by a few months, and it did no more to further the rights of gay men than the earlier organization had.

Nevertheless, the correspondence also shows a less well-known side of Gerber. Occasionally, he dropped his guard and revealed a softer, vulnerable, even endearing character that he guarded assiduously and that few would suspect existed. He wasn't actually the loner that he portrayed himself as being. He had been in at least two long-term relationships with younger men, both of which ended before he turned thirty, and spent much of the rest of his life hoping to find love again. Once he felt comfortable exchanging personal details with boyFrank and McCourt, he let his hair down and admitted, "There is nothing more beautiful than mutual love, naked in bed, with kissing and embracing the other person. With me it does not matter 'how one goes off,' the main thing is the embrace and kiss." Unfortunately, he never found anyone who suited him and who returned his interest. Instead, he resorted to picking up strangers in movie theaters or parks or, more often, hiring male prostitutes.

All in all, Gerber's letters to Manuel boyFrank and to Frank McCourt reveal a very complicated and dedicated human being. Despite losing virtually everything he had in 1925 and launching the stunted Society Scouting Sex Superstition in 1944, he spent the rest of his life trying to figure out a way to "ameliorate"— Gerber's word—the plight of homosexuals. After he resigned himself that he couldn't achieve the goals he had set for himself, he threw his support behind the Mattachine Society and ONE Inc., two organizations founded in the early 1950s that were dedicated to the fight for equality for queer people, by becoming a member of each, donating money to them, and writing articles for the magazines ONE published. He lived through and was involved in four distinct periods of queer history: the pansy craze, the post-pansy panic, the Lavender Scare, and the gay rights movement, which often overlapped one another. It was obvious Gerber spent his life working on behalf of the queer community and was an icon of strength and foresightedness, a beacon from the gloomy

1930s through the menacing 1950s and for a short time beyond. Certainly, if any gay man's life and efforts deserved to be recognized by a biography, his did.

The treasure trove of Gerber and Gerber-related items at ONE exist because boyFrank saved most of the letters he exchanged with Gerber and McCourt. He understood Gerber was valuable to the homophile movement, an early term for what would be known as gay liberation, and he begged Gerber on several occasions to write a book about his experiences and ideas for future generations. "You have, you must realize, . . . much, much to say," he told Gerber. "Your opinions, the conclusions of many years' experience and thinking, constitute a kind of wealth. Won't you share it?"

If writing a book was too laborious a prospect for Gerber, who had already written four, boyFrank suggested that he "write letters, essays, stories, or frag-ments—but preserve them and let them be published some time," and to show his sincerity, he volunteered to preserve Gerber's ideas: "If you make letters to me the form of your self-expression, I will keep them carefully, prevent anybody's seeing them . . . , and help in any other way I can." boyFrank had already begun saving most of Gerber's letters to him, but with these statements made the day after Christmas 1944, he began to watch over them and, consequently, Gerber's legacy. boyFrank had intuited the items would be important for future queer people.

boyFrank kept the correspondence for thirty years when, in March 1974, he sent it along with other Gerber-related items to historian Jim Kepner. Kepner believed "boyFrank's . . . copies of the four Gerber books were broken up into pages or groups of pages, unnumbered and not individually identified as to source, and filed with a few here and a few there in miscellaneous envelopes under quite capricious subject-headings" and then disappeared. How Kepner and boyFrank met one another is unclear, but Kepner wrote to Jonathan Katz, "We," referring to the staff members of ONE, "learned of these entirely through [Fred] Frisbie and Boyfrank," both of whom knew Gerber and about his activ-ism and were members of ONE. Kepner had been collecting items important to queer history since 1942 and added what boyFrank sent him to his archive. In 1994 Kepner's archive and ONE's merged, and it was at ONE where I learned about the letters thanks to Manuel boyFrank and Jim Kepner.

This biography owes its existence to boyFrank and Kepner's foresight and marks the fiftieth anniversary of the death of Henry Gerber, the man many have called the father of the gay rights movement, the often-unsung hero of the queer community whose lifelong work on our behalf cannot be overestimated.

PART I

CHICAGO

1 | "I HAD NO IDEA THAT I WAS A HOMOSEXUAL"

DESPITE HIS EARLY SEXUAL EXPERIENCES with boys his own age, Josef Henrik Dittmar, who would later change his name to Henry Joseph Gerber, didn't know that he was a homosexual on the day he arrived at Ellis Island from Germany with his sister Anna. Some of the boys he grew up with in Passau, his hometown, aimed the derogatory term *Spinatener* at one another in jest and, more pointedly, at one of the town's bachelors. Years later, Josef explained that *Spinatener* meant "spinach man, spinach probably referring to passive pederasty,"* but as he was crossing the Atlantic Ocean, whatever it referred to had nothing to do with him or with what he and other boys were up to.

Josef began a period of sexual experimentation with boys, and occasionally girls, when he was five, and then, he disclosed, "At the age of 7 or 8 I had a boy friend with whom I practiced 'friction' by him lying on the floor and me getting on top of him and pressing up against his crotch and getting pleasurable feelings. We never undressed. At the age of 11 a boy showed me how to masturbate," and he liked to brag, "it would have been impossible . . . for the old nosey priest to pry it out of me and to squawk to my parents."

Sex wasn't his only pastime in those days. He also learned to play the organ, piano, and violin, and took lessons in "harmony and singing." He showed talent at the piano and was "pestered" by his friends who wanted him to play at their dances.

---

* In a diatribe against German sexologist and gay rights activist Magnus Hirschfeld, the "Bavarian 'humorist' Ludwig Thoma" described Hirschfeld as "'the Apostle of Sodomy, the spinach specialist.'"

Then, when he was sixteen, about the time that "society wants boys to get interested in girls," Josef began dating. He never had any sexual activity with them, and the experiment was short-lived. One after another, the girls rejected him, so he focused on boys, rationalizing his interest in them by telling himself "women are no good anyhow. My father and mother hates [sic] each other and their marital life was very unhappy. My older brother got himself in trouble with a girl and had to marry her after he knocked her up, and so on all sides I saw the folly of heterosexuality and soon began to think that I was lucky to have escaped this curse." His escape from heterosexuality and other difficulties took him across the Atlantic Ocean.

As Josef and his sister Anna stood on the deck of the SS *George Washington* a light, gray drizzle veiled the Statue of Liberty. They had first traveled overland by train from Passau, near the Austrian border in Bavaria, in the southeast of Germany, to Bremen, a port city in the northwest, where they boarded a ship. The SS *George Washington* set sail for the United States on October 18, 1913. They travelled third-class, cramped into very close quarters with thousands of other Germans headed for the United States. Heavy thunderstorms drenched the ship as it crossed the Atlantic, pitching violently over the surging waves, but luckily, it didn't meet up with any hurricanes. They arrived at Ellis Island nine days after their departure, on October 27, 1913, tired but safe and excited—and lucky. No sooner had the ship dropped anchor than a hurricane formed in the North Atlantic, the fourth of the season.

Once the ship docked, soldiers herded the Dittmars and the other travelers onto barges that accommodated about seven hundred people each and ferried them to Ellis Island. Finally on dry land, they walked single file under a canopy to the entrance of the immigration station and into the building's Great Hall, a cavernous waiting room. Mothers and fathers steered their children ahead of them. Infants cried. Toddlers wailed. Teenagers and young adults who were still single made eye contact with one another. A few even smiled, an instant's flirtation. Some of the immigrants were with their families. Many arrived alone. Dozens of different languages from across the globe, spoken by some "1,900 people [who] passed through the immigration station" each day, knotted into one roaring babble. The station was elbow to elbow with people—and anxiety. The immigrants knew that not everyone who arrived would be allowed to stay. Two years earlier, over five thousand arrivals were barred from entering the United States because of their mental or physical ailments.

In the Great Hall, thousands of newcomers stood in dozens of single-file lines with two different medical officers in charge of each line. The first officer checked the immigrants' eyes, ears, and hearts and took note of how they stood and walked, looking for any obvious physical symptoms of disease. The second officer double-checked the first's inspection.

Both Gerbers passed the officers' scrutiny with flying colors and climbed the stairs leading to the registry room. There, officials assigned them identification numbers and asked them the same questions that the authorities in Bremen had asked as they waited to board the ship. These included their "name, age, destination, race, nativity, last residence, occupation, condition of health, nearest relative or friend in the old country, who paid his passage, whether" she was ever "in United States before, whether" he was "ever in prison, whether" either of them was "a polygamist or anarchist, whether" they were "coming under any contract labor scheme, and" their "personal marks of identification such as height, and color of eyes and hair."

After waiting almost five hours, authorities gave Josef and Anna the go-ahead to enter the United States, and they returned to the first floor to exchange the money they had brought with them—each had fifty dollars in deutsche marks (together, nearly $3,000 in today's currency) in their pockets—and to buy tickets on the Baltimore and Ohio Railroad. The next day, they left from the Communipaw railroad terminal in New Jersey and, two days later, arrived in Chicago. A family friend, Fritz Bauer, had invited them to live with him until they could get on their feet.

Bauer had immigrated to the United States with his family when he was eleven years old. A bookkeeper, he lived at 1901 Davis Avenue* in West Town, a neighborhood west of the Loop, one of Chicago's fastest-growing districts and a favorite destination for German immigrants since the mid-1800s. Twenty-one-year-old Josef and nineteen-year-old Anna would be among the newest arrivals to settle there.

No one knows the specific reason why Josef and Anna left their family and friends in Germany, but the social conditions there may have driven them to emigrate. By the time each of them was born, Josef on June 29, 1892, and

---

* Davis Avenue was renamed Moreland Avenue.

Anna two years later, to Josef and Maria (née Reissler) Dittmar, the largely Protestant German Empire believed that the Catholics living in their midst were more loyal to the pope than to Kaiser Wilhelm I. The anti-Catholic sentiment had quickly developed into prejudicial laws in many German states, among them Bavaria, and while the prejudice had waned in the years before the Dittmars emigrated, the change was only slight. They were Catholic, and over the years, their family and Catholic friends and acquaintances had felt the brunt of anti-Catholic sentiment. Moreover, Josef's sexual involvement with other boys had gotten him expelled from school and fired from jobs. Germany's antisodomy law, commonly referred to as Paragraph 175, allowed authorities to fine and imprison homosexuals. Living in Passau had become risky.

In 1911 Josef had moved on his own to Antwerp, Belgium, most likely to find work after losing his jobs in small-town Passau when his sexual involvement with other teenagers and young men had surfaced. Belgium was far more liberal when it came to same-sex sexual relationships than any German state. In Antwerp he changed his name to Romaine Neubauer, perhaps to distance himself from his past in Passau, and found employment with Nicholas Dieze, but he got into trouble with the law for forgery and theft, and the police arrested him in mid-November. According to the Antwerp Police Department's daily report dated December 22, 1911, the authorities deported him, and he found himself back in Passau, shamefaced.

The police force in smaller towns, such as Passau, often invoked Paragraph 175 whenever they suspected a man of being homosexual, but Josef wasn't about to give up his sexual trysts. As far as he was concerned, sex was just sex, and his preference for other boys and young men was neither here nor there. He was lucky that the police hadn't used Paragraph 175 against him when he was a teenager, and he may have even owed some of that luck to his father, one of the town's lawyers whose influence with the police would have been substantial. Nevertheless, as Josef grew older, living in Passau became increasingly risky, and barely a year after being deported from Belgium, he packed his bags for the United States.

Besides, Josef (and perhaps Anna) had been smitten with "wanderlust," a term given in the late nineteenth and early twentieth centuries to a "longing for new experience. It is the yearning to see new places, to feel the thrill of new sensations, to encounter new situations, and to know the freedom and the exhilaration of being a stranger" that some individuals experienced. No sooner had Josef and Anna arrived and got settled in Fritz Bauer's home than Josef packed up again and set out, hitchhiking to the West Coast. Like hundreds of other young men in the United States and Europe, he was eager to see as much of the world as possible before he found himself a job and put down roots. Whether he made it all the way to the West Coast is unclear, but getting rides by standing on the side of highways with his thumb in the air ended up being a cinch for him and, in at least one case, added more than a little spice to his life.

On a highway in Kansas, in the middle of proverbial nowhere, a good-looking teenager pulled over and offered him a ride. During their chit-chat, the teenager hired Josef to stack wheat on his father's farm. That evening, Josef "slept in the bunkhouse" with the teenager and his boyfriend, and a large Englishman in his thirties. After lights out, the "boys did not hesitate to invite" Josef into their bed. He later bragged that what they did would have embarrassed even the famous sexologist Richard von Krafft-Ebing. Josef never divulged what the Englishman did during the boys' ménage à trois.

By the end of the year, Josef was back in Illinois, but not living at Bauer's home in Chicago. He rented a room at 507 Stone Street in Joliet, a city southwest of Chicago. Although the fifty dollars he had brought with him to the United States was a substantial amount, he knew it wouldn't last forever. With no other options open to him, he enlisted in the army for a monthly salary of thirty dollars (more than $850 in today's currency), a place to lay his head, and three square meals a day.

President Woodrow Wilson had already declared the United States neutral in the conflict escalating in Europe, preferring to let the European countries that were involved settle their problems with one another without interference. Like many other Americans, Josef reasoned that the fray in Europe would never reach all the way across the Atlantic Ocean. Enlisting in the army would be no worse than joining the Boy Scouts.

There was a hitch in his plan, however. The federal government wouldn't allow just anyone to join the army. It rejected those with mental disorders and "intoxicated persons; deserters . . . ; persons who have been convicted of felony;" or anyone "who is not a citizen of the United States or Porto Rico, or who has not made legal declaration of his intention to become a citizen." Josef had been in the United States for less than a year, but he had heard that immigrants who enlisted got citizenship automatically, another reason to join. He filled out and submitted the forms that declared his intention to become a citizen, which was just enough to allow him to sign up for the US Army in Joliet a few weeks after New Year's Day 1915.

Assigned to Company A of the First Infantry Division of the Regular Army, Josef quickly found himself bound for Hawaii with other recently enlisted men, and by the end of January, he had settled into the day-to-day routine of Schofield Barracks, seventeen miles outside Honolulu. All went well for him during his first year in Hawaii, but on February 5 of the following year, the base hospital admitted him for an undisclosed illness. Given Hawaii's tropical climate, Josef may have contracted either typhoid, yellow fever, or malaria, and he remained hospitalized at the base for nearly two weeks.

On Valentine's Day, the base physicians ordered him to board the USAT *Logan* bound for San Francisco. After the ship docked, the admissions office at Letterman General Hospital found him a bed. He remained hospitalized for nearly two months before he was well enough to leave. His physician released him on April 5, and on that same day, he received his discharge from the army.

Not looking forward to returning to Chicago's frosty spring weather and feeling his wanderlust rekindling, Josef set out to see what California had to offer. He hitchhiked south from San Francisco to Newbury Park, some forty miles west of Los Angeles, and remained there for two months. He worked on a ranch owned by Ed Borchard and then, a short time later, for a man named Philbrook who kept beehives on Borchard's land. During his free time, Josef rode horseback, exploring the area. By June he had become restless again and took to the road, hitchhiking all the way to New York. In New York, without a prospect for a job, he enlisted in the navy, mustering out three months later.

While Josef was away, Anna met George Meixner, the son of German immigrants, and they married on June 1, 1915. George made a living delivering ice to homes and businesses. The couple rented a house at 3452 North Oakley Avenue in a neighborhood called Bricktown. George's widowed mother, Theresa, and his younger brother, Leo, lived with them.

After his brief stint in the navy, Josef drifted back to Chicago and moved in with Anna and her new family. He found work in the mail room of Montgomery Ward at 618 West Chicago Avenue. In those days, Montgomery Ward was a mail-order department store offering dry goods to rural families across the United States and wouldn't open an actual brick-and-mortar store until 1926. He hated his job, calling it a "slave pen," but while working there, he met other gay men who introduced him to Chicago's burgeoning homosexual underground.

In March 1910, at the behest of a large alliance of local churches, Mayor Fred A. Busse convened a committee that he charged with looking into and reporting on vice in Chicago. Called the Vice Commission, its head, Walter T. Sumner, dean of the Episcopal Cathedral of Saints Peter and Paul, sent men into the city to investigate prostitution, alcohol and drug use, child abuse, police corruption, criminals, and any other immoral behavior they might come across. By accident, the unnamed investigator had stumbled onto "colonies" of

> men who are thoroughly gregarious in habit; who mostly affect the carriage, mannerisms, and speech of women; who are fond of many articles ordinarily dear to the feminine heart; who are often people of a good deal of talent; who lean to the fantastic in dress and other modes of expression, and who have a definite cult with regard to sexual life. They preach the value of non-association with women from various standpoints and yet with one another have practices which are nauseous and repulsive. Many of them speak of themselves or each other with the adoption of feminine terms, and go by girls' names or fantastic application of women's titles. They have a vocabulary and signs of recognition of their own, which serve as an introduction into their own society.

"Most of us," the investigator later recalled, "had thought of Chicago as being a place particularly inhabited by virile people, rather of the Western variety. . . . They all recognized that there was a lot of homosexuality in Berlin, but there wasn't a soul on that commission who thought for a minute there was any extent of it in Chicago."

As historian Gregory Sprague explained, the investigator had pointed a spotlight on approximately "twenty thousand active homosexuals" living in

A political cartoonist imagined Chicago's vice as a gigantic octopus—a creature foreign, strange, and unknown to most Chicagoans and, therefore, dangerous—its shadow thrown across the city and its tenacles in every aspect of life. *"The Octopus on the Lake," in F. M. Lehman and N. K. Clarkson,* The White Slave Hell, or With Christ at Midnight in the Slums of Chicago *(Chicago: The Christian Witness, 1910), author's collection*

Chicago's shadows. Those whom the investigator had discovered were female impersonators and other men who wore makeup and brightly colored suits and often bleached their longish hair but didn't wear female clothes. Another group, often married and fathers and considered *normal* by the effeminate men, looked and acted like any non-queer man in Chicago. They visited the effeminate homosexuals' haunts, various saloons, parks, and street corners on the sly. Because they weren't effeminate, they fit seamlessly into society and went unrecognized as homosexual. Consequently, they were invisible to the investigator and wouldn't have been included in the estimated thousands who lived, worked, and loved in the Windy City.

The gay men whom Josef befriended initiated him into the late-night goings-on at Bughouse Square, the nickname of the small plot of grass dotted with trees and benches that was officially known as Washington Square Park. It took up the block opposite the Newberry Library in Chicago's homosexual mecca, Towertown, on the Near North Side. Almost any night of the week, men sauntered up and down its sidewalks, making themselves available to the advances

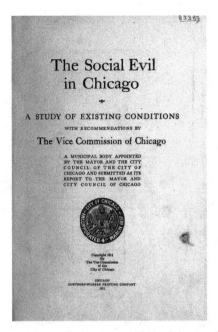

In 1911, the Vice Commission of Chicago published the results of its investigation into such social evils as prostitution, gambling, drug addiction, alcoholism, and homosexuality. The iniquities it investigated were so loathsome to society that the US Post Office declared the book obscene and banned it from being distributed through the mail. *Chicago Vice Commission, The Social Evil in Chicago: A Study of Existing Conditions (Chicago: Gunthorp Warren, 1911), author's collection*

of others. Some gave their charms freely. Others charged a dollar or two. Josef was delighted by the possibilities that Bughouse Square provided, especially meeting the young men he found there in all seasons who would "do anything" he wanted "for a little cash." In short order, he belonged to a network of sexually adventurous young men, taking the "active role" during sexual encounters.

One winter night as Josef strolled through Bughouse Square—the evening in question was "pretty cold"—he caught the attention of another young man. The "fellow asked me for a match," a common way for one gay man to break the ice with another man whom he hoped was homosexual and available. Josef was interested and replied, "It is pretty cold tonight is it not? To which came the simple reply. 'The only place in such a weather is in a warm bed.'" The two left together in search of one.

Another encounter didn't end as happily. One evening, he and a friend met a young man who was amenable to a ménage à trois. As it

Bughouse Square, officially Washington Square Park, became a popular cruising site for gay men for many decades before and after Josef Dittmar discovered its allure. *Courtesy of the Chicago History Museum, Chicago Daily News Collection, DN-0000005B*

turned out, Josef thought the pick-up was "swell" in bed, and the three made a date to meet again in a few days. When they reunited, the man "brought along a pal and both of them got nasty" and tried to rob Josef and his friend, but failed. Josef never revealed how they thwarted the robbers.

In the meantime, the fray in Europe between, on one hand, Great Britain, Russia, and France, and, on the other, Germany and Austria-Hungary, had heated up. By 1917 Germany had committed several acts of aggression that President Wilson couldn't ignore. These included German U-boats torpedoing and sinking several US merchant ships, as well as their attack on the RMS *Lusitania*, an ocean liner, killing over a thousand passengers. He reversed his decision about keeping the United States neutral in the European conflict and enlisted Congress to join its European allies to fight against Germany. On April 6 Congress declared war.

Two months before his twenty-fifth birthday, Josef and his brother-in-law, George, went to their local selective service board and registered for the draft in accordance with federal statutes. Josef's registration card reveals that he was five feet, eight inches tall and slender with blue eyes and blond hair. He declared himself a conscientious objector, or CO, a term used to designate a man who refused to carry arms or otherwise take an active role in war. Three years younger than Josef, George asked for an exemption, maintaining that he was the only support for his wife, Anna, and his mother. Men who were married or who were sole supporters of family members were often excused from military duty.

At about the same time, Josef was arrested, either when he was on the hunt for a bedmate or was caught in flagrante delicto with another man. The officer charged him with "disorderly conduct," a catch-all used for many types of illegal sexual activity. He was fined ten dollars and released, but the incident left him with another police record and made him reconsider his risky sexual activities in Bughouse Square and elsewhere. To keep himself on the straight and narrow, he developed something like a moral code that would inform his conduct for the rest of his life: First, he wasn't interested in pornographic photographs, claiming he was not excited by them. Second, he drew the line when it came to picking up men in public toilets. He knew of too many cases in which homosexuals were blackmailed by restroom pick-ups or beaten and left unconscious on the filthy floors. Third, he maintained that he was not the least bit interested in having sex with men he didn't know. Consequently, he often turned his nose down at men who were attracted to pornography, who cruised public bathrooms, and who had sex with strangers, while at the same time, he all-too-often failed to follow his own code. If given the chance, he ogled the photographed bodies of naked men, sought sex in park restrooms and on elevated train platforms, and more often than not, bedded strangers.

The arrest also gave him a good reason to move out of his sister and brother-in-law's home and into his own apartment. He had met a young man and fallen in love, and he wanted to settle down. Besides, in the long run, having a mate, rather than relying on pick-ups and male prostitutes, was the surest way of keeping out of the police's grasp. Josef never identified the young man with whom he fell in love but described him as the "romantic type." In his study of the Gold Coast neighborhood of Chicago, which included Towertown, sociologist Harvey Warren Zorbaugh described a "romantic type," a young man who rented a "vermilion kitchenette apartment, with a four-poster bed hung with blue curtains and an electric moon over it. When he has his loves he gets violently domestic, tailors, mends, and cooks." While Josef worked nine to five at Montgomery Ward, his young lover attended to the "cooking and the usual duties of a wife." He never revealed how long they lived together, but within a year or so Josef found himself confined to an insane asylum.

Beginning as early as the mid-nineteenth century through the first half or so of the twentieth, the authorities had the legal power to institutionalize men and boys for being homosexual. Leading physicians and alienists (an early term for psychologists), the police force, and most of ordinary citizens believed that homosexuality was a symptom, if not an actual type, of insanity.

It's unclear in which of the three insane asylums in or near Chicago Josef was confined or by whom, but he was arrested, appeared before a hearing, and sentenced by court order to one of them. The Meixners could have begun the proceedings because Anna had the legal authority to confine him, but that seems unlikely. Josef remained close to her and George throughout his life, and if they had institutionalized him, he would have severed the relationship. Equally questionable is the possibility of his having institutionalized himself or that the police did. Police typically arrested gay men and let the court decide the punishment, which could be as long as a ten-year term in prison, in many ways a much more substantial punishment than confinement in an institution. It seems likely, then, that the parents of Josef's young lover discovered their relationship, complained to the authorities, and had him confined.

Josef had been in the asylum for over a year when, on June 28, 1919, the countries involved in World War I signed the Treaty of Versailles. Despite the end to the fighting, the United States was in the grips of a "paranoia" that developed over the fear of German spies hiding within its borders. The Alien Enemies Act of 1798 allowed authorities to ban male German nationals from specific areas of the country and to mandate that they register with the government. It didn't take long for "police round-ups" of German immigrants to be commonplace, their "arrest . . . a humiliating experience" that "could lead to loss of employment, social standing, housing or all three."

The authorities gave Josef the opportunity to choose his fate. By law, they could either designate him an "enemy alien," a term assigned to immigrants from a country with which the United States was, or had recently been, at war, and he would be imprisoned indefinitely at Fort Oglethorpe in Georgia, or they could free him *if* he reenlisted in the US Army that was then occupying the enemy countries, Germany and Austria-Hungary.

The practically minded Josef considered internment and weighed its advantages against reenlistment. He reasoned that, like the army, internment would provide "three free meals a day . . . and safety and security" plus the bonus of "all the young Dutchesses [sic] in camp," referring to the young men who, he

During and after World War I, a pall of suspicion fell across the United States, causing many Americans to become distrustful of German immigrants and even their American-born children. New York Herald, *March 28, 1918, courtesy of the Library of Congress, Prints & Photographs Division, LC-DIG-ppmsca-07746*

hoped, would be sexually available to him. Nevertheless, Josef chose to reenlist. The military offered him everything that internment did but with the added opportunity to travel, at least occasionally. His hitchhiking trip to the West Coast, his travels to Hawaii with the army, and his hitchhiking from Southern California to New York hadn't satisfied his wanderlust. Stationed in Europe, he could request brief leaves and travel all over the continent.

Released from the insane asylum, Josef temporarily moved into the two-story house at 3312 North Hoyne Avenue in Chicago that his sister and brother-in-law had recently rented. Theresa and Leo were still living with them. True to his word, Josef set out to reenlist a few months later, but he soon discovered that there was a glitch that complicated the process. Unlike his first enlistment in 1914, he had professed to being a conscientious objector during his draft registration. To be granted CO status officially for his new enlistment, he had to take the train to Camp Grant, northwest of Chicago, to present his case to the camp's commander and to undergo a "psychological examination" that "covered a wide range and was intended to reach into the utmost recesses of the . . . mind."

Josef had two platforms from which he might argue his case with the commander. He could base his claim on either religious grounds or on his personal sense of morality and ethics. If he chose the first, he would be announcing that his religious conviction excluded him from all military service, while if he chose the second, he would be declaring that his philosophical beliefs allowed him to enlist but only as a noncombatant. He had long abandoned any adherence to religious doctrines, and besides, he had already served in both the army and the navy. No one at Fort Grant would have believed that he had suddenly become so religious that its dictates wouldn't allow him to carry a rifle. Instead, he argued from an ethical standpoint—and won. He officially became a conscientious objector, and the camp's administration assigned him to the army's medical division.

Through his friends and experiences in Chicago, Josef learned that there was a word for men who had sex with other men, *homosexual*, and that he was one. While it may seem unbelievable that he could claim, "I had no idea that I was a homosexual," he was referring to the word, a label, not to the act of men engaging in sex with other men. He was no different than most people at the time. Historically speaking, "although sexual acts between two people of the same sex had been punishable through legal and religious sanctions well before the late nineteenth century," society in general "did not necessarily define individuals as homosexual per se" or had even heard the word *homosexual*. The words they knew and used—*pervert, degenerate, sodomite*, and others—defined queer men as criminal or sinner. Josef didn't believe he was either. He had already grappled with social convention because of his sexual orientation and was aware of the legal mess that he could find himself trapped in if he weren't always on his toes. What he didn't know then was that his decision to reenlist instead of being imprisoned put him on a path that would lead him to standing up for his and other homosexuals' rights, a track that no one could ever have imagined in 1919, least of all the twenty-one-year-old Josef who hadn't even heard the word *homosexual* in German or English before he arrived in the United States six years earlier.

2 | "I HAD ALWAYS BITTERLY FELT THE INJUSTICE"

ON JUNE 28, 1919, representatives from both sides of the war in Europe signed the Treaty of Versailles that ended World War I, and Josef wouldn't be dodging bullets and bombs or scrambling for a gas mask along with the soldiers who carried rifles. Best of all, the moral climate in many European cities had begun to be less critical of homosexuality and, in general, more accepting of it. Josef Dittmar could not have joined the army and headed back to Europe at a better time, but reenlisting wasn't the only major decision he made.

At some unknown point between the day he was released from the asylum and the day he reenlisted, Josef changed his name again, to hide the fact that he had been institutionalized for being a homosexual. In the early twentieth century, anyone who wanted a new identity simply moved to a new location and used whatever name they had selected. Slipping from civilian life into the military was a perfect time for him to metamorphose into someone else. He no longer went by Josef Henrik Dittmar. He anglicized his given names and switched their order, becoming Henry Joseph, then he dropped his last name, a common enough surname in Germany, and adopted *Gerber* to replace it. It's possible that his sister Anna's father-in-law had inspired his choice. Christian Meixner made his living as a leather tanner, and in German, *tanner* is *Gerber*.

On October 2, 1919, after leaving Camp Grant, Henry Joseph Gerber headed for Jefferson Barracks, a few miles south of St. Louis, to reenlist. From there, the US Army transported him to Camp Merritt just outside Hoboken, New Jersey. During the war, nearly three million doughboys

17

passed through Camp Merritt on their way to or from combat. It became so famous among the troops as a gateway that they created a sobering slogan that highlighted its intense traffic *and* the impending doom that they faced: HEAVEN, HELL, OR HOBOKEN. They would be killed in battle and go to heaven, or they would be killed in battle and go to hell, or they would survive the gunfire, the bomb explosions, and the poisonous gas and return to Hoboken alive, passing through Camp Merritt on their way home to civilian life.

The following summer, Henry received his orders. He was to ship out to Coblenz (now Koblenz), Germany, where he would join the American Army of Occupation and work in the base hospital in whatever capacity the administration needed. On July 12, 1920, he and 616 other enlisted men marched for four and a half miles under cloudy skies, in eighty-four stifling degrees of heat, and through soggy humidity to a ferry waiting for them at the Old Closter Dock.

The ferry took them to Hoboken's pier 2, where, exhausted, dehydrated, and dripping sweat, they boarded the USAT *Cantigny*. The ship set sail at 4:40 PM and headed for Antwerp, Belgium, at fifteen knots, slightly more than seventeen miles per hour. Besides its crew and the newly enlisted men, the ship carried several dozen officers and sixty-three civilians who were visiting their officer husbands, fathers, or sons stationed in Germany. It also transferred three tons of clothing, six tons of household supplies, eight tons of mail, ninety-six automobiles, four motorcycles, and two-hundred eighty-three caskets, all destined for the American troops in Germany.

The weather over the Atlantic Ocean was calm, the skies clear, and the USAT *Cantigny* crossed without incident. After what seemed like an eternity to Private Gerber, the ship first docked at Antwerp for a few days. With a police record there, albeit under a different name and, by now, eight years old, Henry wasn't going to risk getting into any trouble and laid low while in port. From Belgium, the ship sailed south and docked at Bremen, its last port of call and the same port from which he and his sister had emigrated from Germany seven years earlier.

From Bremen, Henry took a train to Coblenz in the southwestern corner of Germany, picked up the keys to a private room, as mandated by the army's regulations for conscientious objectors, and then checked in at the base hospital center for his assignment. He didn't end up working in any medical capacity. Instead, he became the sole proofreader for the base newspaper.

The *Amaroc News* (an acronym formed from American Army of Occupation) was issued daily to soldiers across the region of Germany occupied by American forces. It had been operating since the previous July, nine months before Henry joined its staff, and it was so popular among the troops that it quickly became self-sustaining. It reprinted articles from all major US newspapers as well as reports on local events. In his opening remarks, its editor promised that the paper would "not refight the war. We all know, every soldier in the army knows that his division, his regiment, his very squad is the best that fought in the late unpleasantness. So what's the use. That issue [is] a closed incident." Instead, he "hoped to maintain an elevated moral tone and to boost morale in the AFG"—the American Forces in Germany—by "quelling rumor," fostering "a spirit of competition" by "boosting sports," and "though the paper promised to avoid 'preachment,'" by championing "good conduct and 'manliness.'"

While Henry was aboard the *Cantigny*, the White House announced that the president would reduce the number of troops stationed in Germany. A few days later, the first group of doughboys left Coblenz. Twelve days after that, another division left, and soon, the number of American soldiers dropped from 250,000 to 20,000. As the majority of troops were pulling out of Coblenz, visitors arrived, including some of the families of officers stationed there and three hundred West Point graduates who toured the base. The comings and goings not only frustrated the doughboys still stationed in Coblenz but, for many, intensified the long periods they spent waiting for their orders to leave. They began to feel worthless, stagnant, forgotten, and restless.

Almost immediately, the *Amaroc News* became an outlet for the soldiers's aggravation by publishing scores of cranky letters addressed to the editor and poems that echoed what the letters said. One doughboy's poem approached the situation with humor:

> I want to go home, I want to go home,
> We crossed the sea to fight Germanee.
> The war is finished so what good are we?
> We want to go home.
> (Repeat until exhausted.)

—a sentiment shared by all too many others and echoed in this more serious poem:

> We're here because we can't get home,
>   The ocean is too wide,
> If it was narrow as the Rhine,
>   We'd swim to the other side.
>   . . .
> So we're waiting, waiting, waiting
>   Until the ocean's dry,
> Then we'll hike back to God's country.
>   To Mother and mince pie.

Compounding the doughboys' anxiety was the recent order the army issued that banned any sort of contact with civilians except during official military operations, but its underlying target was the doughboys' sexual relationships with Coblenz's Fräuleins. The army wasn't concerned just because sexual activity with the former enemy, who might be spies, could be dangerous and often considered treason but also because of the near-epidemic cases of venereal diseases among the troops. It ignored soldiers' liaisons with one another or with male civilians.

Before the outbreak of World War I, the US military hadn't fully addressed homosexuality in its ranks. The Articles of War of 1916 vaguely "addressed the issue of homosexual conduct" and its only prohibition against same-sex activities was "limited to assault with the intent to commit sodomy." For the most part, the US military was virtually blind to homosexuality, and few officers could imagine that any man among his troops would "preach the value of non-association with women." German or French soldiers? Of course! But never an American soldier. The ignorance on the part of officers made any homosexual in their troops safely invisible to them and, consequently, safe from persecution. Instead, as historian Douglas F. Habib has reported, the army issued a report "on homosexuality within the *German* population" in January 1921 (italics added). It theorized that there were "increased statistics of homosexuals in a country where Oscar Wilde always had followers" and that "sexual perversities would occur more frequently amongst the most nervous of German races, viz. the Prussians," but kept mum about homosexuality among the doughboys.

By the turn of the twentieth century, "one of Berlin's police commissioners" had "estimated the total number of gay men to be in excess of 100,000," and it had grown exponentially over the next few decades. As the investor for the Vice Commission of Chicago had said, there *was* "a lot of homosexuality in Berlin" before World War I, and Berliners showed a distinctive amount of tolerance toward homosexuals. During the war, a thick fog of extreme conservatism settled over civilian life, but by the time Henry was stationed in Germany, it had lifted considerably. "Das lila Lied" ("The Lavender Song"), considered the first anthem of homosexual liberation, was extremely popular, was sung at live performances in hot spots across the city, and was even available as a recording. How Henry found out about Berlin's accepting atmosphere is unknown, but as soon as he could get a furlough, he found his way there to enjoy all that it had to offer, thanks, in large part, to Magnus Hirschfeld.

Born in 1868 in in Kolberg, Prussia (now Kołobrzeg, Poland), Hirschfeld, who was homosexual, began practicing medicine in Magdeburg, Germany, when he was twenty-six. The trial of Oscar Wilde in 1895 for "gross indecency" weighed heavily on him. He moved his practice to Berlin the year after Wilde's imprisonment and began focusing his practice on human sexuality, particularly homosexuality, which resulted in his cofounding the Wissenschaftlich-humanitäres Komitee (the Scientific-Humanitarian Committee) with three other Berliners and working for the repeal of Germany's antisodomy law, Paragraph 175. The publication of his first three books— *Die Transvestiten* (*The Transvestites*, 1910), *Die Homosexualität des Mannes und des Weibes* (*The Homosexuality of Men and Women*, 1914), and the three volumes of *Sexualpathologie* (*Sexual Pathology*, 1917)—earned him a reputation among his colleagues as a brilliant sexologist, but his research wasn't simply theoretical in nature. He based his ideas on the case histories of his very real and troubled young patients. One such case affected Hirschfeld acutely.

The parents of a young army lieutenant were forcing him to marry, and he left Hirschfeld a note on the eve of his wedding: "Please could you educate the public on the bad fate of people like me who are not fit for marriage. Please tell the public everything about us." Then he shot himself and died.

Through Hirschfeld's consequent research on suicide among homosexuals, he discovered that queer men committed suicide more often than heterosexual men, which led him to establish the Institut für Sexualwissenschaft (Institute of Sexual Science or Institute of Sexual Research) in 1919 and to house its offices in an "opulent villa" in central Berlin. It opened its doors to the public on July 6, 1919, just three months after Henry arrived in Coblenz. The institute "promoted sex education, contraception, marriage guidance counseling, advice for gay and transgender people, the treatment and prevention of sexually transmitted diseases, gay law reform and women's rights. It saw over 20,000 people a year" and, in fact, became known throughout Europe as a haven for queer people. The now-famous Lili Elbe was one of the institute's first transgender patients.

Hirschfeld's Institute of Sexual Science attracted physicians, medical students, and other medical personnel from across Europe who found information on sexual matters there that was unavailable elsewhere. Its museum was popular among tourists because of its exhibits of "fetishes, fantasy pictures, and photographs" that surprised and even amused Henry and others, including Christopher Isherwood, W. H. Auden, André Gide, and Sergei Eisenstein. Because of its size and content, the Wall of Sexual Transitions was one of the museum's premier displays and caught the eye of everyone who visited. Divided into "four quadrants," the wall presented photographs of "hermaphrodites in the upper left, forms of androgyny in the upper right, homosexuals in the lower left, and transvestites in the lower right." The institute also sponsored lectures and other public programs.

The institute quickly became the hub of the homosexual rights movement in Germany and especially in Berlin, one of the most accepting cities in Europe. Through Hirschfeld's efforts, and with the determination of other gay rights advocates, "raids on homosexual gathering spots" became "unlikely," "arrests" of homosexuals "were relatively uncommon," and the "enforcement" of Paragraph 175 "had become unusual." Henry, who hated the sexual hypocrisy that he had run up against in the United States, felt a heady sense of liberation when visiting Berlin.

Nevertheless, the freedom Berliners enjoyed was fragile and constantly threatened. In 1920 the officers of the Ministry of Justice began working to revise Paragraph 175 into a harsher law. The proposed revision, called Paragraph 325, would change the legal punishment for any type of sex between men from a relatively light five-year sentence to a five-year sentence in a penitentiary with extremely hard labor. Infuriated by the harsh proposed changes, Hirschfeld led a protest against the change to a standing-room-only crowd in an assembly hall on the evening of February 7, 1921. The proposal failed to find support in the Ministry of Justice and died, but whether Hirschfeld's efforts had anything to do with its demise is unclear. What is known is that the rally he led was the first gay protest in recorded history.

Berlin had added hundreds of homosexual bars, cafés, and nightclubs to its nightlife, and they became headquarters for men seeking others for sex, including male prostitutes, but men were also available in Berlin's scores of cruising spots, of which the

> most famous was the so-called gay path (*Schwuler Weg*), a particular trail through the city's largest park, the Tiergarten. . . . According to Hirschfeld, there was at that time a homeless homosexual man, often referred to as the "Tiergarten Park Butler," who sat on a bench near the entrance to the gay path. If one approached him and asked to buy a "ticket," he would ask for ten cents and then relate which areas were safe from police observation and other kinds of useful information.

Men congregated at several specific spots in the park, including the "classical statue of a marathoner." The garden was only a short walk to Hirschfeld's institute, and Henry undoubtedly sought out male companionship there as he had back home in Bughouse Square.

It's doubtful that Henry, who neither drank nor smoked, patronized any sort of gay club during his visits to Berlin, but if he did, he would have found the *Dielen*, which "were just bare bones pick-up bars—dimly lighted joints," to his liking. The crowd at the Adonis Diele, for example, "consisted largely of young laborers who were out of work; they would sit, playing cards and waiting for customers, their shirts open to the navel and sleeves rolled up." They charged the men who wanted more than just gazing at them. According to a study begun by Richard Linsert, one of Hirschfeld's young colleagues, rates for male prostitution ranged from "fifty pfennig to ten marks and more." Athletes who became prostitutes received the highest fees and included an "'athletic boxer,' Hugo G., and Karl W., a competitive swimmer . . . ; both reported receiving ten marks or more per sexual act." With at least "25,000" male prostitutes available to him in Berlin, Henry had no trouble finding those who struck his fancy.

Some of the male prostitutes adopted specific clothing to attract customers. Although Henry was attracted to men younger than he, he wasn't a pedophile, so he wouldn't have been attracted to Berlin's substantial community of "Doll-Boys," who were typically "under 14" years old, or the "Line-Boys," who were "from 15 to 19" years old and wore "peaked schoolboy hats and short pants to appear considerably younger" than they were. "Bubes (or 'Butchers')," on the other hand, were "handsome, well-built, working-class men," such as the habitués of the Adonis Diele, who were from about twenty years of age to a few years older—Henry's ideal.*

Berlin's male prostitutes held a particular, but not exclusive, allure for Henry—not because they were necessarily more physically attractive or more sexually adept than the men he noticed in the parks, on the streets, in shops, or on the trains he took to and from Berlin, but because of their no-strings-attached approach to sex. He met them, had sex with them, paid them, and that was that. After his experiences with his young lover, Henry wasn't the least bit interested in establishing a relationship with another man—not then, anyway.

Nonsexual activities were also available to Henry. *Urnings*, an early term in Germany for *homosexuals*, produced and acted in plays presented to strictly queer audiences and staged extremely popular "gay balls" with as many men in drag as not. A "French observer of the city around the turn of the century" explained that "gay balls were held often several times a week in different clubs during the festive season between October and Easter. On some nights, one could even find more than one ball being held somewhere in the city."

---

* American homosexuals also had labels for different men. A *female impersonator*, for example, was a homosexual man who dressed in women's clothing either to perform on stage or to attract *normal men*. *Trade* usually denoted men who claimed to be heterosexual but who would have sex with a homosexual for money. Many who made a living or supplemented their salaries as trade were actually gay men pretending to be straight. A man who was *dirt* may have been trade or simply a heterosexual or homosexual man who blackmailed his male sexual liaisons. Some terms indicted specifics about men's bodies, such as the phrase *blind meat*, which indicated that a man had not been circumcised, or *kosher meat*, which meant that a man had been. Homosexuals even had a name for heterosexuals: *jam*.

Having easy access to young men and male prostitutes wasn't the only windfall for Henry when he first set foot in Berlin. "As many as twenty-five gay and lesbian magazines" that included articles about various aspects of homosexuality, personal ads, and even photographs of naked or nearly naked young men "crowded the German market" during the 1920s and early '30s and were "readily available at newsstands to anyone who wanted them." Several were aimed at a very specific readership, among them a "satirical magazine, an S/M specialty mag, and several lesbian ones. So visible were the gay magazines" on newsstand shelves "that a public health officer . . . railed publicly against their corrupting effect on youth, who would be lured," he believed, "by nude coverboys" and "by the personal ads" printed in their pages "into the enslavement of cocaine and prostitution." They also helped to expand their readers' vocabulary. Henry reported that he learned a "few terms from the homosexual magazines," including "auntie, a homosexual of later vintage."

To Henry's delight, several of the newsstand magazines published well-written, informative articles about homosexuality. *Der Eigene*—the "title loosely translates to 'The Self-owner' or 'His Own Man'"—was the most famous and longstanding of the magazines. Founded in 1896 and published continuously, if irregularly, during World War I and until 1933, it served as a "forum on homosexuality, and encompassed scientific, literary, artistic, and historical articles," as well as "poems, news bulletins and photographs of stunning, naked young men." It also printed the "personal ads" that the "public health officer . . . railed" against.

Personal ads were a safe way for gay men to meet one another. The streets and parks were full of dangers, particularly teenagers or young men bent on gay bashing. In personal ads, men described themselves and their desire in carefully guarded short notes. The "beauty of gay personal ads . . . was that they could be written relatively anonymously and in coded language" such as this example from *Der Eigene*:

> Aristocrat, young, belonging to the oldest noble family of Hungary, independent but bound by the free development of his inner nature by social circumstances, inspired by upstanding sympathies and passionate love for the beauty of nature and art, is looking for connection to a likeminded person as a travel partner, friend, secretary, or reader. . . . Discretion a matter of honor!

Der Eigene, the longest-surviving magazine published for gay men, offered its readers news articles and essays on topics of interest to them along with photographs of nude and seminude young men. *Author's collection*

"Art," "discretion a matter of honor" punctuated with an exclamation mark, and "likeminded person" suggested the writer was gay. The phrase "bound by the free development of the inner nature by social circumstances" was his testament that society had confined his natural disposition, something that would have spoken loudly to another gay man. The use of personals in Germany "peaked in the 1920s," during Henry's stay in Coblenz.

Because he had private quarters on the base in Coblenz, Henry could safely subscribe to some of the magazines he had first seen on Berlin newsstands. He preferred the monthlies that published photographs of nude young men, and undoubtedly *Der Eigene* was one. By that time, it had gained a reputation because of its "homoerotic illustrations and aesthetics." It's likely that Henry even responded to a few of the personal ads he found in it. If the ads, the cruising lanes, and the *Dielen* were a treasure map for Henry's libido, Hirschfeld's Institute of Sexual Science, with the lectures it sponsored and the exhibits it assembled, offered a feast for his intellect.

It's unclear when Henry first visited Hirschfeld's institute or even if he ever met the renowned physician, but the institute and its founder's advocacy for homosexual rights had a profound effect on him, as did the work of other activists such as Friedrich Radszuweit. The wealthy Radszuweit fought for homosexual rights and the abolishment of Paragraph 175 from 1923, when he founded and ran the Bund für Menschenrechte (League for Human Rights), until his death nine years later. Radszuweit's league, a "social and political organization for homosexual men, women, and for male and female transvestites," boasted a membership of "tens of thousands" of supporters. Although known for his league and the homophile magazines he published, principally *Die Insel* (*The Island*), he also produced one of the earliest phonograph recordings to directly address gay themes: "Bubi laß uns Freunde sein" (Bubi, let's be friends).

Adolph Brand, best known for publishing *Der Eigene*, also influenced Henry, and like Hirschfeld and Radszuweit, he founded an organization, Gemeinschaft der Eigenen (Community of the Special), in 1903 to advocate for homosexual rights. It has been characterized as "more of a literary circle" than a political body that "met weekly at Brand's house . . . to recite poems, listen to readings, and discuss matters important to the group." In 1920, during his trial for "peddling pornography and soliciting sex through" *Der Eigene's* "personal ads," Brand stopped its publication and issued *Freundschaft und Freiheit* (*Friendship and Freedom*), which he and his authors used to condemn the "forces of political conservatism in the young [Weimar] republic, especially devotees of the old monarchy and the powerful political hand of Catholic and Protestant churches." Henry found Brand's denunciation of religion and its stranglehold on politics a booster to his own growing atheism.

To Henry's knowledge, nothing like the endeavors of Hirschfeld, Radszuweit, and Brand, to name but a few of the vanguard, had ever been attempted in the United States.* In fact, while Henry marveled at their work, he couldn't

---

* According to historian Jonathan Ned Katz, another German immigrant, Presbyterian minister Carl Schlegel, advocated for homosexual rights as early as 1906–1907. Certainly others, still unknown today, sought equality for gay men before Henry.

imagine anyone taking the lead in the United States to advocate for homosexual rights or even willing to join such a movement "for the defense of 'our kind.'" The difference in the way the two countries approached homosexuality struck him profoundly. As he put it,

> I had always bitterly felt the injustice with which my own American society accused the homosexual of "immoral acts." I hated this society which allowed the majority, frequently corrupt itself, to persecute those who deviated from the established norms in sexual matters.
>
> What could be done about it, I thought. Unlike Germany, where the homosexual was partially organized and where sex legislation was uniform for the whole country, the United States was in a condition of chaos and misunderstanding concerning its sex laws, and no one was trying to unravel the tangle and bring relief to the abused.

The "chaos" and "misunderstanding" that Henry observed was the lack of uniformity in laws across the United States. Each state formulated its own regulations for sodomy, its own understanding of who homosexuals were and what *homosexual* meant, and its own punishments, including fines and prison terms. What might be strictly policed in, say, Wyoming might be ignored in New York. Consequently, gay men found themselves mired in a legal morass.

If Henry didn't know what *homosexuality* was when he immigrated to the United States, his experiences in Berlin opened his eyes. Homosexuality was so common among human beings, he discovered there, that it could only be considered natural and that laws against it were illogical and hypocritical. As important, he discovered that challenging the so-called antisodomy laws was possible, albeit feasible only if someone were willing to take the first step. That step—the most important—was organizing. One person had little hope of making a difference, but tens of thousands could change history. He vowed to himself that, as soon as he returned to Chicago and found a job and a place to live, he would do what he could to help the plight of homosexuals in his adopted homeland—a promise he kept.

3 | "TO PROMOTE AND TO PROTECT"

MOST OF THE SOLDIERS in the American Army of Occupation looked forward to going stateside and picking up their civilian lives where they had left off. As the *Amaroc News* put it, the "American soldier is returning home to take his place at the head of affairs of the nation. He is going home with the ideas for which he fought firmly fixed in his mind, and he intends to see that they are carried out. It is to be hoped that there are none so unwise as to . . . attempt to divert him in any way from this purpose." Henry's sorties into Berlin had given him "ideas" that also needed to be "carried out."

Henry hadn't seen any of his family in Germany for nine years, so in 1921, while waiting to return to the States, he took the train to Passau, more mature and world wise now than in 1913, when he and Anna emigrated. His early life in Passau with his devout Catholic parents had been far from ideal. They hadn't bothered to hide their animosity toward one another from Henry or his brother and sisters, a situation that was exasperated by the trouble he had often gotten into with the law, with school authorities, and even with employers because of his sexuality. His brother added to the turmoil when he got a girl pregnant, which led to a hurried marriage to restore the peace. Fortunately, his family had made it through World War I without too many hardships. His nephew, now twelve, was only a toddler of three when he last saw the boy.

Then, two years later, in January 1923, camp commander Major General Henry T. Allen received a directive to prepare for a complete withdrawal of the remaining troops in Coblenz. Allen recalled every soldier on leave or furlough. The years of anticipation and anxiety were almost over. But not every soldier was eager to leave. For some, the army had given their lives a purpose, a direction, something they lacked as civilians. For others, who were more practical, it afforded them three square meals a day and a place to lay their heads at night. For still others, their sweethearts or wives were German. They didn't want to leave them behind but didn't want to uproot them, because they were sure to face anti-German sentiment in the United States. For those soldiers, the troop withdrawal was complicated, daunting, and unwelcomed.

By the end of the month, the USAT *St. Mihiel* docked in Antwerp, waiting for the troops' withdrawal. At the same time, the *Amaroc News* began closing its offices and shutting down operations. In its January 23 issue, the *News* reported that ceremonies marking the soldiers' withdrawal from Germany would begin at noon the next day, and at 3:45, soldiers would board the train from Coblenz to Antwerp. To mark the event, Julian B. Claff, the editor of the *Amaroc News*, rounded up his staff and posed for a photograph with them.

The *Amaroc News* printed its last issue on the day the troops boarded the train, as its editor took care of last-minute duties, such as canceling the *Amaroc's* subscription to the International News Service and writing letters of recommendation for the Germans on the paper's staff. Claff wrote a final report dated February 1 in which he noted that all the staff had left except for him and "one enlisted man, Private Henry Gerber, who remained to liquidate the paper." As the base at Coblenz shut down, Henry earned "thirty-six [dollars] a month with an extra allowance of eighty cents a day" that went toward his rent and meals because he had to live off base.

Once stateside, Claff published an article about the *Amaroc News* in which he mentioned Henry long before he identified any other staff member. Claff's second sentence reads, "Hank Gerber came in on the George Washington with General Allen and eighty more die-hards." Henry's place in the article and his nickname, Hank, suggests that he was liked by Claff and the other staff members. The black-and-white of the staff taken during Henry's last days in Coblenz appears at the end of the article.

Henry had volunteered to remain behind and help liquidate the *Amaroc News* because he was conflicted about going home. He didn't have a job waiting for him in Chicago, nor was there a special someone holding his breath, anticipating Henry's return. He had found acceptance in Berlin, basked in the freedom that he had found there, and felt safe with men like Hirschfeld, Radszuweit, and Brand wrestling with Germany's law on behalf of the homosexual community. Buying gay magazines publicly at newsstands and attending public lectures about homosexuality had become commonplace for him. He had gotten accustomed to seeing gay men out and about, unconcerned about being noticed, and being able to approach other men on the streets and in the parks with little fear of being arrested and sentenced to lengthy prison terms. In short, returning to the States meant abandoning the freedom he had enjoyed in Berlin. It's no wonder that he delayed leaving Coblenz as long as he could, but he couldn't postpone the inevitable forever.

On February 20 he took a train from Coblenz to Bremen and boarded the SS *George Washington*, the same ship he and Anna had taken to the United States a decade earlier. It sailed at midnight and arrived at Hoboken on March 3. After a bout of cold and cloudy weather, the sky cleared as the ship docked, the west wind bringing warmer temperatures. Once in port, Henry claimed on the List of United States Citizens form that he had been born in Chicago because, having been threatened with being an enemy alien three years earlier, he wanted to ensure that would never happen again. He also lied about his age, shaving three years off his date of birth.

Once he was back in the States, Henry was so eager to get to the work of liberating homosexuals that he "purchased his way out of the Army," something "soldiers up until World War II" could do. Nevertheless, he took his time getting back to Chicago. Where Henry lived and what he did during the remainder of March and all of April is unknown, but by May he was in Washington, DC.

The District of Columbia had an active, if covert, gay subculture when Henry arrived. Queer men sought out one another in the darkened balconies of vaudeville and movie houses in the "tenderloin district," including the "Strand, Leader, Rialto, Central, and Contralo on Ninth Street, the Columbia and Metropolitan on F Street, the National on E Street, and Keith's on Fifteenth." Keith's had the extra advantage of being in the same building as the Riggs Turkish Bath, which had a substantial gay clientele. On warm, clear nights, Lafayette Square, a small park within a stone's throw north of the White House, was another favorite cruising spot and had been since 1885, and nearby Pennsylvania Avenue and Ninth and F Streets were almost as popular. Henry found Lafayette Square as beguiling as Bughouse Square and spent a great deal of time there, strolling up and down its paths hoping to stumble upon an attractive young man—or, sitting on its benches, trusting that he could lure one to him. One of the young men he met, Carter Bealer (a.k.a. Jeb Alexander), kept a diary in which he mentioned Henry.

Bealer claimed that he was only attracted to "young, middle-class white men who were 'not obvious'" and spurned older men, such as the "stout spectacled idiot of 45" who "flopped down at the other end" of Bealer's bench one night and tried to make conversation with him. Despite his preferences, when Henry approached him, the twenty-three-year-old Bealer agreed to accompany the thirty-one-year-old from the park to the "Department of the Interior Building on C Street, Northwest" where Bealer let Henry masturbate him. They continued to run into one another at the park, but each time Henry tried to talk Bealer into another tryst, he ignored Henry's propositions and even "made flimsy excuses to get rid" of him. Henry finally told him, "I don't know what you're looking for, but I know it's not me," and yet he was smitten, kept making innuendoes whenever they ran into one another, and became a "damned nuisance'" in the process.

Henry didn't stay in the nation's capital for long. He took the Washington-Chicago Express, the least expensive train, out of DC, and eighteen and a half hours later, he arrived in Chicago. Anna and George urged him to move into their home at 3312 North Hoyne Avenue, and having nowhere else to go, Henry agreed to move in temporarily to regroup. George's mother, Teresa, was still living with them, but Leo, George's brother, had died of unknown causes three years earlier when he was only twenty-two. Refusing to live off his sister and her family and eager to have his privacy, Henry began looking for a job immediately.

On July 10, 1923, Frank H. Galbraith, the superintendent of Chicago's post office, hired Henry as a "temporary sub. Clerk at the Lakeview Station" post office. His first day on the job was August 23. He earned sixty cents an hour (or ten dollars in today's currency), and two months later he was promoted to a full-time position delivering mail, making $1,400 a year (or more than $23,000 in today's currency). Each year thereafter until 1925, he continued to get raises. On October 1, 1924, his salary increased to $1,500 and then, the following January, to $1,800 (about $25,000 and $30,000, respectively, in today's currency). He also trained to become a notary public.

Henry maintained the lies about his birth and age. On his job application for the post office, he claimed to have been born in the United States and, again, subtracted three years from his actual age. Anti-German sentiment was at an all-time high by then, making his second lie about his place of birth understandable, but trimming three years off his age again was simply vanity. As far as his supervisors knew, he was still in his twenties.

On April 1, 1924, Henry wrote a letter to Galbraith explaining that he had developed a "tenacious case of tonsillitis." He faced an operation, and, needing time for recuperating afterward, he asked for permission to use his vacation time for the procedure and recovery. The next day, Henry received a response from a clerk in Galbraith's office. He hadn't followed protocol. The clerk filled out the necessary paperwork for him requesting "sick leave for five days beginning March 31," and if Henry needed more time, he could take the nine vacation days that were due him, beginning April 5 and concluding with April 17. Henry signed and returned the form with his physician's note validating his request for time off.

Henry hadn't been honest in his note to Galbraith. His physician, J. W. Plater, who worked for the Illinois Social Hygiene League, a clinic in Towertown, was more forthcoming when he submitted a brief report to Galbraith about Henry. Plater informed Galbraith that Henry had developed not tonsillitis but syphilis. Plater recommended that Galbraith excuse Henry from work indefinitely, but as it turned out, Henry only needed a few weeks to be cured. The league's superintendent, Bernard C. Roloff, wrote a letter to Galbraith's office on April 26 and summarized Henry's treatment: "Henry Gerber . . . has already had nine successive treatments and in our opinion is not contagious nor infectious and could safely be taken back to work. He should continue treatment however, to prevent a recurrence of his disease." Roloff also commended Henry, who "wisely came" to be treated "quickly after his infection was noticed." Henry claimed he had tonsillitis to cover up the fact that he had contracted syphilis orally, and the sympathetic Roloff did what he could to veil Henry's sexuality by suggesting he had been infected inadvertently. Roloff was banking on Galbraith's ignorance of the fact that syphilis is only contracted through sexual contact.

Galbraith gave Henry the go-ahead to return to work and resume his duties on Monday, April 28. Five months later, Henry received the results of his first job evaluation. Daniel T. Hickey, his supervisor, ranked him at "98 per cent" for his previous year's work. If Henry had felt any anxiety over his future, all was well now. He had passed his first evaluation with flying colors, Roloff had camouflaged the real source of his syphilis, and Hickey wouldn't be firing him for being homosexual. Henry had been lucky. His physician was liberal. One of Henry's gay friends may have recommended Roloff or, perhaps, the fact that the doctor's office was in Towertown, ground zero for Chicago's liberalism, tipped him off.

Chicago wasn't as carefree for queer men as Berlin was, and yet the Windy City had developed a liberal atmosphere in reaction to the conservatism of the war years. By 1919, just after Henry left the asylum to serve in the American Army of Occupation in Germany, the Jazz Age, also known as the Roaring Twenties, swept across the United States, bringing with it a sudden, intense political and social liberalization. Artsy, politically savvy bohemians (artists, writers, young people, and politically liberal or radical older ones) were adamant about shaking off whatever conservatism clung to them and, in Chicago, congregated in the Near North Side neighborhood dubbed Towertown. It extended west from the Water Tower at Michigan Avenue for close to a mile. While its boundaries were "always fuzzy," most Chicagoans agreed that it was bounded by "the wealthy Gold Coast to the east and what was called Little Italy to the west. Its main drags included Wabash Avenue and Ohio, Erie, Huron, Superior, Pearson, Chestnut and State Streets. Some of the bohemians lived as far west as LaSalle Street, or in fringy areas outside Towertown proper."

Historians often mark 1879, when "reading tournaments" were staged at McCormick Hall on North Clark Street, as the year in which Towertown began to attract Chicago's bohemians. Within a dozen years, the *Dial* and *Poetry*, two important literary journals, emerged in the Village and attracted writers of all genres to its inexpensive rooming houses. At the same time, artists flocked there and set up their studios in cheap rentals. Suddenly, Towertown was the "geographical center of what was perhaps the most vital literary and artistic upsurge in the history of the country," later called the "Chicago Renaissance," as well as a haven for queer people, many of them the same writers and artists that were an integral part of the "artistic upsurge." Once the bohemians and their liberal politics got a foothold in the area, it became the neighborhood most welcoming to queer people in the Windy City.

At the same time that Jazz Age liberalism blossomed, the federal government ratified Prohibition, which had been supported by various religious and politically conservative groups. Although it outlawed the "manufacture, transportation and sale of intoxicating liquors," huge numbers of Chicagoans ignored the new law and patronized speakeasies and the scores of cabarets that served alcohol on the sly. Young women, called flappers, and their male counterparts, labeled sheiks, swelled the crowds. Many flappers and sheiks could not have cared less about politics, but they were devoted to having a good time, drinking heavily, dancing to jazz—and rejecting convention. The word *jazz* perhaps best puts the decade into proper perspective because, by at least 1918, it had come to mean "sexual intercourse," according to the *Oxford English Dictionary.*

The confluence of the bohemian movement, the jazz-related culture, and Prohibition set the stage for an unexpected and unique change: the very visible appearance of gay men in a new guise, the pansy or fairy. Although some pansies appropriated a few telltale signs of what the dominant culture thought of as effeminacy, they weren't female impersonators, as many of the men whom the Chicago Vice Commission's investigator had discovered nearly a decade earlier were. They expressed themselves visually as part male (their clothing) and part female (the dabs of makeup that they wore and their mannerisms). The pansy was not simply visible to Chicagoans in certain quarters of the city; he was also a transgressive and easily identifiable figure.

Flappers and sheiks, whose chief slogan was "free love," couldn't reject homosexuals because, like them, they clashed with society's predominant sexual taboos. If, by mainstream standards, gay men were deviant, they were no more deviant by those same socially sanctioned standards than the young women who bobbed their hair, raised the hemlines of their dresses, demanded equal rights, and lost their virginity before marriage—or the young men who stood beside them, cheering them on. The progressive politicos, who staunchly supported equal rights for all citizens, had to accept them as equals or be branded hypocrites and the politics they espoused void.

Now able to appear in public, homosexuals attended the performances at Towertown's cabaret, vaudeville, and legit theaters; held, attended, and performed at drag balls and appeared fully dragged out at masquerades; sponsored and attended lectures about all sorts of cultural ideas and events, among them homosexuality; recorded popular music; had their own radio programs; and otherwise dropped their camouflage to be themselves in ways they had never been able to before. Towertown—and a few other Chicago hot spots, principally the South Side's Bronzeville—became their havens.

Being accepted by the bohemians wasn't the sole reason queer people flocked to Towertown. The large number of them crammed together there made it possible for them to be completely ignored by their neighbors and to live in virtual anonymity, unlike the small towns many had left behind, where one's personal business easily became everyone else's. Not a soul would notice anything a gay man happened to say or do, and those who did notice wouldn't bother to respond or interfere. Or if they did notice, they just might join in. Historians have dubbed this period of marked gay visibility and acceptance the pansy craze.

That isn't to say that the pansy was completely free from societal restraints. Laws still regulated their behavior, but the cop on the beat in Towertown, the Loop, and other permissive districts looked the other way when they became aware of a pansy in their midst. The public was divided. One gay man recalled how heterosexual men he knew at the Subway, one of Chicago's many queer-friendly bars, reacted to the pansies among its customers: "Some of my friends said, 'I get a kick out of kidding with them'; others said, 'I feel sorry for them.' Most of them say, 'I would kick the shit out of them if they tried to make me.'" Yet the pansy had become so much a part of the fabric of Chicago life that, when two male investigators for the Juvenile Protective Association checked into the Sterling Hotel at 1859 West Madison Street to investigate a prostitution ring based there, the desk clerk thought that they might be having a sexual tryst and, without a second thought, asked them, "Two rooms, boys, or one?"

Before he reenlisted in the army in late 1919, Henry knew about the freedoms that Towertown afforded gay men, but as Chicago historian Gregory Sprague reported, "Although Gerber was aware of Chicago's gay subculture, he did not appear to have participated in it on a regular basis." Since he himself didn't drink or smoke, he wasn't interested in spending his money on drinks for possible pick-ups in cabarets or on cover charges for drag balls. He was too sober-minded and practical, and with Hirschfeld, Radszuweit, and Brand as his inspiration and the pansy craze in full swing in Chicago, he was sure that the time was ripe for change.

While living with the Meixners, Henry had to toe the line, but as soon as he began earning a salary from his position at the post office, he moved out of Anna and George's home and into one of the small rooms on the second floor of a rooming house at 1719 Crilly Court. Crilly Court lay in one of the "fringy areas outside Towertown proper" in a neighborhood now called Old Town that was populated by German immigrants and a small percentage of African Americans. His room was big enough for only essential furniture: bed, bureau, night table. His landlady cooked his meals and washed his clothes. He ate with the family and shared the living room with them.

The area into which Henry moved was substantially less expensive and far grittier than Towertown. It didn't offer cultural events like those held at the Dill Pickle, a "political forum, theater, lecture hall, and nightclub" and a "hub for radical politics and art, where anarchists and labor agitators could spar or collaborate with playwrights, poets, painters, and journalists" or like those sponsored by the Seven Arts Club, a "roving lecture forum that took up temporary residence in a variety of 'alley garages and hotels'" and presented "lectures by 'Prostitutes and Queens, as well as scholars,'" nor did it boast any popular cafés or cabarets such as the Green Mask Inn or the Erie Cabaret. Instead, Henry's new neighborhood was known for its "collection of flophouses, boardinghouses and seedy tenements." His neighbors included two popular bordellos that stood sentry on either end of the block on which he lived.

Henry became friends with some of the men he met while cruising Bughouse Square and other places, and he mentioned to them how they had to organize if they wanted to change their lot in life. To his dismay, many told him point-blank not to do "anything so rash and futile" as trying to organize them, but he wasn't dissuaded. His motives weren't entirely altruistic, either. He wasn't the least bit ashamed to admit that, if he were successful, he would be "known to history as deliverer of the downtrodden, even as Lincoln" was, and besides, if he "succeeded" he would also "benefit" from his efforts.

Despite the doomsayers, he invited a handful of the men he had met while cruising the streets to his place to discuss organizing. He had already come up with a name for them, the Society for Human Rights, a nod to Friedrich Radszuweit's League for Human Rights. A few joined his cause, and because Henry's tiny bedroom would have accommodated only one or two visitors, they met in the basement of his rooming house where there was room for dozens, and its two outside doors allowed men to come and go in secret.

When Henry first met John T. Graves, Graves was a "preacher who earned his room and board by preaching brotherly love to small groups of Negroes" at St. John African Methodist Episcopal Church. Identified as African American in both the 1910 and the 1920 censuses, the forty-six-year-old minister shared his apartment at 4105 South Dearborn Street with twenty-year-old John L. Sullivan, a white man who was a plumber for a church that may have been Graves's congregation, and with thirty-nine-year-old Abraham Sutton, also an African American, who was a waiter in a railroad club car. Graves and Sutton joined Henry's Society, and Sullivan may have too. Sutton hoped the Society would stand up for him because his "job . . . was in jeopardy" after his bosses learned he was gay. Proud of the fact that he wasn't a racist, unlike many of the men he knew, Henry visited the men's apartment on many occasions and described it as a "sort of hang-out" for gay men where Henry had "met many colored boys," a hint that he had engaged in sex with at least some of them.

Graves became the president of the Society for Human Rights, the first African American to head any gay organization in the United States, and moved to the Near North Side, into a room at 1151 Milton Avenue.* Ellsworth Booher, the society's treasurer, lived in the same boarding house, but whether they lived together is unknown. Al Meininger, its vice president, lived at 1044 North Franklin Street. One of the society's trustees, Henry Teacutter, lived in Henry's building on Crilly Court. All the members were close to Henry's age or older, and given Henry's penchant for younger men, it's unlikely that he had any sexual interest in Teacutter. One of the society's other trustees, John Slather, lived on the South Side, at 1836 East 101st Street, and another, Fred Panngburn, lived out of state, at 5855 University Avenue, Cleveland, Ohio. Besides Sutton, the society's membership included at least several other men. One, Franz Spirk, immigrated to the United States the year before Henry formed the society. Like Henry's young lover, Spirk was a "romantic type," but unlike most of the society's other members, he had a steady job with a satisfactory salary. He was a clerk in a bank.

Henry outlined his plan for the Society for Human Rights at their very first meeting. Their first objective was to enroll more members. They would never succeed if their ranks included only those at the meeting. Once they garnered both financial and moral support from others, they would sponsor lectures examining the attitudes that society had developed about homosexuals and homosexuality and publish a monthly bulletin, *Friendship and Freedom*, which Henry named after Adolph Brand's magazine, to educate other gay men and the public at large. It would serve as a "forum for discussion" of topics such as the pansy's public "behavior." Henry firmly believed that advocating for "self-discipline" would "win the confidence and assistance of legal authorities and legislators" who would support the society's efforts and eventually understand "the futility and folly of long prison terms for those committing homosexual acts."† The group would also advocate "against the seduction of adolescents."

---

* Milton Avenue was renamed Cleveland Avenue.
† In Illinois at the time, homosexuals could be imprisoned for a minimum of one year and a maximum of ten.

One of the major topics of discussion during their first meeting was whether they should brand the "organization a purely homophile Society," i.e., accept only gay men and "exclude the much larger circle of bisexuals." At the time, many homosexuals, including Henry, thought *bisexual* didn't necessarily refer to those who were attracted to both sexes but to those who married women and fathered children to hide their homosexuality. If a bisexual's secret life was discovered, he could be blackmailed or betrayed to the police, along with anyone else who happened to be associated with him. Allowing bisexuals would be extremely risky, and the members agreed to exclude them for the time being.

Henry also discussed legitimizing the society, which meant they needed a charter of incorporation from the state of Illinois. He reasoned that it would bode well with potential members and financial supporters if the state government approved it. Several days later, Henry asked Hickey, his supervisor at the post office, if he could recommend a liberal lawyer to draw up the paperwork for incorporation. On December 8, 1924, Henry, Graves, and Meininger visited attorney James J. O'Toole's office at 1327 North Clark Street, south of Henry's rooming house, where O'Toole gave them the application form for incorporation. Henry filled it out. Two days later, O'Toole notarized the application, and Henry mailed it to the secretary of state. He paid the ten-dollar application fee himself and, undoubtedly, O'Toole's bill as well.

When filling out the form, Henry had to include the society's objectives and was rightly concerned that if he mentioned anything about homosexuals, the secretary of state would reject the application. To protect the society, Henry used vague terms to disguise its objectives. The society had been formed, he stated,

> to promote and to protect the interests of people who by reasons of mental and physical abnormalties [*sic*] are abused and hindered in the legal pursuit of happiness which is guaranteed them by the Declaration of Independence, and to combat the public prejudices against them by dissemination of facts according to modern science among intellectuals of mature age. The Society stands only for law and order; it is in harmony with any and all general laws insofar as they protec [*sic*] the rights of others, and does in no manner recommend any acts in violation of present laws nor advocate any matter inimical to the public welfare.

Gerber applied to the state of Illinois to have the Society for Human Rights and paid the ten-dollar application fee himself. It was signed by the organization's officers. *Courtesy of the Illinois State Archives, Secretary of State (Corporations Division), Dissolved Domestic Corporation Charters, May 2, 1849–March 7, 1980, record series 103.112*

On December 10, 1925, the Society for Human Rights became the first legally incorporated homosexual organization in the United States. *Courtesy of the Illinois State Archives, Secretary of State (Corporations Division), Dissolved Domestic Corporation Charters, May 2, 1849–March 7, 1980, record series 103.112*

To give the society a whiff of respectability, Henry included Graves's title *Reverend* in the list of officers, and Graves likewise included it with his signature.

The secretary of state approved the application on December 10, 1924, the first time a gay organization was given an official charter by any state in the union. Henry, whose address on Crilly Court was the group's official address, immediately set about collecting materials from newspapers and other publications to reprint in *Friendship and Freedom*, but he ended up writing many of the articles himself. The only hitch he faced was getting the bulletin printed. It took time and effort for him to find a printer willing to do the job, and then only after Henry assured him that he wouldn't have any problems with the law because they wouldn't be publishing anything that could be misconstrued as obscene.

Produced on a shoestring, *Friendship and Freedom* debuted in early 1925, the first gay-focused magazine to be published in the United States. It opened with an "article on 'Self-control,'" followed by "a poem by Walt Whitman, and an essay 'Green Carnations'" that Henry translated from *Die Freundschaft* (*Friendship*), one of the many gay-focused magazines popular during Henry's stay in Coblenz. Henry announced in the debut issue that the society planned to use the money generated by subscriptions to fund financially strapped gay men and help them find jobs.

Henry mailed copies to homophile groups in Europe to announce that the society was joining the movement to advocate for homosexual rights and, with his name and address on the masthead, to promote himself internationally as an activist. Henry made sure to put Magnus Hirschfeld's institute on *Freedom and Friendship*'s mailing list. Two years later, when Hirschfeld published an essay entitled "Die Homosexualität" ("Homosexuality") in a book on sexual practices, he included a photograph of nearly twenty gay publications, gifts from their publishers to the Institut für Sexualwissenschaft. Captioned "Homosexuelle Zeitungen und Zeitschriften" (homosexual newspapers and magazines), the photograph included Henry's *Friendship and Freedom* in the middle surrounded by European publications.

To debut his activism, Henry began writing letters to the editors of newspapers and magazines whose pages included negative comments about sex-related issues, among them homosexuality. He mailed several to the editor of the *Chicago Daily Tribune* before one was finally published in its March 2, 1925, issue under the title "Are Indecent Shows Realistic?" From the get-go,

Sexologist Magnus Hirschfeld included this photograph of over a dozen gay publications, among them Gerber's *Friendship and Freedom*, in his essay "Die Homosexualität" ("Homosexuality"). The photograph was captioned "Homosexuelle Zeitungen und Zeitschriften" (homosexual newspapers and magazines). *Author's collection*

Henry accused the editor of refusing to publish his earlier letters, and having gotten that off his chest, he got down to business. "I may have funny ideas," he wrote, "but I believe I am not as stupid as some of your contributors, as, for instance, the one who says that in Kansas grass grows when farmers say prayers." His disregard for religion would intensify and became a staple in his future writings.

The point of the letter wasn't to argue for or against the fare of theatrical productions, including vaudeville, but to ask, first, why people waste their time going to *any* theatrical production, indecent or otherwise, and second, why it was anyone's business which type of production theatergoers chose to attend. The word *indecent*, he instructed the editor, was relative, noting that, what might be considered improper by one person, might not be for another. Henry even explained that licentious shows were popular because people thought the so-called respectable ones were hypocritical.

So far, his letter was serious, but besides a very logical mind and a keen sense of right and wrong, Henry had a funny bone. Henry added, "If I want to hear 'spiritual' things I go to the Salvation Army and get an hour's 'inspiration' free," although Henry had never stepped foot in a Salvation Army building his whole life. He concluded it tongue in cheek: "Doubtlessly numerous people of the neurotic class call *The Tribune* an 'indecent' newspaper, but nevertheless it is the World's Greatest Newspaper." "The World's Greatest Newspaper" was the *Tribune*'s well-known tagline.

Henry's excitement over the commencement of his activism was short-lived. He soon realized that the doomsayers were right. Most of the men he knew weren't as ready as he was to put everything they had—family ties and friends, social acceptance, and their jobs—on the line, and so attracting new members was beyond his reach. The "average homosexual," Henry learned, "was ignorant concerning himself. Others were fearful. Still others were frantic or depraved. Some were blasé." Even the few men who cheered Henry's efforts in private believed "as long as some homosexual sex acts" were "against the law, they should not let their names be on any homosexual organization's mailing list any more than . . . bandits would join a thieves' union."

Henry even went so far as to contact heterosexual Chicagoans, especially well-known physicians, hoping they would endorse his efforts and buttress his cause, but they were concerned about their social standing and what associating themselves with his group might do to them and their careers. Others simply didn't understand the need for the society. The "big, fatal, fearful obstacle seemed always to be the almost willful misunderstanding and ignorance on the part of the general public concerning the nature of homosexuality," Henry soon learned, and "what people generally thought about when" he used the word *homosexual* "had nothing to do with reality." They thought he was referring to the makeup-wearing, flamboyant pansy because they didn't know that "masculine" homosexuals existed.

Extremely frustrated by his experience, Henry quoted Friedrich Schiller: "Against human stupidity even the gods fight in vain." Despite the negativity he faced and the frustration he felt, Henry soldiered on. He scraped up enough money to launch a second issue of *Friendship and Freedom* just weeks before the law wrenched the proverbial rug out from under him.

4 | "INFECTING GOD'S OWN COUNTRY"

HENRY'S SUPERVISOR EVALUATED HIS JOB performance a second time in April 1925. Hickey continued to be pleased by the quality of Henry's work and raised his score by a point, putting him in the ninety-ninth percentile, as close to perfect as anyone was likely to attain. He had job security and, as important, had moved out of his room on Crilly Court and into one at 34 East Oak Street, only a few blocks from Lake Michigan. The move put Henry smack dab in the middle of Towertown and all it had to offer men like him. His new boardinghouse was only a three-block walk to Bughouse Square and a four-block walk in the other direction to Oak Street Beach and its esplanade, another well-known hot spot for men wanting to pick up other men. Most of all, the organization that he had been thinking about for over six years was up and running, albeit on wobbly legs. All was well in his life—or so it seemed.

Chicago was in the grip of one of its many heatwaves on Saturday, July 11, but the breeze off the lake gave the Chicagoans who lived near it, like Henry, a little respite from the swelter. Late that evening, Henry strolled to the Loop despite the heat. The Astor, a movie theater at 12 South Clark Street, was a popular haunt for men who typically cruised the balconies, which ushers usually ignored when they made their rounds. He didn't get home until 2:00 AM Sunday morning, and by then, he was dead-tired and ready for sleep.

He was about to climb into bed when he heard pounding on his door. Because it was so late, he presumed his landlady had some emergency and needed to speak to him. He opened the door without a second thought. To his surprise, several men barged in. One, a detective, immediately demanded, "Where is the boy?" Henry

44

was taken aback. He didn't understand what the detective was talking about. He was alone and in a small room. Anyone could see there wasn't another soul there.

A reporter from the *Chicago American* followed the detective in as did a couple of uniformed policemen. The detective ordered one of the policemen to arrest Henry and the other to search his room. No one showed him a search warrant. While the reporter took notes, the policeman discovered Henry's files for the Society for Human Rights, his diaries, his diploma from his notary public training, and his typewriter. They hauled Henry and all his property to the police station at Chicago Avenue and LaSalle Street where he was surprised a second time that night. Al Meininger and Rev. John Graves were at the station being booked, along with a young man named George whom Henry had never met before. After the mug shots and the fingerprinting, the police locked them up in separate cells for the night.

The next day, Monday, news about the arrests of the three men broke. The short article of 152 words that the reporter wrote for the *Chicago Evening American* mangled the facts but got the names of the society's three officers correct. Entitled GIRL REVEALS STRANGE CULT RUN BY DAD, the article was published without a byline. One of the police officers gave Henry his copy of the paper, and Henry read that Meininger's daughter, twelve-year-old Betty, had walked nearly a mile from the Meiningers' apartment at 532 North Dearborn Street to the Chicago Avenue police station on Saturday to ask an officer on duty there "why her father carried on so." She told the officer that men visited him for "afternoon and night . . . séances" during which they engaged in "strange rites." Her questions raised the officer's curiosity and gave the police a reason to raid Meininger's apartment. When they pushed their way through his door, the article continued, the police found Meininger, a thirty-seven-year-old married father of four, with Graves and Henry, both of whom lived in Henry's former rooming house on Crilly Court. It identified Henry as the "publisher of the cult paper, Friendship and Freedom."

When he wrote about the incident nearly forty years later, seventy-year-old Henry corrected the article's errors but also got several facts wrong. Henry lived on Oak Street and was alone when police arrested him there, not at Meininger's. He recalled that the reporter was from the *Examiner,* but because both it and the *Chicago Evening American* were known for their sensational headlines and stories, it's understandable that he confused the two. He believed that the article was front-page news, when in fact it appeared on page eleven.

Henry's arrest wasn't nearly as important a news item to the paper's editor as it was to Henry.

Henry felt betrayed by Meininger. He had pegged Meininger as an "indigent laundry queen," a phrase that Henry had learned in the army and then again while he was among gay friends in Chicago. Soldiers used "laundry queen" for men who were assigned laundry duty, but among homosexuals it referred to a man who padded his crotch with articles of clothing to enhance his "bulge." Instead of being homosexual, Meininger was one of the "bisexuals" that Henry and members of the Society for Human Rights had agreed to exclude from the organization because of the problems they might bring to it. Meininger had brought the law to their doors, exactly as the members of the society had feared "bisexuals" would.

That same morning, the police allowed Henry to make a phone call, and he contacted Hickey to tell him that he had been arrested. He couldn't tell Hickey exactly why because he hadn't been charged with anything yet. Months before, Henry had translated a philosophical tract from the German for Hickey, and he felt he owed Henry a favor. Besides, Henry was one of his best employees. The ever-sympathetic Hickey told him not to worry. He would simply note in Henry's files that he approved Henry's absence, and that would forestall any suspicion or gossip about what had happened to him as well as protect his job. A few hours later, a police officer led Henry to court. Graves, Meininger, and George were already there, and during the proceedings, Henry learned the backstory behind his arrest, which contradicted much of the newspaper account.

Meininger's daughter hadn't contacted the police to complain about her father's activities with other men. That was the reporter's way of drumming up animosity against the prisoners. His wife had contacted a social worker, the same woman who had been assigned to the poverty-stricken family by a social agency in Chicago, and complained to her about Meininger's sexual trysts with other men. The social worker, whom Henry called a "hatchet-faced female," testified against him. The night before, she had studied Henry's diary intensely to prepare herself for taking the stand and found what she believed would be a damning admission in it. "I love Karl," she read aloud to the court and, according to Henry, "out of context." He had always been careful not to write anything in his diary that authorities could use as evidence against him, but she had discovered the one statement that could be misconstrued. Her role in the proceedings was to explain the negative effects that Meininger's "strange cult" had on his family, and if the court accepted the social worker's weighty testimony, as Henry knew it probably would, he was doomed.

During the 1920s, much of a social worker's attention focused on what was then considered "family disorganization," or the breakdown of the family structure that often occurred, they believed, because of poverty and circumstances seemingly unique to urban life. Various conditions had a negative effect on the family—violence within the home, alcoholism, addiction, sexual abuse, hunger, the lack of medical help, unemployment, and even child labor—and caused it to disintegrate little by little, and that disintegration, in turn, caused an unraveling of the fabric of society as a whole. Meininger's sexual activities with other men, the social worker testified, was a symptom of his family's disorder. Only by removing those responsible for the family's troubles—Meininger, whose sexual trysts were damaging his family, and Graves and Henry, who were the other leaders of the "cult"—would Meininger's wife and children be saved.

Henry was no fool. He had lost jobs, was expelled from school, and had run-ins with the legal authorities over his same-sex sexual conduct in Passau and Chicago. He couldn't help but notice that the judge and the prosecution winced when the social worker testified and knew then that the narrow-minded judge was convinced of his guilt.

Although the three words the social worker read from Henry's diary were damning, the officer who had barged into Henry's room the night before submitted a powder puff to the court as further evidence of Henry's homosexuality, making the situation even worse. The detective testified he had found it in Henry's room, but Henry protested loudly, denying that he had never owned one and that he had never used makeup. The detective was trying to defame Henry by suggesting that he was a pansy. Whether the detective had planted the powder puff in Henry's room the night he arrested him or added it to the evidence later is unknown, but the judge ignored Henry's denial.

Powder puffs and other make-up and accessories used by men had already become firmly associated in the public's mind with the pansy. On January 16, 1916, for example, Brooklyn police raided a saloon and arrested six gay men and the heterosexual bartender. The police officers claimed the men they arrested wore makeup and had powder puffs in their possession although witnesses at the subsequent hearing testified the police lied. Nevertheless, the court convicted the seven for disorderly conduct and gave each a six-month sentence. A decade later, screen superstar Rudolph Valentino was branded homosexual in the *Chicago Tribune* because of a powder dispenser.

Quintessential matinee idol and, considered by many, the most handsome man in Hollywood, Rudolph Valentino faced a backlash because of his role in *Monsieur Beaucaire*, the 1925 Louis XV costume drama. In it, he wore obvious makeup and flamboyant costumes. Many considered it an "overtly feminized role," and when, the year following its release, Valentino and his wife divorced, the public began to speculate that he was gay and their marriage had been what was called a "lavender marriage," one arranged to camouflage his homosexuality.

An editorial published in the *Chicago Tribune* in the summer of 1926 poked fun of Valentino's sexuality, implied that he was gay and, because of his role in *Monsieur Beaucaire*, blamed him for being the reason why a "face-powder dispenser" was installed in the men's room of an unidentified Uptown ballroom, probably the Aragon, which opened four days earlier. The editorial opened peacefully enough, describing the coin-operated dispenser, but then exploded into a homophobic rant.

"Homo Americanus!" its writer railed, with *homo* referencing homosexuals, before turning his readers' attention to the matinee idol: "Why didn't someone quietly drown Rudolph Guglielmo, alias Valentino, years ago?" Then he revealed what drove him to such an outburst in the first place: "And was the pink powder machine pulled from the wall or ignored? It was not. It was used. We personally saw two 'men'—as young lady contributors to the Voice of the People are wont to describe the breed—step up, insert coin, hold kerchief beneath the spout, pull the lever, then take the pretty pink stuff and put it on their cheeks in front of the mirror." The incident reminded him of an earlier one: "Another member of this department, one of the most benevolent men on earth, burst raging into the office the other day because he had seen a young 'man' combing his pomaded hair in the elevator. But we claim our pink powder story beats his all hollow."

Was the fact that some men were using powder or combing their hair in public, the editorial asked, evidence of the "degeneration" of society

> into effeminacy [and] a cognate reaction with pacifism to the virilities and realities of the war? Are pink powder and parlor pins in any way related? How does one reconcile masculine cosmetics, sheiks, floppy pants, and slave bracelets with a disregard for law and an aptitude for

crime more in keeping with the frontier of half a century ago than a twentieth century metropolis?

Although the editorial was published without a byline, its author has since been identified as John Herrick.

Incensed by the editorial, Valentino challenged Herrick to a boxing match to prove which of them was "more a man" in a letter to the editor published the next day in the *Chicago Record-Herald*. Addressed "To the Man (?) Who Wrote the Editorial Headed 'Pink Powder Puffs' in the Sunday Tribune," Valentino threatened to give Herrick "the beating you deserve" and taunted the writer: "I will meet you immediately or give you a reasonable time in which to prepare, for I assume your muscles must be flabby and weak, judging by your cowardly mentality, and that you will have to replace the vitriol in your veins for red blood—if there be a place in such a body as your's [*sic*] for red blood and manly muscle." Herrick chose not to respond to the actor's challenge, but his attack on Valentino shows that, despite the pansy craze then in full swing, not everyone in Chicago had gone gaga over gay men.

The judge at Henry's hearing hadn't said a word about the powder puff the detective supposedly discovered in Henry's room, but at the end of the session, he wondered aloud if Henry had violated the Comstock Act by sending *Friendship and Freedom* through the mail. He had looked over the confiscated copies of *Friendship and Freedom* and deemed it obscene and was cuing the prosecution to add another charge against Henry.

In 1873 the US Congress passed a law officially known as the Act of the Suppression of Trade in, and Circulation of, Obscene Literature and Articles of Immoral Use. It was commonly referred to as the Comstock Act after Anthony Comstock, who had founded the New York Society for the Suppression of Vice. A rabid, congressional lobbyist, he had worked to get the law enacted. It defined obscene quite broadly to include "erotica; contraceptive medications or devices; abortifacients; sexual implements, such as those used in masturbation; contraceptive information; and advertisements for contraception, abortion, or sexual implements."

Comstock and his followers stretched the definition so wide that it would also be applied to "prize fighting, intercollegiate football, [and] the ballet," and they relied on it to prosecute anyone who mailed, for example, a print of a painting in which a nude man appeared, a letter referring to a park where gay men congregated, or a bodybuilding magazine to another person. It even allowed postal inspectors to open and freely read any person's mail on the suspicion that its contents might be obscene. Relying on the Comstock Act, post office officials even deemed the Chicago Vice Commission's report, *The Social Evil in Chicago*, obscene because of the subjects it had investigated and discussed in the book, and they refused to allow the commission to distribute it through the mail.

On top of everything else, Comstock was a particularly vicious homophobe. Once, when asked what he thought of "lessening sodomy law," he railed that

> inverts* are not fit to live with the rest of mankind. They ought to have branded in their foreheads the word 'Unclean.' Instead of the law making twenty years' imprisonment the penalty for their crime, it ought to be imprisonment for life. . . . They are willfully bad, and glory and gloat in their perversion. Their habit is acquired and not inborn. Why propose to have the law against them now on the statute books repealed? If this happened, there would be no way of getting at them. It would be wrong to make life more tolerable for them. Their lives ought to be made so intolerable as to drive them to abandon their vices.

It's no wonder then that *obscenity* was one of the charges that was "most frequently used against queer people, along with sodomy, masquerade, and disorderly conduct."

Henry denied that anything in *Friendship and Freedom* could be construed as lewd, but the judge couldn't have cared less. The fact that the first issue of *Friendship and Freedom* included an article on Oscar Wilde, whose life of "gross indecency" continued to upset most conservative people even thirty years after his conviction, was enough for the judge to consider the magazine offensive on the face of it.

The judge called for a continuation. They would meet again the following Thursday. He adjourned the trial with a swift bang of his gavel against his bench, and the authorities led Henry and the three others out of the courtroom and into a black Maria that transported them to the Cook County Jail. He and Meininger shared a cell, but Graves was jailed in the section reserved for African Americans. Overwhelmed with guilt over having gotten himself and

---

* *Invert* was another term for *homosexual*, and *inversion* for *homosexuality*.

his friends into legal trouble, Meininger broke down and, once he composed himself, told Henry how they came to be arrested.

When the police arrived at his apartment, they found him with George, whom he had picked up, and took both into custody. While searching the place, they ran across a copy of *Friendship and Freedom* and confiscated it. George wilted under police questioning at the station and admitted to having sex with Meininger, and then as he was being questioned, Meininger confessed to having sex with men and explained the purpose of the Society for Human Rights and *Friendship and Freedom*. He gave them Henry's new Oak Street address.

Henry was so angry at Meininger that he refused to speak to him and began chatting with one of the prisoners in the next cell who recommended a "'shyster' lawyer" who specialized in "doubtful cases" and would be able to get Henry out on bond. He phoned the lawyer, who agreed to represent him and suggested that they meet the next morning when he would counsel Henry on his rights and the strategy that his defense would take.

The following Thursday, July 16, the four men appeared with their lawyer before the same judge, and this time, inspectors from the post office showed up to testify against them. As the four prisoners and their lawyer waited for the judge to appear, one of the inspectors whispered to Henry that "he would see to it" the four "got heavy prison sentences for infecting God's own country" with their perversion.

Once the judge appeared and the trial began, Henry's lawyer, who was primed for a fight, demanded that the judge release the prisoners because of the flimsy evidence against them. Not to be confronted by a defense lawyer, the judge told him to "shut up or be cited for contempt," and the lawyer backed down, his tail between his legs. More submissive now, he asked the judge to release the four men on bail. He agreed to and set the bail amount at $1,000. The judge adjourned the proceedings almost as soon as it had begun, scheduling a continuance four days later.

Finally released on bail after five days behind bars, Henry headed straight to the Lake View post office. He wanted to get back to work and to put the mess he was in as far behind him as possible—for the time being, anyway. Unfortunately, Hickey greeted him with bad news. The postal inspectors had notified Frank Galbraith about Henry's arrest and homosexuality, and Galbraith unofficially ordered Hickey to suspend him. In a huff over his suspension, Henry charged over to the editorial offices of the *Chicago Evening American* and demanded that the editor retract the story because of the fabrications in it. The editor promised to but didn't follow through. Henry wanted to sue the newspaper, but he had spent a large amount of his savings on the lawyer and didn't have the funds. The postal inspectors had notified US Assistant Postmaster General John Bartlett in Washington, DC, about the hearing, and on Friday, July 17, at 8:44 PM he sent a telegram to Chicago's postmaster, Arthur C. Lueder. He didn't mince words: "Suspension without pay Henry Gerber authorized pending final action." Henry's suspension was official, and the cards were finally, irrevocably stacked against him.

In the meantime, one of Henry's friends took it upon himself to contact a different lawyer. The new attorney charged Henry the same amount as the first one, but he had a better reputation and more political clout in Chicago. When they met to discuss the case, the new attorney told Henry not to worry about his next court appearance because "everything had been 'arranged' satisfactorily." As it turned out, he told Henry the truth. He had pulled some strings, and when the four men went to their third hearing, on Monday, July 20, they were surprised to find themselves in front of a new judge. They were in luck. The talk on the street, Henry later learned, was that the second judge was a "queer himself."

No sooner had the proceedings begun than the new judge chided the prosecuting attorney for ignoring the law of the land and bringing to court someone who had been arrested without a warrant. He ordered the postal inspectors to return Henry's confiscated property and promptly dismissed the case.

The prosecuting attorney stopped Henry as he tried to slip out of the courtroom and admitted, "I had nothing on you, but the boy who had been rooming with the preacher had confessed to having sex with him." He had confused Graves and Meininger. Nevertheless, Henry, who had been confounded when the detective who barged into his room and demanded to know where Henry's boy was, now understood what the detective meant. He had assumed that, like Meininger, Henry would be in bed with a teenager when he knocked on Henry's door. The prosecutor wasn't the only one to corner Henry before he could leave. The arresting detective demanded to know, "What was the idea of the Society for Human Rights anyway? Was it to give you birds the legal right to rape every boy on the street?" Henry shoved past him without replying.

Henry's new lawyer had also worked behind the scenes to get the commissioner to agree not to charge the men with sending obscene materials through the mail. Everything had been taken care of as far as the legal issues were concerned, and so for the next few weeks, Henry tried to take "life easy" and recuperate "from the mental shock of having been in the clutches of such Unholy Inquisition." Despite the judge's order, the only thing the authorities returned to Henry was his typewriter. His diaries and all the files of the Society for Human Rights disappeared, either lost or destroyed.* He was also waiting to hear word from the post office about whether he would be allowed to return to his post office job.

The days passed by at a snail's pace and became weeks with nothing for Henry to do but run Meininger's betrayal of him over and over in his mind. He had visited Meininger only once, long before the arrest, and was under the impression that the society's vice president lived alone in a single room as so many of the other men he knew did, but besides the room where he entertained men, Meininger rented an apartment for his family. Henry thought the woman whom he had noticed in the hall was Meininger's neighbor, not his wife, and didn't give her a second thought.

As far as Henry was concerned, Meininger had gotten him "mixed up in . . . stupid bitches' affairs," and that "bitch's indiscretion" had dragged the Society for Human Rights "into the dirt." Making the embarrassing and destructive episode even worse for Henry was the fact that he had spent virtually every cent he had saved on lawyers to represent him as well as the others, including Meininger and his pickup, George. Making matters worse, Meininger pleaded guilty to disorderly conduct because he had been caught red-handed with George and was fined ten dollars. Because he didn't have a cent to his name, Henry even paid that.

But Henry had to face one last indignity. Once the other members of the Society for Human Rights learned that Henry had been arrested, they vanished without a trace. They were "only interested in getting as many pieces of trade as possible and [had] no solidarity or interest in helping others." He was bewildered that the very same people he had hoped to help turned their backs on him.

Regardless of how angry he was at others, he was angrier at himself. He had misjudged the situation. He thought the nine would be enough to work to repeal the antisodomy laws. They weren't. He had underestimated the fear that the very people he had hoped to help lived with day after day. It was a monolith

---

* Historian S. Chris Hagin contacted the Chicago post office in 1983 hoping to locate information on Henry's confiscated property and was told that in the 1970s it had destroyed its old records. I tried to get copies of Henry's case from both the Chicago Post Office and the Chicago Police Department through Freedom of Information Act requests and learned the same thing.

in their lives that he somehow hadn't taken seriously enough. He had also been blind to the fact that for an organization of any sort to succeed it needed a substantial budget. Most of the men who had joined the Society for Human Rights weren't employed or, if they were, their salaries hovered at the subsistence level.

On August 10, two weeks after the judge dismissed the case against Henry, Bartlett wrote Chicago postmaster Arthur C. Lueder again. He explained that the postal inspectors who testified at Henry's trial reported the trial's proceedings to him. He determined that "Mr. Gerber is not a suitable person for retention in the service" and "authorized" Lueder to fire him "for conduct unbecoming a postal employee . . . effective August 13, 1925." He reminded Lueder to be sure to let Henry know about his firing in writing.

As far as Henry was concerned, the straw that broke the camel's back was Lueder's letter to him. He had been fired because he was a homosexual, as the communication from Bartett and others made clear, and in the minds of Bartlett, Galbraith, and Lueder, he was guilty of unimaginable perversions. Despite his near-perfect job evaluations, he lost his livelihood. Worst of all, he had fallen victim to the very indictment that he hoped the Society of Human Rights would end.

That same day, Henry replied to Lueder's letter. He mentioned that although he had lived on Crilly Court when he was first hired, he had then moved to Oak Street, the last address the post office would have had for him in its records. He had just moved again, this time to room 374 of the Lexington Hotel at Twenty-Second Street and Michigan Avenue, and he could be contacted there. He also reported that he had lost his ID badge. He kept his letter professional and brief and neither complained about nor objected to his dismissal.

The Lexington Hotel became infamous when Al Capone set up his headquarters there and, a short time after that, was converted into a brothel, but Henry didn't stay there long enough to learn about either. He was officially unemployed now and virtually penniless, because someone he trusted had lied to him. Full of optimism and hope when he left the army in 1923, cynicism settled on him almost overnight. By September 8, he had moved back into the Meixners' home, his safety net.

The fiasco of the Society for Human Rights—Meininger's blatant lie, the disloyalty of the other members of the group, the apathy of the gay men in general, and the underhandedness of the police and officers of the court— haunted and soured the thirty-three-year-old Henry for the rest of his life.

PART II

NEW YORK

5 | "WHICH WAY DO YOU TAKE IT, AND FOR HOW MUCH?"

HENRY HAD HAD IT WITH CHICAGO. He was angry with everyone and everything there, but mostly, he was angry with himself. What was he thinking by "picking up fairies on the street" and making them "presidents or vice-presidents?"— a reference to Graves and Meininger. He made up his mind to pack his bags and get as far away from Chicago as possible. The question he faced now was *Where?*

He had gotten used to the freedom that he had when he lived on Crilly Court and then when he lived in the middle of the gay mecca when he rented on Oak Street. Gay men were accepted there, could be themselves, and could find sexual companions at the drop of a hat. Now that the pansy craze had taken hold across the nation, other large cities would certainly afford him the same sort of liberty and advantages.

San Francisco had been a wide-open city for many decades. He was there nine years earlier, when he was hospitalized at Letterman General, but all he had seen of the City by the Bay was his hospital room and the halls that ran from one ward to the next. In those days, Henry was still naive about homosexuality in general and, more specifically, where to go to meet men. San Francisco had the Black Cat Café, where men could enjoy pansy acts and drag queen performances or pick up male prostitutes; the Presidio, where men cruised each other and male prostitutes loitered; and other places where gay men congregated. Washington, DC, offered its own allures. He had stayed there for a few months after he left the army in 1923. He had lost his naïveté by then, and it hadn't taken him long to learn about Lafayette Square, where he met younger, good-looking men like Carter Bealer, and the movie houses on

Ninth, Fifteenth, and F Streets, where he found scores of available and eager sex partners. Despite his attraction to both San Francisco and Washington, DC—as well as Boston, Philadelphia, Los Angeles, St. Louis, New Orleans, and dozens of other cities, all of which had a thriving and relatively visible gay community—he finally came to a decision. His new home would be New York.

The largest city in the United States, New York abounded with the type of cruising spots that Henry fancied. One of the most favored by gay men was Central Park, where, as historian George Chauncey reported, "In the 1920s, so many met on the open lawn at the north end of the Ramble" to pick one another up "that they nicknamed it the Fruited Plain." Washington Square Park was another very active cruising site, especially along its western perimeter, which the locals nicknamed the "meat rack." Riverside Park was yet another, serving as a headquarters for sailors and their admirers. Union Square, a fourth, was very popular. A fifth was Forty-Second Street in Times Square. There were many more. Henry was sure he would have no problem satisfying his penchant for cruising parks and picking up men.

In addition to all the advantages that New York offered him, a friend from his stint in Coblenz, Alva Lee McDonald, lived in Brooklyn with his wife and child. He and Henry had kept in touch, and McDonald assured him that he would do what he could to help pave the way for him, including helping him to find a job. In fact, he already had a lead on one that would be perfect for Henry.

Six years earlier, McDonald boarded the USAT *Northern Pacific*. He was headed to Camp Meade in Maryland with scores of other new recruits. Shortly after a brief stint there, he transferred to Coblenz and wound up in the *Amaroc*'s offices, where he became a reporter and where he and Henry became friends.

McDonald was something of a go-getter, and he hit the ground running. No sooner had he arrived in Coblenz than he began networking, making himself known around the base. He helped found the first American Legion chapter in Germany and became a member of its executive committee, as well as a member of the board of directors of the Sergeant's Club and the official historian of the post. However, his interests weren't confined to the base. Despite the army's injunction against fraternizing with the locals, McDonald met a Fräulein, Marie Christine "Carma" Hecht who lived in Coblenz, and they were married on June 3, 1922. He was forty-four years old. She was twenty-seven.

They had a son who was born at the Augusta Maternity House in Coblenz shortly before the army began to withdraw its forces from Germany. It's apparent that he enjoyed his time on the staff of the *Amaroc News* and with the American Army of Occupation in general because he named his son Don Amaroc McDonald. He was one of the soldiers who wasn't exactly looking forward to returning to the States. Like many other doughboys who had married Germans, he was concerned about the prejudice his war bride and newborn son might face.

McDonald and his family boarded the USAT *St. Mihiel* on January 25, 1923, along with thousands of other soldiers, scores of whom also had families with them, and at 5:00 PM the *St. Mihiel* raised anchor and set sail. The McDonalds were bound for Savannah, Georgia, and from there the army transported them to Fort Moultrie, in Charleston, South Carolina, where they lived for a few months. By September McDonald received new orders. He and his family transferred to New York where, with his background on the *Amaroc News*, he began working on the staff of the *Recruiting News*, a magazine published by the US Army Recruiting Publicity Bureau, as a feature writer. His first article for the magazine, "Dan, the Old Timer," a short personality piece, appeared the following month.

A heatwave ravaged New York that June, but by the time Henry stepped off the train at Penn Station in September, the weather had made a complete turnaround. The temperature had dropped significantly, some thirty degrees, into the midsixties, and as the days turned into weeks and the weeks into months, autumn would be one of the coldest in New York's history. The winter would be even worse, with highs in the teens and lows in the single digits for weeks on end. Such frigid weather might have kept someone less determined to resume his sex life at home and out of the cold, instead of cruising the parks and avenues, but not Henry. After all, he had found an amiable young man in Bughouse Square one winter's night only a few years earlier, and a little cold wasn't going to stop him.

Once Henry arrived, deciding where he would live was relatively straightforward. As he had done several times in the past, he gravitated to the district where a large number of German immigrants had settled, this time in Kleindeutschland (Little Germany), a neighborhood on the Lower East Side. The area had long been the center of German immigrants' lives, although by the time Henry arrived, many of them had left the neighborhood, pushed out by an influx of Jewish immigrants. Being among other Germans suited him, and the neighborhood was as cheap a place to live as anywhere in Manhattan. He found a room to his liking at 116 East Eleventh Street.

Making his new digs even more attractive to him, Henry would live on the doorstep of Fourteenth Street, one of the city's popular strips for cruising. As early as the 1890s, "East Fourteenth Street between Third Avenue and Union Square was one of the preeminent centers of working-class gay life and of homosexual street activity in the city" and had been dubbed "the Rialto." It remained the principal cruising spot for men interested in male prostitutes until Times Square stole that distinction from it in the late 1920s. Henry found Fourteenth Street, a short three-block walk from his room, very inviting, and it took him no time at all to get settled into his new place and begin cruising there.

Alva McDonald was a godsend. Henry was eager to get his derailed life back on track, and when McDonald invited him to his apartment in a brownstone at 1166 Dean Street, Henry was eager to drop by. McDonald told Henry the Recruiting Publicity Bureau needed Henry's proofreading expertise and offered to introduce him to the man in charge. Henry had enjoyed his work proofreading the *Amaroc News*, a skill that few had, and he was excited over the prospect of working in publishing again. True to his word, McDonald gave copies of Henry's recommendations, including one from Julian Claff, to the colonel and introduced the two a few days later. The colonel wanted to hire Henry on the spot, but his hands were tied. Every man on the staff of the Recruiting Publicity Bureau had to be in the army. He couldn't hire Henry unless he reenlisted. Henry wasn't going to let something so inconsequential get in his way, and so he hurried to the US Army Recruiting Station and signed up for another stint. He began work at the Recruiting Publicity Bureau almost immediately.

The bureau was the brainchild of Major A. G. Rudd, who became its first director. Headquartered in the Army Building at 39 Whitehall Street, which also housed the recruiting station, the bureau was initially organized to disseminate news pertaining to soldiers and army life, but it quickly evolved into a department dedicated to recruiting exclusively. Rudd wanted to hire soldiers who had experience working on newspapers, but finding them was difficult. When Henry joined the staff of the Recruiting Publicity Bureau, he became the third soldier in its offices whose background included time on the *Amaroc News*. Besides McDonald, the trio included Cedric R. Worth. Like McDonald, Worth joined the bureau shortly after returning stateside.

Henry continued to live on East Eleventh Street until the end of 1925, when he packed up and moved north to 144 East Thirty-Fourth Street, on the southernmost boundary of Murray Hill. From there, Henry had an easy walk to the New York Public Library at Fifth Avenue and Forty-Second Street. He spent hours working on his own projects in the library when he wasn't proofreading others' work at the bureau. He had always had an interest in writing, and after he published his letter "Are Indecent Shows Realistic?" in the *Chicago Daily Tribune*, he was hooked and began writing short essays on a variety of topics. When he wasn't in the library's stately reading room, he followed his other interests nearby. Bryant Park, another popular place to cruise, was adjacent to the library, and a few blocks farther north lay Times Square.

"Times Square," as historian George Chauncey pointed out, was "one of the city's most significant centers of male prostitution," as well as one of Henry's favorite cruising sites. It drew two distinctly different types of male prostitutes. One was composed of "well-dressed, 'mannered' and gay-identified hustlers serving a middle-class gay-identified clientele" who "met their customers as the latter left the theater and walked home on the west side of Fifth Avenue from Fifty-second to Fifty-ninth Streets." The second group, the "effeminate (but not transvestite) 'fairy,'" or pansy, "sold sexual services to other gay men and to men who identified themselves as 'normal'" and could be found along 42nd Street between Fifth and Eighth avenues.

Despite the liberty the pansy craze afforded gay men in New York, or perhaps because of it, not everyone was happy about them overrunning Times Square or their visibility throughout Manhattan. Police charged 238 men with "homosexual solicitation" in 1918, but the number of arrests nearly tripled, "to over 750," by 1920 and "averaged round 500" annually during the pansy craze.

On February 4, 1923, the police cracked down on homosexuality in Greenwich Village. "Every tearoom and cabaret," the *New York Times* reported, "was visited" by a "party of ten detectives" who took "what they thought were five women and eight men" in custody. As it turned out, "one of the 'women' was a man who was "familiarly known . . . as 'Ruby'" and was "charged . . . with 'disorderly conduct for giving what police termed an indecent dance.'"

Claiming to speak on behalf of many theatergoers, the *Brevities*,* one of New York's bestselling, weekly scandal rags, began to complain loudly about the "impudent sissies that clutter Times Square." To attract readers to its many other

* The *Brevities* was alternately known as the *Broadway Brevities*, the *Broadway Brevities and Society Gossip*, and the *New Broadway Brevities* during its fourteen-year history.

articles in which writers shook their fingers at the Big Apple's homosexuals, the editor of the *Brevities* streamed lavish, extravagant headlines across its pages using ambiguous words and phrases loaded with assonance and consonance. Sexy Sailors Blow! one bawled, and added in a smaller font, "Bawdy Boys Run Riot on High Seas as Fags Stir Emotion of Rollicking Rover; Gay Decks Reek with Lust When Briny Deep Bohunks Practice Funny Business." Others bellowed, Fag Balls Exposed, calling attention to a gay masquerade ball, and Pansies Blow U.S., which described a supposed mass exodus of them to Europe.

Its salacious headlines weren't the tabloid's only draw. Homophobic articles, even more lewd than the headlines, that were published virtually every week helped to rev up sales. In January of the year before Henry arrived in New York, for example, it published the first installment of a "thirteen-part series, 'A Night in Fairy-land,' an exposé of gay and lesbian nightlife in Manhattan" that was a succession of "sensational articles" using "lurid" descriptions of gay men's "pick-up rituals."

The *Brevities'* fare wasn't limited to the written word. It also published dozens of cartoons making fun of the pansy.

To help fill its coffers, the *Brevities* also ran ads for novels dealing with gay life, such as the anonymously penned *Confessions of a "Pansy"*:

> Tear off an hour, sink into an armchair, grab-a-hold of "Confessions of a Pansy," and forget your culture. It takes you right into Pansy-land. Read of the unbelievable activities at Pansy Parties, Drags, etc. Their degenerate actions and methods frankly exposed. The ins and out of their queer practices related in startling understandable language. Their code of morals and inhibitions that they guard so zealously, exposed in PLAIN words. Enter Pansyland in all its delight-ful and frightful orgies. Darn right, we'll send it in a plain wrapper.

The *Brevities* even ran a series of so-called confessions by a variety of underworld characters, including "The Fag." Caught "red-handed with a lad" from the neighborhood when he was fifteen, the Fag admitted that his "old man gave" him "a good tanning, and a few weeks later" he "ran away from home and beat" his "way to New York"—an age-old story. At last, he found happiness in the Big Apple. "The pickings are perfectly glorious here," he admitted because he didn't have any "trouble selecting" his "sweeties, and are

The *Brevities*, a tabloid in New York (1916–1925), published a series of sensationalized articles purportedly about gay nightlife entitled "Nights in Fairy-Land" that stoked homophobia even as it revealed gay life and culture. This cartoon is from the September 1924 issue. *Author's collection*

they nice!" The week before "The Fag" appeared, *Brevities* had featured a female prostitute's account of her life, and the week after, a murderer's.

Even as the *Brevities* described queer life in Manhattan, Times Square, where many of its titillating and misleading articles were set, quickly became one of Henry's favorite cruising spots. He was "always sure" to find "a ringer and not a dud" there, and because so many of the men congregating on the sidewalks were prostitutes, it was "safe to walk up to anyone and say: 'Which way do YOU take it, and for how much?'" Henry wasn't interested in picking up pansies or effeminate men who, he thought, were "usually psychopathic individuals" but preferred straight-acting, younger men. For Henry, "anyone over 22 or 23—at most 25" was "entirely out of question," and he was never "the passive type" during sex.

SWISH!

"Oh, isn't there some mistake?"
"Sez you."

From the *Broadway Brevities* (June 6, 1932), one of the many cartoons that appeared in tabloids during the 1920s and '30s that poked fun of the "pansy." *Author's collection*

Henry began keeping a diary again to take the place of the old one that the detective who arrested him in his room on Oak Street confiscated, and in it, he kept a record of his sexual exploits. He claimed that he experienced an average number of "about 4" orgasms "a week." While taking full advantage of being close to Bryant Park and Times Square, Henry also hired a "string of 'prostitutes'" and scheduled them to show up at his place on "certain days of the week and parties* would ensue. Henry had a hearty, abundant sex life, and yet he hoped that he would one day find his perfect, elusive mate. All the men he met were "too self-centered" to be someone he might settle down with, and

---

* *Party* was gay slang for a sexual encounter.

besides, they were only interested in a quick, "purely physical" time with him. He didn't delude himself into believing that cruising or male prostitutes offered him anything more than sexual gratification, either, or that he should be embarrassed over it. The ultimate pragmatist, he was realistic about his situation:

> There are thousands of boys in New York who make a living by peddling their bodies, just as their heterosexual sisters. After all, when you buy your meals in a restaurant you do not consider it a shame for the chef to sell his meat; and all you care is to see that your hash is well browned and the potatoes French fried if that be your speciality [*sic*].

Henry's humor shines brightly in such ambiguous language he employed to hide his real meaning. He used *meat* for "penis," *browned* for "anal intercourse," and *French* for "oral sex"—all slang terms that gay men in New York, Chicago, San Francisco, and most other large US cities would have known.

By the time Henry joined the bureau's staff, Rudd had moved its offices to Governors Island in Upper New York Bay between Battery Park in Manhattan and Brooklyn. The island had been a military prison with offices, warehouses, barracks for its soldiers, and homes for the officers and their families, but many of the buildings needed to be modernized or torn down and replaced with new ones. Rudd began renovating the island's base in the mid-1920s, which included adding new barracks. Those that had been built right after the Civil War had fallen into dilapidation. He added a new public school as well as a YMCA, a movie theater, and a club restricted to officers.

With his experience with the mail in Chicago and proofreading for the *Amaroc News*, Henry's new position at the Bureau was a good fit, but Henry didn't just spend his days reading the proofs of the *Recruiting News* or news releases. The bureau published posters, some using original artwork, others incorporating black-and-white photos, but all captioned with at least a few words. The bureau's most recognizable one showed Uncle Sam pointing directly at the viewer with the caption. "I want you for the U.S. Army. Enlist now." The image was original art by James Montgomery Flagg, and it was one of the many items Henry approved before it went into production.

In his second year at the Recruiting Publicity Bureau, the *Amaroc News'* editor gave Henry the opportunity to write for the bureau's weekly magazine. His article "The Evolution of the Army Ration" appeared in the July 1, 1927,

Gerber, second from right, worked at the Recruiting Publicity Bureau for two decades. Besides his official role as proofreader there, he headed a correspondence club, Contacts, and produced *Commentary* and *Chanticleer*, two of the club's publications, using government equipment and supplies. *Stanley J. Grogan, "Army Publicity and the People: The Chief of the Army Information Service Explains the Function of the Department," Recruiting News, December 15, 1931, 14*

issue of the *United States Army Recruiting News*. That year, President Calvin Coolidge authorized a much-needed upgrading in soldiers' rations, and Henry's article was meant to draw attention to the soldiers' good fortune. Tracing the changes in the rations that the US Army provided its troops didn't come close to the subject he typically wrote about—the repression of sex, especially homosexuality, in the United States—but he rolled up his sleeves and got to work. It's obvious from the details he wove into the narrative that he used the New York Public Library for much of the information in the article.

Beginning with the "old theory that only a man fed on rum and meat would make an ideal defender of his country," Henry outlined the slow evolution of rations from the post-Revolutionary days, when the army commanders allotted each soldier "the straw upon which he slept and the candle with which he found his way after taps" as well as "one pound of bread or flour, one pound of beef or three-quarters of a pound of pork and a gill of rum." The article was the most public of all his contributions to the *Recruiting News*, although he slipped a tidbit to Roy Humphries, the writer/artist of its Did You Know That— column, a weekly composite of illustrated trivia. Henry told him that

"Frederick the Great, King of Prussia, searched the world for the tallest men for his bodyguard." During his time with the American Army of Occupation in Coblenz, likely during his sorties to Hirschfeld's institute, Henry learned that the Prussian king was a homosexual, and he knew why Frederick had sought out towering men to surround himself. He must have chuckled to himself, knowing that, with his tiny contribution to Did You Know That—, he had pulled one over on the army, gave the gay monarch some publicity, and signaled to gay readers—mostly soldiers—that one of their kind worked for the *Recruiting News*.

Henry's article on army rations wasn't the only piece he wrote, but it was the only one to be published. He had sent essays and letters to the editors of many of the more important newspapers and magazines in the United States, only to be met with silence or a rejection slip. It didn't take him long to realize that he was wasting his time with American publications, and he began to submit his essays to Radszuweit's *Blätter für Menschenrecht*. Unlike his American counterparts, Radszuweit accepted Henry and his views with wide-open arms.

Henry's first German publication came in the magazine's October 1928 issue. In his "Englische Heuchelei," Henry renounced the English critics who attacked Radclyffe Hall's *The Well of Loneliness*. The following year, his "Die Strafbestimmungen in den 48 Staaten Amerikas und den amerikanischen Territorien für gewisse Geschlechtsakte" appeared in the same journal. In it, he examined the antisodomy laws throughout the United States to show how inconsistent they were. In 1930 his exposé about the penalties men faced when convicted of same-sex sexual activities in the United States, "Zwei Dollars oder fünfzehn Jahre Zuchthaus," appeared in *Das Freundschaftsblatt*, another of Radszuweit's publications.

Henry couldn't have been happier that he had found a home for his work in the German magazines published by one of the principal leaders of Germany's gay liberation movement. With a circulation of "over 50,000 copies," *Blätter für Menschenrecht* had a huge readership, and being among its contributors not only put Henry in the spotlight of an important pro-homosexual group but also gave him an international audience.

Then, in 1932, after waiting for a breakthrough in his writing career, Henry struck it rich, or so he believed. The editor of the *Modern Thinker* published Henry's long essay—nearly ten printed pages—"In Defense of Homosexuality." He had written it in response to W. Béran Wolfe's "The Riddle of

Homosexuality," which appeared in the magazine's April issue. Wolfe believed that homosexuals could be cured through psychotherapy, but Henry saw it as only one more way in which homosexuals could be persecuted.

With his psychoanalytical perspective, Wolfe had argued that by engaging in sex with other men, homosexuals could dodge the responsibilities of heterosexuality and, consequently, labeled homosexuality a neurosis. Henry argued back that the extraordinary stress under which homosexuals lived, which was created by living in a society that punished them for being themselves, created their anxiety. He wondered,

> What heterosexual would not turn highly neurotic were his mode of love marked "criminal" were he liable to be pulled into prison every time he wanted to satisfy his sex urge—not to speak of the dangers of being at all times exposed to blackmail by heterosexuals who prey upon him, and the ostracism of society? Were he not clever in pretending to be "normal," he would lose his place of employment quickly. This constant insecurity and danger from all sides would drive anyone into any number of neuroses.

Despite the obstacles and dangers that they faced, Henry was certain that the typical homosexual wasn't at all interested in a cure and simply wanted to be left alone to enjoy life as much as possible.

Henry tackled many of the then-important theories about homosexuality, including the belief that it was caused "by social conditions" or "determined by 'early childhood experiences,'" by "the segregation of the sexes" in schools or in "the army, navy, labor and prison camps," and by "masturbation." He ridiculed the idea that men chose to be homosexual, a prescient stand to take in the 1930s.

Published in 1932 as the country was sinking further and further into the Great Depression and when gay men could be imprisoned in New York City for as long as twenty years and lose family, friends, jobs, and social standing simply because they were homosexual, Henry's essay was revolutionary. Publishing it, even in a liberal magazine like the *Modern Thinker*, was extraordinarily brave, but Henry wasn't about to lose his freedom and everything he had worked for. He pseudonymously signed his article "Parisex," a word that, at the time, suggested an individual who enjoyed sex without wanting to reproduce, and hoped that none of the magazine's staff would snitch on him to the Dr. Wolfes of the world.

Visionary, revolutionary, and brave, Henry had a strong sense of humor that was evident in much of his writings, all sharp and reserved, never sloppy or slapstick. He was fond of intelligent conversation, reading, and classical music, characteristics which he also sought in his friends. An introvert, he had never gone in for the type of nightlife that so many other gay men craved: the cabaret shows, the speakeasies, or the drag balls. He described "solitude" as "the greatest blessing of man," adding he could "get along without 'friends'" and preferred "to be alone rather than waste my time with morons who have nothing to say and only have learned a few phrases, such as 'You said it,' 'You are damd [sic] right,' 'Search me.'" His nightlife was private, quiet, and often revolved around those places where he could meet potential bedmates. Henry spent the next two years commuting from his place at 144 East Thirty-Fourth Street in Manhattan to his nine-to-five on Governors Island and, on various nights, cruising for sex in any part of town where he heard that men roamed.

In the meantime, Major Rudd's plan to modernize the base was nearly complete, including the new barracks. Named Liggett Hall, it opened in November 1929 and provided the soldiers stationed on the island with "three square meals a day" and a "comfortable, healthful home." They had access to the base's YMCA, its pool, and a movie theater. Henry knew firsthand one other aspect of living in the barracks on Governors Island that recruiting officers never mentioned in their spiels: over 1,300 men, most of them young and many handsome, would be living there. Some would be gay or, at least, they would be open to one relieving them of their pent-up sexual energy. Historian Jim Kepner discovered that one of Henry's roommates in Liggett Hall was a man "younger" than Henry "who may not have been Gay but who was at least familiar with the subject." It's unknown if they were sexually or romantically involved with one another.

When he reenlisted in 1925 to work at the Recruiting Publicity Bureau, Henry received medical and dental insurance, steady employment with punctual and consistent paychecks even if he were put on sick leave, and clothing (sets of uniforms) to wear during the days he was on the base. Once construction on Liggett Hall was completed, Henry considered moving in. Living there would add room and board, a considerable savings, to his other benefits. His only other expenses would be the ferry and subway fare to and from Manhattan; the cost of occasional meals at restaurants, a show, or a concert; or the few dollars that the men he picked up in Times Square would charge him for sex.

It didn't take him long to make up his mind—and not simply because of what living in the barracks offered, but also because of the financial disaster that had just befallen the country. On Thursday, October 24, 1929, the stock market took a nosedive, and within five days Wall Street collapsed. As the economy tanked, the United States fell headlong into the Great Depression.

The "overconfidence in stock market investments during the Roaring Twenties" had "created an unsustainable asset bubble" that burst that Thursday. The sudden shift from, in the Roaring Twenties, a decade of affluence in which economic growth was at an all-time high to a decade of poverty and blight was overwhelming for most Americans. "Wages fell 42%" as "unemployment rose to 25%" and "more than 11 million people" lost their jobs.

The effect of the crash spread worldwide. In Germany, for example, the economic crash devastated the gay rights movement. Despite Hirschfeld's and like-minded activists' long struggle to get Paragraph 175 rescinded, it remained in place. Fortunately for Henry, the crash had little, if any, effect on his life. His salary was fixed at $21 a month ($350 in today's currency), most of which he was able to save.

Liggett Hall had just opened in time for him to move in, and Henry packed his clothes and possessions again, the third time since leaving Chicago. Living in the barracks wasn't exactly "comfortable" or even "healthful," as the recruiters always promised, but "stark and functional." By the end of November, the weather turned frigid, but the freezing weather barely registered with Henry. As far as he was concerned, the bitter winter and the austere and practical accommodations were fine. The huge influx of young soldiers moving into the barracks with him brightened and warmed up his life tremendously.

In 1928 or '29 Henry joined a correspondence club, Contacts, which had been organized by Merlin Wand—his real name, not a pseudonym—who lived in a small town in Pennsylvania.* Correspondence clubs, also known as pen pal clubs, had a long history, evolving from what were initially called

---

* Wand's sexual orientation is unknown, but as census reports reveal, he was married with two children, a boy and a girl.

matrimonial clubs that helped men and women find a mate with the objective of marriage. By the early twentieth century, they developed into requests for correspondents who were interested in friendship or romance and even sexual encounters, but not necessarily marriage. They were very similar to the personal ads that Henry found in *Der Eigene* and other German homophile magazines.

Like other correspondence club directors, Wand distributed lists of new and renewing members' self-descriptions to all members on a regular basis, typically monthly. Wand assigned each member a number, and those who received a list could write to another member by sending a letter to them in a sealed envelope addressed to the other member's identification number and putting the sealed envelope into another one addressed to Wand. Wand then mailed the letter to the designated member, who responded or ignored it as he or she saw fit. In any event, Wand and the other directors wouldn't know if they were corresponding or, if they were, what the two discussed. Such machinations were necessary to keep the director safe from prosecution under the Comstock Act.

Potential members of Contacts filled out a form on which they identified their political allegiance; if they were particularly interested in art, literature, travel, etc.; and personal data, including their age, marital status, and occupation. They were invited to submit a brief self-description, revealing anything they wanted to about themselves or the individuals with whom they hoped to make contact. Wand published the descriptions of all new and renewing members in a monthly newsletter, *Commentary*. It also included a list of books members were willing to loan one another and, occasionally, brief articles and stories members had written.

Wand began Contacts in 1926 after he realized that his job as a chemist for the Radio Corporation of America (RCA) left him with a considerable amount of spare time on his hands. He founded it for

> those intellectuals who are mentally marooned, either in the hinterlands where culture and refinement of thought have not yet penetrated, or who are not able to find the right intellectual milieu in a big city where the methods of standardization have been applied also to the ideas of people, whose stereotyped, herd physiognomies make it an almost futile task to find mentally fit companions.

He ran ads for Contacts in the classified sections of various magazines and newspapers across the country, especially those, such as the *New Masses* and the newspaper *Haldeman-Julius Weekly*, that were published for socialists. Since the late nineteenth century, socialists had supported the homosexual rights in Europe and the United States, and many of the major gay sexologists, among them Edward Carpenter, Havelock Ellis, and John Addington Symonds, were socialists.

Wand's ad in the *New Masses*, for example, opened with the eye-catching headline CONTACT WITHOUT FRICTION! and read, "Are you mentally isolated? 'CONTACTS,' literary correspondence club, puts you in touch with versatile, unconventional minds. No formalities. Books loaned free to members. Membership fee. $2.00, year. Particulars free. (Stamp please). Write. MERLIN WAND, Manorville, Pa." *Versatile* and especially *unconventional* would have caught a gay man's attention. Many would have wondered if Contacts had a gay membership, and some even mailed the membership fee of two dollars to Wand in hopes of finding out. Henry was one of them.

Although his sex life was very satisfying, Henry joined Contacts hoping, like many of its members, to meet his ideal mate, but he had another reason. He had just formed the Army Correspondence Club. Henry's club was obviously meant to attract soldiers, and undoubtedly men in the other branches of the armed forces, as well as men who wanted to meet them. With the membership lists that Wand would send him, he planned to syphon at least a few of Contacts' members into his. He invited the men whose self-descriptions caught his eye, men who only wanted to correspond with other men or who used certain words or phrases that signaled, to those in the know, that they were gay, to join his club. Terms such as *art lover, interested in physique photography, broad-minded,* or any mention of homosexual writers, such as Whitman or Wilde; of gay artists, such as DaVinci; or of gay sexologists, such as Edward Carpenter, were dead giveaways. He even advertised it in *Reader's Digest.* To entice men to join, he offered free memberships initially, yet he wasn't even able to induce two dozen men to join. The few who did weren't enough to make it worth Henry's effort financially, and he disbanded the Army Correspondence Club a short time later.

Wand changed jobs in 1929 and almost immediately realized that his new position left him with virtually no time to devote to Contacts. He announced in *Commentary* that he had to discontinue the club and hoped one of its members would volunteer to take it on. Henry, who had begun saving a considerable amount of money by moving into Liggett Hall and had just decommissioned the Army Correspondence Club, "came to the rescue by volunteering to keep the club alive till someone could be found to carry on the work" permanently. He ran the club for only a few months when, in 1930, Stanley Altman stepped forward and took over as its director with Wand's blessings.

Altman lived in Albany, New York, and had just formed his own correspondence club, Pioneers, but he hadn't attracted many members. He combined the two and kept Contacts as its name, hoping that the original Contacts' reputation and its sizeable membership, enhanced by Pioneers' membership, would attract more members. He was wrong. By the end of the year, he was ready to call it quits. Henry believed Altman abandoned the club because he lost his job and the Great Depression was in full swing, but records show that, if Altman did lose his job in 1930, he quickly found another, working as an office clerk during the early years of the Depression.

When Altman announced his decision to terminate Contacts, a contingent of members who remembered Henry's successful tenure as the club's interim director asked him to return to its helm. At first, he wasn't sure he should, but he couldn't help but find the clamor for his return a bit flattering. After much hesitation, he finally agreed to manage Contacts again permanently. He didn't change a thing about the club, not even the motto Wand had created for it— "The Only Correspondence Club for the Mentally Marooned"—or its logo. It depicted a mysterious, wizard-like figure with the hood of the cape he wears pulled over his eyes and a grin, or grimace, on his lips. He leans over a globe that has been turned so that North America shows. One can only wonder if the figure was meant to depict Merlin the wizard in the Arthurian tales and served as a sort of totem for Merlin Wand.

Just in case the authorities caught wind of what at least some of the pen pal club members were up to, Henry didn't use his barracks address on anything associated with the club, not on *Commentary*, not on Contacts' letterhead, not on anything else. Instead, he rented a post office box at Cooper Station, often referred to as New York's D Station. He was covering his tracks and swore he was never going to be an easy target for the postal authorities again. If they wanted to drag him into a police station and lock him up as they had in 1925, they would have to work like the devil to find him.

Contacts' letterhead displayed a wizard-like figure looming over a globe, probably representing its founder Merlin Wand. Gerber continued to use the image on his stationery during his tenure as Contacts' director. *Courtesy of ONE Archives at the USC Libraries*

6 | "ESCAPE FROM THE BUGHOUSE OF THIS FAIRYTALE KULTUR!"

HENRY'S WORK AT THE BUREAU wasn't taxing and left him with more than enough time to devote to Contacts. He told members he wasn't making any profit from the club and that he used what he accrued from membership fees for expenses: "23%" went "for postage, 29% for advertising, 25% for office supplies and 23% for printing." Nevertheless, Henry wasn't on the up-and-up with them. They had no way of knowing that, because he worked at the bureau, he had access to the most up-to-date office equipment—"addressographs, graphotypes and mimeographs"—all the office supplies he needed, and even free franking. He even worked on Contacts in the bureau office, not in his room in Liggett Hall.

Henry's only actual expense was the cost for posting ads for it in some of the most widely read magazines of the day, among them *American Mercury*, *Saturday Review of Literature*, the *Nation*, and the *New Republic*. These charged more for ads than many others did, and Henry liked to brag that Contacts could afford to advertise in them, while less prominent groups such as the Mixers in Detroit, the Friendship Club in Spokane, and the Star Friendship Exchange of Virginia couldn't. He pocketed the membership fees that he didn't spend on advertising.

Under his direction, Contacts' membership exploded, or so he claimed. He reasoned that people interested in joining correspondence clubs wanted to be members of the largest ones possible. The more members a club had, the more chances they had in finding that special and elusive "ideal friend." His ads in the *Saturday Review of Literature* and the *American Mercury*, for

COMMENTARY

Published monthly by CONTACTS, correspondence club for the mentally isolated intellectuals, Box 91 Station D, New York City

Volume V No. 1   April, 1935   Commentary 67

Among Our Competitors

IT WOULD BE impossible, of course, to analyze here the thousands of correspondence clubs in this country. Generally, they are either plain matrimonial rackets, using the proverbial rich old widow as a bait; or clubs for stamp collectors and other fiends; or they are literary correspondence clubs. As far as the American Mercury, the Forum, and the American Spectator magazines are concerned, we have no competitors, for the smaller clubs could not afford such expensive ads.

The Saturday Review of Literature, the Nation, and the New Republic, are the only other mediums in which we advertise, and in these we find from time to time the following three clubs, which are competing with us:

    a) The Mixers, Detroit, Michigan, operated by Georgia Smith;
    b) The Friendship Club, of Spokane, Washington, also operated by a woman;
    c) The Star Friendship Exchange, in Richmond (or Roanoke) Virginia.

THE MIXERS saw the light of day only about a year ago. Unlike the other two clubs, Georgia Smith openly admits that in the year of the club's existence she has gained 70 members from an initial outlay in advertising of 70 cents. Her ads in a recent number of the Review were exactly seven words, which would indicate that the good lady is either a mystic or addicted to numerology. Perhaps her lucky seven will soon add another seven times seven members. But she is no longer advertising in the Review. Perhaps she finds that even 49 cents spent on ads is too costly. Her club is frequented by elderly men and women, mostly women. One of her special features is the chain-letter. 5 or 6 members make up a chain. One starts a letter and sends it to No.2 who adds her wisdom and then sends it on to No.3, until all members have added their say, when the voluminous chain is again returned to No 1 to make another circuit, etc. etc. One objection to that might be that the postage charges might in time become excessive. Georgia Smith, I am informed, also conducts a mental dude ranch or some sort of resort and the members are asked to board with her. The Mixers have recently raised their membership fee to keep alive in this cruel world of fierce competition. Compared to her 70 members for the last year, Contacts has enrolled 436.

THE FRIENDSHIP CLUB in Spokane, which I believe operated as U.S. Postal Friendship Club in the East some years ago, charging $1 for an address, has now come down to 5 addresses for a dollar. The addresses are "carefully selected to suit the demand of the member." The circular of this club, which came to my desk recently through one of our New York members who wrote for it, consists of a small multigraphed page full of high-sounding boloney about the pangs of "loneliness of spirit, mind and heart"—it does not mention the much more painful loneliness of the last dollar in our pocketbooks—. The word "marriage" is nowhere mentioned, but the fact that the application blank demands information as to height, weight, color of eyes, hair, complexion, nationality and religion, plainly shows that it is a scheme for matching up lonely spinsters or widows with equally lonely males who are unable to find a wife out of 60,000,000 females in the United States, or depend on the Friendship Club to make the "right selection."

Members of Contacts received *Commentary*, a monthly mimeographed bulletin, that included articles, lists of books members could borrow from other members, and the self-descriptions of new and renewing members. *Courtesy of ONE Archives at the USC Libraries* example, used eye-catching language and the club's steady growth to attract members:

> Surrounded by Millions of Cracked Brains, the products of our moron civilization! CONTACTS, correspondence club for the mentally isolated, connects you with over 1,000 debunked people. Free book exchange. Send 3¢ stamp for Prospectus 4C. Contacts, Box 91 Station D, New York City.
>
> "More Fun than the Theatre," writes a new member of CONTACTS, correspondence club for the intellectually isolated, with 1200 cultured members in all parts of the world. Uncommon books loaned free. Send 1¢ stamp for Prospectus E. Contacts, Box 91, Station D, New York City.
>
> "Not a Brain Cell in a carload of skulls." Is your human environment like this? CONTACTS connects the mentally marooned with over 1300 intelligent people, everywhere. Uncommon books loaned free. Send 3¢ stamp for literature. Contacts, Box 91, Station D, New York City.
>
> CONTACTS, an unusual correspondence club for unusual people, connects you with 1800 members the world over. Unusual books loaned free. Send 3¢ stamp. Contacts, Box 91, Station D, New York City.
>
> Are you without congenial contacts? Then the services of CONTACTS, the Clearing House of Friendship, will interest you. 2400 members enrolled since 1927. Write for free details. Contacts, Box 91, Station D, New York City.

The snappy copy that Henry wrote for the advertisements could have come from any of New York's public relations firms, and through it, his coded language spoke loud and clear to any gay man who happened to run across them. He began several, "Contacts, an *unusual* correspondence club for *unusual people*" (italics added). In the bodies of others, he mentioned that *Commentary*'s booklist offered members "unusual" and "uncommon" volumes to borrow. He used his favorite spiel over and over, daring potential members to "escape from the Bughouse of this fairytale kultur!"—or some minor variations of it. Using *bughouse* was an inside joke for Henry. Another term for *mental institution*, such as the one in which he had been confined, it also reminded him of Bug-house Square, his favorite cruising spot in Chicago.

It's very likely that, although the membership grew over the years, Henry greatly exaggerated it, and yet he maintained that he had no intention of turning the club into a "very large and nondescript" mega-organization that every Tom, Dick, and Harry could join. Instead, he wanted to fill it with "liberal and truly cultured members of the world's intellectual elite." At the same time, he was aware that the "very nature" of a correspondence club that was meant to appeal to a more-than-ordinarily intellectual element would necessarily exclude a "mass membership, for the masses generally shun all intellectual enterprises and are afraid to be different from and superior to their fellow morons." So he wasn't unduly concerned about its membership—except, of course, when it came to those men who were interested in contacting other men.

In the materials he sent to prospective members, Henry also claimed that local chapters of Contacts had sprung up in New York, Philadelphia, and other large cities, and he assured them that others were being formed all over the country. The chapters met "to exchange ideas, enjoy friendly chats, lectures, or musical or social entertainment." He offered to help anyone create their own chapter by putting them in touch with the "official representative of Contacts" who lived in their vicinity, but he was crystal clear that neither he nor Contacts was "officially connected" with any of the "local chapters." He was protecting himself from being arrested for any shenanigans that the chapter members were up to.

From the outset, he hoped that Contacts could become an important, if camouflaged, organization for gay men. Although not as altruistic in its goals as the Society for Human Rights, it would nevertheless provide them with a means of contacting one another, for exchanging ideas and information, and for supporting one another, which had been among his objectives with *Friendship and Freedom*. He was purposefully radicalizing a tradition that had been established decades before by other pen pal clubs, but the Comstock Act complicated matters.

Emboldened by the antiobscenity law, the postal authorities paid close attention to all correspondence clubs and resorted to underhanded means of corralling homosexuals. As historian John D'Emilio discovered, "Postal inspectors subscribed to pen pal clubs" and "initiated correspondence with men whom they suspected of being homosexual in order to obtain confirming evidence. Once confirmed, post office officials then placed tracers on the victim's mail in order to locate other homosexuals." Eventually, they arrested the victims of their snares.

The threat of the Comstock Act hung over Henry, and he did everything that he could to disguise Contacts as a matrimonial club by making sure he included a large number of women on his membership rolls. Their presence not only added a layer of camouflage to hide his homosexual members but also ensured that heterosexual men would join, adding a second layer of heterosexual respectability. He once quipped that he found "'normals' and 'perverts' peacefully laying down side by side in Contacts and the only friction that may be is no doubt carried on furiously in private letters," adding a sexually charged allusion to the biblical lion and lamb resting together peacefully.* Nevertheless, he was bothered by the game he had to play to keep the law off his back.

As was the practice with directors of other correspondence clubs, Henry assigned each member an identification number, and only he knew the identities of the members who had set out to correspond with others. When new members' self-descriptions arrived, he kept track of which male applicants seemed gay to him, and these became an "inner sanctum" of the club. "Probably a few men made homosexual contacts through 'Contacts,'" one of its former members recalled. Henry wrote to many of them himself and even shared the information with a select few. He told one of the members that "1744 and 2573 are allright," by which Henry meant they were homosexual, and "so are 1156 and 2389, 1925, 671." Members who were especially eager to find pen pals could even pay to have their self-descriptions run in several issues of *Commentary*, not just when they joined or renewed.

Certainly, sex was at the top of the list of what Contacts' gay, and most of its heterosexual, members were most interested in. It was at the top of Henry's list too. "To me," he said, "Contacts was a means of getting something *myself*. That it has helped others to find friends is very laudable." To identify other gay men, new and renewing Contacts members signaled their sexual orientation in their self-descriptions. A twenty-six-year-old Canadian, who was unmarried and made his living as an "art model," listed his interests as "posing, writing, nude art, equitism, biography, philosophy, sexology," while a forty-year-old

---

* In Isaiah 11:6 it's actually a leopard that lies down with a kid and a wolf that lives with a lamb.

bachelor, a "college teacher," included "inversion, music, literature, . . . psychology of the abnormal, theatre" in his and emphasized that he "preferred" contact with "male correspondents." Both men used coded words to indicate their homosexuality. Being an "art model" would have suggested that the Canadian posed in the nude, perhaps even enjoyed being naked in front of others, and to underscore the idea of male nudity, he included "posing" and "nude art" in his interests while his curiosity about "sexology" signaled his own homosexuality. Similarly, the professor's interest in "inversion," the "psychology of the abnormal," his hope for "male correspondents," and being a bachelor at forty years of age marked him as gay too. Contacts appealed to "quite a lot of men" who "subscribed with the idea of finding male friends interested in the same subjects as themselves," and many listed physique photographs and physique photography as one.

Magazines devoted to physical culture, an early term for *bodybuilding*, included black-and-white physique photographs in their pages to illustrate the results of exercise routines. Photographers who took and sold pictures of them advertised their wares in the back pages of the magazines, often marketing them as "anatomical studies" for "poor students of the arts who could not afford a live model" and were supposedly meant to express a "reflection of the Greek ideal" of "meticulously proportioned" men. Like the classical Greek and Roman statues that the models often imitated, they usually posed naked in the studio, although they might also wear posing straps during the session. As the photographer developed the film, he added a fig leaf or shadow to hide their genitals of those who posed nude or painted posing straps onto the actual pictures. Purchasers could easily flick off the painted-on straps with their fingernails. The models' nudity enhanced the eroticism of their muscularity, and physique photographs became collectibles among many homosexuals.

By the time Henry took over Contacts, physique photographs and magazines had become something of a mainstay in the homosexual subculture. As early as the 1880s, Eugen Sandow, considered the father of modern bodybuilding, began the tradition of bodybuilders posing nude for physical culture photographs. Sometimes he wore skintight boxers, but more often than not he posed nude with a fig leaf painted on later. He published them in a magazine he produced, *Sandow's Magazine of Physical Culture*, to illustrate his articles on building specific muscles, and he sold them to his fans at his many live performances while touring the United States and Europe. English man-of-letters Edmund Gosse bought a set of them and snuck his collection, which he described as a "beautiful set of poses showing the young strongman clad only in a fig leaf," into the funeral of poet Robert Browning at Westminster Abbey to peek at during the service when he got bored.

Soon after, the American health guru and bodybuilder Bernarr Macfadden followed Sandow's lead, publishing his own magazine, *Physical Culture*, which has been described as "part diatribe against medical doctors, part instruction in calisthenics and nutrition, part mouthpiece for a growing national interest in sports and exercise," and "part pornography." Many declared the magazine pornographic because Macfadden and others whose photographs graced its pages were often nude with their backs to the camera or with their nakedness otherwise hidden. Accused of introducing perversion into the physical culture world, Macfadden fought back by denouncing homosexuals and complaining that "his advocacy of muscular development *might* provide fodder for male sexual fantasies" (italics added), but that wasn't his intention or fault. He thought of homosexuals as "painted, perfumed, . . . mincing youths ogling every man that passes" them. He was referring to the pansy, not understanding, or pretending not to know, that not all gay men wore makeup or acted effeminately.

Keeping his blinders firmly in place, Macfadden sponsored the first-ever contest for the World's Most Handsome Man in 1921. It was not a bodybuilding competition at all but a beauty contest for men. The hands-down winner was a young, Italian immigrant, Angelo Siciliano. As a young man, Siciliano had taped one of Sandow's pictures on his bedroom mirror and, with Sandow's body to inspire him, worked diligently to mold his body into something similar to his hero's, or so one of the myths that surrounded him explained. To capitalize on the contest, Macfadden published a four-page spread in *Physical Culture* to introduce the stunning young Italian to his readership. The Adonis also hoped to capitalize on his new-found fame and gave himself a new name suitable for his profession. Henceforth, he would be known among his colleagues and fans alike as Charles Atlas.

The spread, which Macfadden appropriately captioned "The World's Most Handsome Man," appeared in the October 1921 issue of *Physical Culture*. The first photograph of the lot, a three-quarters shot of Atlas from the back, takes up the entire page. Naked except for a pair of thick socks rolled down ever so slightly, Atlas exudes "more than a whiff of eroticism." The spread not only revved up sales for Macfadden but gave his young protégé a leg up in the physical culture world.

The following year, Macfadden sponsored another competition, the World's Most Perfectly Developed Man. He was on the lookout for a bodybuilder this time. Atlas entered the second competition and won it too. Between competitions, the Adonis developed a line of physical culture courses and began announcing their availability in large ads published in *Physical Culture*. With the second competition under his belt, Charles Atlas became a superstar of the physical culture world, posing naked for professional physique photographers who painted posing straps on each and then sold them by mail order to fans of naked, extremely buff men.

Suddenly, the extremely thin boundary that had once separated muscle building from homoeroticism was so blurred that the difference between the two were utterly indistinguishable, and the magazines that published the photographs were described as "house organs for homosexuals," with no pun intended. As historian Greg Mullins has noted, "*Physical Culture* obviously" initiated the homoerotic photograph "into the age of mass produced and mass distributed photo magazines" regardless of Macfadden's denials and regardless of how strenuously he stuck to his guns and claimed that the photographs had "aesthetic value" and aided in "health education." The gay members of Contacts who noted their interest in physique photographs in their self-descriptions couldn't have cared less about aesthetics or education, and the mention of physique photography continued during Henry's tenure as Contacts' director.

Henry had been in charge of Contacts for only a few months when Magnus Hirschfeld announced that he was planning a three-month tour of the United States, beginning with a six-week series of lectures in New York. Hirschfeld had two reasons for the talks. First, he wanted to share his research about sexuality with the American medical establishment and with interested nonphysicians. Second, he was eager to flee Germany's growing fascism.

The Jewish and gay sexologist had had several run-ins with right-wing thugs, beginning in 1920 when, after giving a lecture in Munich, he was set upon by a gang of young fascists and left for dead on the street. The assaults continued off and on for the next ten years as fascism tightened its stranglehold on Germany. When in 1930 Harry Benjamin, a renowned endocrinologist and Hirschfeld's friend, invited him to speak in New York, Hirschfeld saw it as an opportunity to explore the United States firsthand and decide if he should settle there.* He boarded the SS *Columbus* in Bremerhaven on November 15, 1930, and arrived in New York a week later. Benjamin booked a room for Hirschfeld at the newly opened Hotel New Yorker, and almost immediately the sexologist began his lectures at the Labor Temple, the New York Academy of Medicine, and elsewhere.

Hirschfeld usually lectured in German, claiming that his English wasn't good enough for him to communicate properly otherwise, but the truth was that he spoke freely about all sorts of sexual matters, especially homosexuality, to German-speakers, but to English-speakers he was circumspect, focusing on how to best select marriage partners and giving advice on eugenic-based marriages. The difference in his approaches were obvious in articles published in two different newspapers. On one hand, the *New York Times* reported that "Dr. Magnus Hirschfeld ha[d] come here . . . to study the marriage question," with the phrase *marriage question* underscoring heterosexuality. On the other, the *New Yorker Volkszeitung*, a German-language newspaper, announced that Hirschfeld had come to New York to "discuss 'love's natural laws,' a turn of phrase that Hirschfeld frequently used when making the case for the naturalness of homosexuality." Hirschfeld knew that most Americans were less accepting of homosexuality than their European-born counterparts.

After six weeks in New York, Hirschfeld set off on the rest of the tour, traveling across the United States with stops in Detroit, Chicago, San Francisco, and other large cities. By the time he reached the West Coast, he was convinced that he couldn't return to Berlin. "As a freedom-loving person of Jewish descent," he wrote, "it appears to me that living in Germany, if one is not absolutely forced to, has become a moral impossibility. I have resigned myself to the idea that I shall never see Germany, my homeland, again, though it causes me great emotional suffering." He also decided that the United States was not for him, and he continued his tour to Hawaii and then to Japan and other Asian countries. He finally settled in the South of France, where he died in 1935. Despite his high regard for Hirschfeld, it appears that Henry didn't attend any of Hirschfeld's lectures.

As the years passed, Contacts and *Commentary* began to eat up more and more of Henry's free time, not that he was complaining. He enjoyed the work. He

* Hirschfeld had visited the United States briefly in 1893 when he attended the world's fair held that year in Chicago.

printed the *Commentary* in black ink on mimeographed 8½" × 13" sheets of blue paper and wrote all the articles that appeared in it himself. The April 1934 issue, for example, included Henry's "Among Our Competitors," a brief analysis of several pen pal clubs. He based his evaluations on the information that the directors sent him as a prospective member. His comments are Henry at his acerbic best.

The Friendship Club, he observed, was a "small multigraphed page full of high-sounding baloney about the pangs of 'loneliness of spirit, mind and heart'" that did "not mention the much more painful loneliness of the last dollar in our pocketbooks." He decided that Sarah E. Havilandran, director of the Star Friendship Exchange, was prejudiced because she was from the South, and once he read the material she sent him, he was convinced of it: "Sure nuf, Honey, she *demands* in the prospective member's application . . . information as to the prospective's 'Race.'"

The issue also included a list of sixteen books that members were willing to loan to others for the cost of postage. Ten of the sixteen listed belonged to member no. 10—Henry. He had "quite a library of selected volumes" of nonfiction. As the ever-vigilant director of the group, he was quick to note that *Commentary* didn't "handle books considered 'obscene' by the Post Office Department."

Contacts and picking up male prostitutes weren't Henry's only after-hours interests. While living in New York, he had made a number of friends besides Alva McDonald, Cedric Worth, and the men-for-hire he found on Forty-Second Street. A few of his newfound pals were among the soldiers stationed on Governors Island whom he met in Liggett Hall while grabbing chow at dinner time, swimming in the pool at the base's YMCA, or waiting in line for popcorn at the island's movie theater. They included his roommate, whom he identified only as Drexel, and another soldier, Joseph Edward "Eddie" Ferruggia. Just after he moved into Liggett Hall, Henry had breakfast with one of his gay soldier friends, whom he never identified, and the friend's pick-up from the night before, Fred Frisbie.

The twenty-three-year-old Frisbie was eager to fight for gay rights but flummoxed when it came to figuring out a way to do so. During breakfast that morning, Henry recounted his activities with the Society for Human Rights. Frisbie hung on the older man's every word and was outraged when Henry recalled his arrest, trial, and dismissal from his post office job. When the conversation turned to the possibility for forming another organization that might be more successful than the Society for Human Rights had been, Frisbie eagerly joined the discussion.

Frisbie and Henry ended up attending several get-togethers at a gay couple's home. They may have been W. Frank McCourt, a Contacts member, and Charles W. "Chuck" Ufford. Henry spoke about the Society for Human Rights there, too, and several of the men who were present became as fired up by Henry's memories of the Society for Human Rights as Frisbie had been. They pressed Henry to lead them in establishing a gay rights group, and if he wasn't interested in that responsibility, they hoped he would at least counsel them on how to go about organizing. Henry was so "pessimistic" and "bitter" because "the Chicago gay community hadn't come to his support" four years earlier that he refused to have anything to do with organizing or even advising them. One of the men in attendance was already at work founding one of his own, but it appears that it never materialized.

Released from the army in 1932, Frisbie moved to Los Angeles soon after. He had been so impressed by Henry and the discussions about the Society for Human Rights that he never forgot the older activist and their conversations. Nearly half a century after being introduced to him and attending meetings together, he sketched Henry's portrait from memory.

Nevertheless, Frisbie, the gay couple who hosted meetings in their home, and the men who attended the meetings weren't the only friends and acquaintances Henry had made after moving to New York. Not long after Frisbie set off for Los Angeles, Henry set out on a new venture under the Contacts umbrella with four of them, all writers: Jacob Hauser, H. P. Seguin, B. C. Hagglund, and William Chiles. The project that drew them together was the little magazine *Chanticleer*.

Because the staff of *Chanticleer* used Contacts' membership list as a potential subscriber base, Henry served as the magazine's circulation manager. Hauser was its editor, and Seguin, Hagglund, and Chiles were associate editors. In its premiere issue, Hauser described the mimeographed *Chanticleer* as "makeshift" and "impromptu" and its staff as men who "possess that urge for expression which Milton said . . . is 'death to hide.'" He also announced *Chanticleer*'s purpose: "In our despondent and chop-fallen ties there is need of light-loving, life-loving; of the impetuous spirit which over-rides barriers, and has in view the one goal: vitality, a dynamic responsiveness to the world about us, and the world within." *Friendship and Freedom* had been disguised as a magazine for sexual liberation in general, while its true aim was to help gay men. Except for Henry's pieces and an essay by Chiles, *Chanticleer* focused

HENRY GERBER - 1929
drawn from memory
by Fred Frisbie

Fred Frisbie, who socialized with Gerber in 1929, drew this portrait of him from memory decades later. *Courtesy of ONE Archives at the USC Libraries*

on the social-political in general, with a socialist leaning, and even Henry's work didn't recommend homosexuality for anyone but instead showed how hypocritically religious leaders, legal and medical authorities, and society in general dealt with it. Henry was gay, Seguin was bisexual, and the others were heterosexual. What drew the men to band together was their left-leaning politics and their desire to get published, not their sexuality.

The four had found it virtually impossible to get their work in print. Hauser lamented that they were outsiders and didn't have the right connections, and as outsiders, they had to "take the initiative to proclaim" themselves, "following the very sensible advice of Walt Whitman, the noted self-promulgator." In short, *Chanticleer* became a self-publishing enterprise. With a very slim print run that went, primarily, to Contacts members, their proclamations didn't fall on many ears.

Hauser made his living by working in a post office in Brooklyn, New York, and published the first of his sequence of twenty-five poems, "Pagan Psalms and Scenes," in *Chanticleer*'s January issue as well as in each of its next three numbers. B. C. (Benjamin Clarence) Hagglund lived in Holt, Minnesota, where he edited the *Holt Weekly News* and, in his spare time, ran a publishing house that issued collections of poetry, including Hauser's first volume, *Dark Metropolis*. Although a poet, he only contributed short, Marxist essays to *Chanticleer*. Harry P. Seguin, a Canadian, had moved to the United States permanently and made his living as a shopkeeper. He contributed his series of eight "Letters I Would Have Written to Nietzsche" to the magazine. A bisexual who had been a member of Contacts and had met his wife though it, he made a living at a variety of jobs, including working in an airplane factory. Unfortunately, nothing is known about William Chiles's personal life, but among his nonfiction pieces for *Chanticleer* he included "A Heterosexual Looks at Homosexuality" in which he suggested that the laws that criminalized the homosexual should be examined and rescinded.

The four men divided the space for their poems and prose almost equally between them. Seguin's letters appeared in nine of the eleven issues, and both Hagglund's poetry and Chiles's nonfiction pieces appeared in ten. Hauser reserved all but one issue for his poetry, but Henry's reviews and brief essays appeared in every issue that the men published. A testament to the high regard the others felt about Henry's writing—and to the fact that he was supplying the subscribers and the means and materials to print *Chanticleer* as well as probably doing all the hands-on work needed to shepherd it into print—he got the lion's share of the available space.

An avid newspaper reader, Henry was appalled by what he saw taking place politically around him, especially the plight of homosexuals, and he poured out his disgust and concern into the dozen pieces he published in *Chanticleer*. Some were short essays, but others were reviews of current books, fiction and nonfiction. Always direct, atheistic, and left-leaning, he took a no-holds-barred and take-no-prisoners approach in all of them, and yet he sprinkled humor, particularly satire and hyperbole, throughout many. They present his view of society's persecution of homosexuals, the reasons for it, and those who directed and supported it. Linked to religion, by which he usually meant Christianity and especially the Catholic Church in which he had been raised, his writings returned to those themes over and over during the next three decades.

Henry's debut essay, a satire entitled "Theism and Atheism Reconciled," poked fun at Russia, an "avowed atheist country" and how its leaders were "haggling with the president of the Most Christian Nation," the United States, "over diplomatic recognition." Two months earlier, Soviet ambassador Maxim Litvinov and President Franklin D. Roosevelt had squabbled over the United States' recognition of the legitimacy of the Soviet Union's Communist government, and their negotiations were stuck on a point that Henry found ridiculous. The United States wanted the Soviet government to sanction the "sending of American Christian missionaries . . . to the Soviets," and only after it did, would the United States recognize the Soviets' government. Henry joked that the "newspapers forgot to say" whether Litvinoff had "waggishly counterdemand[ed] equal permission for Russia to send atheistic missionaries to America."

Henry forgot all about humor when he confronted "religionists" in "What Is Atheism?" in *Chanticleer*'s third issue. Christians believed, he asserted, that the "universe is run on a harmonious order, and that beauty in life is an indubitable proof of the existence of a wise and benevolent father in the skies," but it seemed to him "that anyone with an open eye can see that the disorder in nature, the downright ugliness of life, prevalent injustice, the terror of wars, murder, starvation, the dishonesty of politicians, and the general suffering of a great majority of people throughout the world, are by no means an indication of harmony and beauty."

After a few paragraphs, Henry focused on the Church's "criminal history":

> Anyone brought up in the stifling air of puritanism or fundamentalism will understand the harm religion has done to mankind. Not only by the age-old association with monarchies, capitalism and its bloody wars, and the exploitation of mankind, the sanctioning of slavery, wars and other regressive measures but by its perverse teaching of the filthiness of the natural function of sex, the churches have made man slave-minded and by its promise of pie in the sky by and by, man has been distracted from his real need, social betterment, here and now.

Henry evoked Mae West in "Moral Welfare" to illustrate his stance against Christianity. The article opened with an epigraph comprising two quotes, one supposedly from Mae West, star of stage and screen and an accomplished playwright and scriptwriter. Henry quoted her as having said, "It ain't no sin," which he followed with a comment supposedly made by Cardinal Dougherty of the Archdiocese of Philadelphia: "It is, too." The epigraph's faux dialogue summarized West's battle with the censors.

Superstar West was a box-office smash, and "'by 1934 more than 46 million Americans' . . . had seen her first two films." Nevertheless, she had had trouble with the censors during much of her career, and in 1926 while staring in *Sex*, a play she had written, she was arrested, charged with "producing an immoral show" and "maintaining a public nuisance," and convicted. She served only eight of her ten-days sentence, getting off early "for good behavior."

The publicity that swirled around West's play inflamed various religious and social groups that, in response, threatened to boycott any movie that didn't meet their standards. To ensure their financial investments, Hollywood moguls agreed to self-censor films and enlisted Daniel A. Lord, a Catholic priest, and Martin J. Quigley to devise the Motion Picture Production Code. Popularly known as the Hays Code after Will H. Hays, president of the Motion Picture Producers and Distributors of America, Lord and Quigley's regulations covered eleven broad subjects that Hollywood couldn't depict on the screen: "crimes against the law," "sex," "vulgarity," "obscenity," "dances," "profanity," "costume," "religion," "national feelings," "titles," and "repellant subjects." As might be expected, Lord and Quigley focused a great deal of attention on sex, gave that subject the Code's largest number of prohibitions, and addressed how filmmakers must depict adultery, scenes of passion, seduction or rape, and homosexuality. They forbade any depiction or suggestion of homosexuality on screen regardless of how slight. Lord and Quigley were doing their best to counteract the pansy craze and shove gay men into the shadowy underground.

Initially, Hollywood followed the Hays Code only halfheartedly, sometimes censoring its films but, more often than not, ignoring the code altogether. In 1933 Dennis Joseph Cardinal Dougherty of the Archdiocese of Philadelphia labeled the motion picture industry the "greatest menace to faith and morals in America today," "declared it sinful for any of the area's 800,000 Catholics to enter a movie theater," and organized a boycott of Hollywood's films in response to its lackadaisical handling of moral issues. Subsequently, "over 300,000 Catholics" signed pledges "to avoid the movies," and "ticket sales dropped around 20 percent." The box office failures put Hollywood on notice, and the film industry tightened down on what film scripts depicted. The next year, West's script for her fourth film, *It Ain't No Sin*, was scrutinized intensely by censors, and they forced her to edit the script so extensively that the film she eventually shot had little in common with the original. She was even ordered to change its title: *It Ain't No Sin* became *Belle of the Nineties*.

Henry was against all "sex suppression," whether religious or legal in origin and regardless of whether the sexual activity being regulated was heterosexual or homosexual, and he believed that a rebellion against the sex taboos was afoot. He listed three reasons for his stance:

The war brought our yokels to France and for the first time they had an idea that sex morality as preached (but not always practiced) by their priests was so much apple sauce and that to live, after all, means to enjoy all the physical and mental pleasures which nature has so plentifully endowed us with. Then there is science which has exposed all the religious superstitions. . . . Last but not least, the economic collapse has put a big dent into the social ideal of monogamy. Millions out of work and existing merely on starvation wages, make it difficult for the average man to establish a home and a family.

But "the average man" didn't stop wanting and having sex. Those who did marry, Henry argued, used birth control to keep from having to support children, although they were going against the Catholic Church's teachings. He defended "poor, misguided Mae West" who had been "declared Enemy No. 1 now that Dillinger is safely put away by a regiment of heavily armed police" because "she has the dangerous delusion that sex was not made so much for procreation as for pleasure." He described the censorship of her film script as a "Hitler edict."

Henry turned his attention from the church to the American press in "Hitler and Homosexuality." Ernst Röhm, the head of the Sturmabteilung,* had been one of Hitler's most ardent supporters since the beginning of the Nazi Party, and throughout their association, Hitler not only knew about Röhm's homosexuality but had "defended" Röhm "more than once," warning "his party comrades against being too squeamish about a man's personal morals if he were a fanatical fighter for the movement.'"

By 1934 Röhm's homosexuality had become an embarrassment to the Nazis, and Himmler, Göring, and others had convinced Hitler that Röhm was conspiring to lead the Sturmabteilung in a coup. Hitler ordered his men to execute any brownshirt they discovered across Germany, and during the evening of June 30, they murdered more than two thousand. Hitler's men caught Edmund Heines, Röhm's second in command, in bed with a young man and executed them, and other brownshirts, on the spot. At the same time, Hitler appeared at a meeting of the leaders of the brownshirts and arrested Röhm. Two days later, Hitler had Röhm shot in his cell.

---

* The Sturmabteilung, or storm troopers, were popularly called brownshirts.

Henry's point was not merely to show Hitler's duplicity when it came to Röhm but also to point out the American press's hypocritical reaction to the Night of the Long Knives, as the massacre came to be called. The "newspapers of America," he wrote, "were strangely compromised by this Hitler story. Should they praise the murderer Hitler for suppressing homosexuals, or should they give credit to Röhm and his homosexual camorra for being the only men in Germany virile enough to attempt to wipe out the unspeakable Hitler? The newspapers condemned both and saved their faces."

Henry imagined that, with the "waning of capitalism and organized religion" in many parts of the world, particularly those countries that then embraced communism or atheism, "the opposition of the governments to homosexuals will also wane, as has been seen by the example of Russia."* Vehemently antifascist and against any government interference with human sexual rights, Henry ended the article with a rare upbeat comment. He envisioned that "homosexuals will go on fighting to rid the world of tyranny."

Along with his short essays, Henry also contributed book reviews to *Chanticleer*, but they weren't simply reviews in the strictest sense of the word. He didn't shy away from including his political beliefs. In "Recent Homosexual Literature," for example, he explained his view on the source of the persecution of gay men in the United States:

> Politicians and priests . . . are in fact responsible for sex suppression in America. Capitalism, loyally supported by the churches, has established a Public Policy that the Sacred Institution of Monogamy must be enforced; and such a fiat is the deathknell to all sexual freedom. Monogamy is the ideal of this state and all deviations from this ideal are strictly suppressed, including free love in all its forms, birth control and homosexuality. For these forms of sexual freedom, if free to practice, would defeat the sacred institution of monogamy.

In the rest of the review, he took potshots at recently published novels. Henry condemned André Tellier's *Twilight Men*, Blair Niles's *Strange Brother*, and Kay Boyle's *Gentlemen, I Address You Privately* as failures because all

---

* Little did Henry know that, although Russia had rescinded its sodomy laws after the October Revolution of 1917, it reinstituted them the very year his essay appeared.

three novels had unrealistic plots and ended on an implausible note. They had been written, he believed, "to convey the impression that ALL homosexuals were potential murders. But that is no more so than if after reading Dreiser's 'American Tragedy' one would come to the conclusion that all heterosexual men would kill their loves, and die in the chair." Henry *almost* praised Edward Scully's *Scarlet Pansy*. He and Scully were friends, and Henry was gratified that Scully ended the novel with his protagonist dying a "hero on the battlefield," but he was nevertheless offended by the explicitness of the sexual adventures of the effeminate main character. Henry concluded that the novel "could be classed as anti-homosexual propaganda, for anyone—even homosexuals—reading the book will lay it aside disgustedly" because of its "filth and swinishness."

In another review, "A New Deal for Sex," Henry revealed that he had enjoyed René Guyon's *The Ethics of Sexual Acts* because Guyon advocated that "it is not the various modes of sex pleasure in practice everywhere that are abnormal, but . . . the sex superstitions, based on religion" that "are perverse." He added:

> Rene Guyon goes deeply into the sexual taboo and its origin, traces it down to ancient tribal rituals and to its final glorification with the invention of Christianity, which, by the way, was founded by two probably sexually impotent persons, Jesus and Paul. Thus it is clearly shown that the whole modern sex taboos in Christian countries . . . are based on the philosophy or rather theology of Christianity, i.e. that it is sinful to enjoy life and that it is pleasant to God that man should suffer in this vale of tears.

His other reviews included an attack on the lyrics of Wagner's *Tannhäuser*, "Tannhaeuser, or the Triumph of the Sex-Cripples Over Passion." Henry admitted that the music is "grand," but he called the lyrics "bunk" and the plot "impossible" because it ends with "the triumph of the church over nature"—the suppression of the free expression of sex, especially homosexuality, by religious and legal institutions. In "More Nonsense About Homosexuals," he flogged La Forest Potter for *Strange Loves*, an investigation of homosexuality based on case studies of men who had sought help from physicians and psychologists, hoping to be cured. Potter's book proved "that the medical authorities in America, of which Dr. Potter is a shining example, are about 100 years behind the times, and . . . that most psychologists in this country are mere yes-men who blindly and obediently follow the current authorized moral code without any regard to common sense or the results of modern scientific research." At the review's end, Henry resolved, "It is only the attitude of Anglo-Saxon society that is *strange*, a society whose mental health has been perverted by socalled [*sic*] Christian morality and its theory that sex is sinful and filthy."

Henry continued in a similar vein in all the other pieces he published in *Chanticleer*, and unfortunately, it was the only outlet for his work. *Chanticleer's* staff hoped that it would become an open sesame into mainstream publishing, but that wasn't to be the case. Its circulation was far too small to reach the literary lions of the day, and those members of Contacts who read it were no closer to the literary hub of the United States than Henry. Hauser was the only one of the quartet to carve out a place in the literary establishment, and it was a tiny niche. Harriet Monroe selected three of his poems for publication in the August 1935 and April 1936 issues of *Poetry*, and in 1936, the Guggenheim Foundation awarded him a fellowship. Chances are that his publications in *Chanticleer* had nothing to do with his good luck. None of the other three editors were as fortunate.

Henry faced a huge obstacle in getting published, one that Hauser hadn't listed in his reasons for publishing *Chanticleer* and one that didn't affect the others. However, Henry was acutely aware of it: "Homosexuality has until recently been strictly taboo and no 'decent' author or publisher considered it fit to mention in print." He wanted to write about the problems facing gay men in the United States, but his progressive views didn't mesh at all with the very conservative sociopolitical views of many editors and publishers, a conservatism that reflected the state of politics in the United States at the time.

That conservativism in all corners of society coalesced into a concerted effort by legal and religious institutions to put homosexuals behind bars. The visible pansy of the 1920s was being forced into invisibility by the church and law enforcement agencies, and by 1934, as *Chanticleer* was being printed, the crackdown was in full swing. Henry put his neck on the block for the second time in his life by publishing openly pro-homosexuality articles—that were just as openly against legal and religious authorities—in *Chanticleer* under his own name and not a pseudonym. Had anyone who received copies chose to sell him out, he might have suffered at the hands of the law authorities even more than he had in 1925. The fact that he took a public, if limited, stance in the midst of New York's, and the country's, crackdown on homosexuals is amazing—and nothing less than heroic.

7

"FOR CHRIST'S SAKE, LEAVE ME OUT OF IT"

WHY HENRY AND THE OTHER MEN who produced *Chanticleer* suspended it after only a year is unclear. It may have been their plan from the beginning, but it may also have been because the burden of the actual production of the magazine fell on Henry's shoulders, as it had a decade earlier with *Friendship and Freedom. Chanticleer*'s eight-page issues demanded a great deal of typing, then mimeographing, collating, and finally mailing, and the work undoubtedly grew burdensome. Having flirted around the Comstock Act for a year because of Henry's essays and reviews may also have influenced their decision. Postal authorities would have considered *Chanticleer* obscene because of his contributions alone, but obscenity was only one problem that faced Henry and other gay men in the 1930s.

For many historians, 1933 marks the demise of the Pansy Craze with the death, on August 10, of Jean Malin, the country's best-known pansy entertainer, as well as the end of Prohibition that officially ended on December 5 of the same year. Nevertheless, pansies didn't suddenly disappear off the streets of large urban centers. The public's understanding of them, however mistaken and naive, simply shifted, and the public's notion of "queer people went from 'novelty'" during the pansy craze to "'threat.'"

The campaign against them that began in the 1930s during the death throes of the pansy craze wasn't the first official movement against them, just one of the more publicized. As historian Jonathan Ned Katz discovered, the "earliest known American crusade against sodomites" began in New York in 1842 and focused on those areas such as "City Hall Park and Broadway," where jobless, often lower-class, younger men prostituted themselves to older upper-class men. By the 1890s anti-vice groups, reformers, and newspaper reporters scrutinized the saloons that "flamboyantly effeminate 'fairies'" patronized and called for them to be closed and their habitués arrested. In 1892, for example, the *New York Herald* called for the city's district attorney, De Lancey Nicoll, to clean-up the Slide, a "degenerate resort" where patrons could enjoy "orgies beyond description."*

By 1910 New York's police chief added a new task to its vice squad, the "surveillance of homosexuals," and shortly after the armistice that ended World War I was signed, raids on other homosexual hangouts, such as the Everard Baths, became common. Five years later the police department gave Terence Harvey the unique role of patrolling areas where men cruised. He was extremely successful, having "arrested 88 (30 percent) of the 239 men convicted of degeneracy in the first half of 1921," the same year in which police were directed to use entrapment to arrest men in Central Park. Within three years, as Henry was trying to get his Society for Human Rights off the ground, New York's state legislature added "'homosexual solicitation'—any solicitation for a 'crime against nature or other lewdness'"—to its statutes as a "disorderly conduct" charge. Other large cities across the country followed New York's lead.

As the pansy became more and more visible on the streets of New York and other large urban centers during the close of 1919 and the first months of 1920, police constantly harassed them, closed a large number of Greenwich Village hot spots, which the authorities had deemed "rendezvous for perverts, degenerates, homosexuals and other evil-disposed persons," and arrested their patrons and managers for "operating a 'public nuisance' and 'disorderly house,'" as well as "openly outraging public decency."

As the Great Depression gripped the country, various New York newspapers egged on the police's antihomosexual campaign by publishing exposés against "Times Square clubs featuring pansy acts" and the "drag balls" that had attracted "thousands" to Harlem, Madison Square Garden, and various hotels where they had been held. In the early 1930s the state of New York established laws against any "bar or restaurant" from serving queer men and women, any play or movie that dealt with gay situations from being produced, and any man who was "trying to pick up another man." The only way for them to

---

* At the time, *orgy* didn't necessarily refer to group sex but to any unrestrained, boisterous, emotion activity of a gathering of individuals.

keep from being nabbed by the long arm of the law was to keep out of sight, as many began to do, and when in public, to be restrained.

The *Brevities'* coverage of queer life took on the aspects of exposés. In one of the first, John Swallow Martin, an ambiguous, campy nom de plume, declared "all the fairy round-ups of recent months," especially the "various raids in Bryant Park, . . . began earlier this year than last" and noted "several raids" had been "staged at 'Frank's Place' in Brooklyn, . . . a plague-spot" where "night after night, but especially on Saturdays and Sundays, anywhere from fifty to seventy-five sailors" appeared along with "from fifty to a hundred men and boys, with painted faces and dyed tresses, singing and dancing." Four months later, Buddy Browning wrote "Fag Balls Exposed"—a title as campy and ambiguous as the author's nom de plume—for the *Broadway Brevities*, claiming that the "third sex is flooding America" with their "gaudy" masquerade "balls," and to prove his point, he claimed that, during the previous week, some "6,000 men, women and oddities" attended the Sixty-Fourth Masquerade and Civic Ball at Rockland Palace at 155th Street and Frederick Douglass Avenue.

The police harassment escalated, and the *Brevities* added another layer to its exposés of homosexuals and fanned the antihomosexual sentiment by linking homosexuality to Germany's fascism, a growing threat in Europe. Fred Schultz inaugurated the *Brevities'* bizarre connection of American homosexuals and German Nazis in his "Fags Ram Heinies!"—another ambiguous and campy title.* In the article, Schultz claimed the "Germans are turning queerer and the [German] Army is getting stronger," warning readers of the Nazis' perversion and aggression as Germany's desire for an empire became more and more obvious to Americans. The unidentified author of "B'way Queers Brazen!" strengthened the link between homosexuality and the Nazis:

New York's hordes of third sexers have descended upon Broadway and Times Square with a whoop and are making life intolerable for normal passers-by. . . . Peculiarly enough, this condition has been brought about by the enormous amount of publicity allotted to the queer Adolph Hitler and his Nazis. Acting on the logic that if one of their members can rule Germany, they have appropriated the Main Stem for themselves. The police should teach them the error of their ways.

---

* *Heinies* was slang for *buttocks* as well as a derogatory word for *Germans*.

Adding one more link to the Hitler-homosexuality connection, the *Broadway Tattler,* another popular tabloid, published an untitled cartoon strip poking fun at Hitler's rumored homosexuality. The cartoonist depicted Hitler giving a speech to the "Beebles uff Chermany" in the first panel, in which he announced that he and his followers will use "sterilization" to "purify our race." Readers at the time would have understood that *sterilization* meant *castration*, which many medical and legal authorities proposed as a cure for homosexuality. In the next two frames, a mincing Hitler reveled that "zex perverts" and "pansies" needed to be exterminated; in the following frames, Hitler was arrested and castrated; and in the sixth and final frame, he speaks in "falsetto."

Henry continued to work on Contacts and *Commentary* in his spare time. To keep the money coming in, he notified members when their memberships were about to expire, and on April 8, 1935, he sent a renewal notice to member no. 1366, a sailor with the coast guard who was stationed in Wilmington, North Carolina. Two weeks later, the sailor sent Henry three dollars (about sixty dollars in today's currency), which paid for a year's membership and allowed him to publish his self-description in four different issues of *Commentary*. The sailor had a curious surname that he spelled just as curiously: *boyFrank*. He sometimes spelled it *Boy Frank*, sometimes *Boyfrank*. He also played with the spelling of his first name, sometimes spelling it *Manuel* and, at other times, *Monwell*, a phonetic rendition. The following September, Manuel wrote Henry to thank him for adding him to the list of new Contacts members, but instead of using the traditional spelling of words, Manuel spelled certain ones phonetically.

Manuel began the letter with a traditional salutation, but then switched to his unique style. "Thanks for yoor noht about my relisting (1366). It waz gratifying to get wun byt before my hook hit the water. Sins then I hav receevd two intelligjent letterz and I only today got around to answering them. Contacts haz certainly dun a good servis in eliminating spais for personz hoo hav interests in common." Manuel was gay, and through his listing in the *Commentary*, he had recently received three letters from men interested in him and whom he found interesting in return.

Manuel's slim autobiography, "His Was a Monkey-Puzzle Family Tree," which he wrote under the nom de plume J. P. Starr,* reveals that he not only

---

* He derived the surname of his nom de plume, Starr, from the outlaw Belle Starr, whom he claimed as a distant relative.

lied about his age, as Henry did, but also rejected his birth name and adopted another one which he used for most of the rest of his life, as Henry also did. He was born on May 21, 1895 (not 1900 or 1901 as he often claimed), in Bales Township, Pottawatomie County, Oklahoma, as Glenn Manning Glass. His father was Henry Perkins Glass, his mother Emma Frances (née Knepper) Glass. He had two older sisters, a younger sister, and an older brother. His great-grandfather, Manuel Boyfrank, a telegraph operator, married an indigenous woman, a member of the Omaha tribe, whose last name was Glass. He was so nondescript and practiced "self-abasement" so successfully that he became known as "Mrs. Glass's husband," and the family began using *Glass* as their surname.*

In his early adolescence he worked on ranches as a cattle drover where he learned about homosexuality. He explained to historian Peter Boag that it was widely practiced among the cowboys he knew. He recalled, "'At first they'd solace each other gingerly and, as bashfulness waned, manually. As trust in mutual good will matured, they'd graduate to the ecstatically comforting 69.' Importantly, cowboys' attraction to each other could be more than just . . . sex" because it "was at first rooted in admiration, infatuation, a sensed need of an ally, loneliness and yearning, but it regularly ripened into love."

A few years later, Glenn set out to find a career, and the town's telegraph operator hired him to work in his office. Because he would be following in his great-grandfather's shoes, he advised Manuel to use his great-grandfather's name, and he did for a while. By 1916 he and his older sister Lucille left Oklahoma to seek their fortunes in San Francisco, where he was known as Glenn Glass officially. They found an apartment and lived together at 1455A Franklin Street. He worked as a clerk and she as a telephone operator.

The war in Europe was heating up, and twenty-two-year-old Glenn enlisted in the army at the recruitment office at 660 Market Street on January 2, 1917. He used Manuel boyFrank when he enlisted. The army assigned him to the 278th Aero Observation Squadron in France, which kept track of movements of German forces and pinpointed artillery locations. He sailed to Europe in December 1917 on the SS *Orduña* and was "wounded twice" and "gassed twice" in France. Manuel and his squadron returned to the United States on the USS *Patricia*, sailing from Brest, France, on June 24, 1919, and docking at Hoboken on July 5,

---

* boyFrank's great-grandfather's father-in-law was Hugh Glass, the central character in the film *The Revenant* (2015).

the same port from which Henry would sail, three months later, to Germany. Shortly after landing, he and the hundreds of other men in the squadron posed together for a panoramic photograph at Camp Albert L. Mills on Long Island, where they were then stationed. He received his discharge papers six months later.

Manuel returned to San Francisco and continued to work as a clerk for the next few years, but civilian life wasn't to his liking. He reenlisted, this time in the coast guard, on September 14, 1927, and was stationed in Port Angeles, Washington. In the early 1930s the yeoman discovered one of Henry's ads for Contacts in the *Saturday Review of Literature* and, hoping that he might ferret out other gay men in its membership lists, he joined. Not long after, he was transferred to the coast guard base in Curtis Bay, Maryland, and that fall, he renewed his membership in Contacts.

On September 9, 1935, Manuel wrote Henry to thank him for listing him in the *Commentary* as a renewed member and, more important, to try to ascertain how trustworthy Henry was before opening up to him. Most of the homosexuals who joined correspondence clubs approached other men slowly and carefully. They had a great deal to lose if they misunderstood a potential pen pal's self-description.

Manuel had read Henry's articles in *Chanticleer*, perhaps even assumed Henry was gay, but had to know for sure. After a few pleasantries and deal-ing with the business at hand, Manuel discussed atheism and religion, two of Henry's ever-present themes, to show him that they were in the same corner intellectually. "With all yu say about churches," Manuel wrote, using his on-again, off-again phonetic spelling, "I am in practical agreement. I am a member ov the American Association for the Advansment ov Atheismim." Then he approached the issue of sex and hinted at his own sexuality. "Wun ov the thingz I hold agenst the church most iz the way it haz maid sex a horror instead ov a utility that awt to be as much a matter ov cours az drinking water. What ryt hav preests to cry "Bastard! Adulterer! Pervert!" and so on? . . . Millionz ov yung personz hav been persecuted becawz they heeded the most urjent promptingz ov their naicherz." He concluded by suggesting that they need to work "to maik respectabel whatever sex behavior peepel wish to follow, long az noboddi iz hurt by it." If Henry hadn't read between the lines before, he couldn't help but do so now.

Regardless of Manuel's overtures, Henry remained very circumspect. Although he responded within a week, he distanced himself from the sailor, sending him a form letter and a packet of material: a history of Contacts, instructions about how members could borrow books from one another, testimonials about what a wonderful addition Contacts had been to members' lives, and other items.

In the meantime, Manuel had moved off-base and into the home of Charles George Maki and his mother, Matilda, at 358 Purdy Avenue on Staten Island. Thirteen years Manuel's junior, Maki had been one of Manuel's shipmates. They had kept in touch and dreamed up a plan to create a commune that they would run together. In his second letter to Henry, Manuel described it in detail, hoping that Henry would allow him to advertise it in *Commentary*.

Manuel and Maki called their group a "convent" and their philosophy behind it a "church for radicalz." Members would live with the Makis and would work around the house to earn what they needed to live, including room and board, but no salary. Manuel stressed that it would be a safe place for homosexuals. Henry's answer to Manuel's scheme was short and emphatic. After thanking Manuel for the informative letter, he got down to brass tacks. "Since I am neither a radical nor interested in religion," Henry wrote, "your radical church would not interest me, still less joining a convent to become a nun; I am too individualistic for that to join any sort of commune-istic enterprise." Nor was Henry interested in recommending other clubs to Contacts' members and for good reason.

A few years earlier, a Contacts member in Oklahoma had come up with a scheme similar to Manuel's, the Society of Seekers, and mentioned it in *Commentary*. Other Contacts members sent him a membership fee, but they lost their money when the organization quickly collapsed. Similarly, Henry had recommended Vincent Burke's nudist magazine, the *Olympian*, to Contact members. Burke never sent the magazine to any of those who had subscribed but pocketed the subscription money. Henry was embarrassed that he had been taken in by Burke and swore, "I am never again recommending anything or anybody as a principle, no matter what it is and I am going to stick to the Contacts idea sole and simple, that is of connecting the intelligent few and the broadminded."

Nevertheless, Henry was willing to do what he could to help Manuel. He suggested that, instead of describing himself in his next listing, Manuel should describe his organization and mention that he was the "chief monkey-monk of the Monkey-monk monastery." Always trying to make a buck, Henry also suggested that Maki should also join Contacts and, after paying his three-dollar membership fee, use his profile to advertise it too. Henry asked only one thing of Manuel in return: "But for Christ's sake, leave me out of it." They stopped corresponding, but that didn't keep Manuel from fantasizing about an organization for men exclusively.

Henry's reticence was well founded. Any group of unrelated people living together, especially a houseful of men, would have drawn the notice of neighbors almost immediately and then of the authorities. He didn't know Manuel at all, and the debacle in Chicago had left him distrustful of men he didn't know well. It was a reasonable reaction to the antihomosexual atmosphere permeating New York. Instead of focusing their attention on the pansy, authorities now had another vile outlaw in their crosshairs.

Fueled by a series of sex-murders of children and intensely publicized by newspapers across the country, a panic erupted, and the "sex criminal," who was responsible for the atrocities, was born. He took on a variety of identities, including "sex fiend," and by the mid-1930s, he had been irrevocably associated with homosexuals despite the fact that the "majority of cases of child 'sex murders' reported by the press involved men attacking girls." Consequently, gay men became the principal and, in many minds, the only perpetuators of all sex crimes. Law enforcement, from the city police commissioner all the way up the chain to the FBI, used the shift in the public's view of the "queer as an effeminate fairy whom one might ridicule but had no reason to fear" to the "image of the queer as a psychopathic child molester capable of committing the most unspeakable crimes against children" as an excuse for cracking down on homosexuals. FBI director J. Edgar Hoover was instrumental in fanning the flames against them.

Rumors about Hoover's sexuality circulated widely during his law-enforcement career. In the summer of 1933, political reporter Ray Tucker scrutinized Hoover's activities, and in his subsequent report, he not only made fun of Hoover for being "Uncle Sam's official snooper" but accused him of using his position to retaliate against those who criticized him. Tucker also took a shot at Hoover's sexuality. Describing Hoover, Tucker publicly hinted at the far-flung belief that Hoover was a homosexual: "He is short, fat, businesslike, and walks with mincing step. . . . He dresses fastidiously, with Eleanor blue as the favorite color for the matched shades of tie, handkerchief and socks." Mentioning how Hoover walked was telling enough, but more coded language followed. Portraying Hoover as dressed meticulously, with the colors of various articles matching, when FBI investigators were known for their shabbiness and lack of fashion sense, was another jab at Hoover's heterosexual veneer. Heterosexual men didn't care about how they dressed, Tucker was sure his readers believed, but queer people did. "Eleanor blue" was associated with the First Lady, Eleanor Roosevelt, who had popularized the color, and by associating him with her favorite color choice, Tucker feminized him, but more important, the color was more lavender than blue, and by 1933 lavender was associated with homosexuals. Tucker didn't have to say that Hoover was gay. His readers could read between the lines.

Outraged by Tucker's comments, Hoover had his henchmen investigate Tucker and corralled his journalist-friends to champion him. A *Liberty* magazine writer, for example, countered Tucker's description of Hoover, claiming the FBI director's "compact body, with the shoulders of a light heavyweight boxer, carries no ounce of extra weight—just 170 pounds of live, virile masculinity." Nevertheless, the *Liberty* article did little to mitigate Tucker's comments, and nine days after Tucker's piece appeared, a scandal columnist for the *Washington Herald* poked fun at the way Hoover walked, declaring that the "Hoover stride has grown noticeably longer and more vigorous" after Tucker turned a spotlight on it.

Changing how he walked into a more recognizably masculine step did nothing to curtail the rumors. One gossip claimed Hoover cross-dressed and had sexual relationships with various men, including a decades-long romantic and sexual relationship with Clyde Tolson, the FBI's associate director and Hoover's right-hand man. Others swore that he had been caught with a young man in New Orleans and had sexual trysts with teenagers in his limousine. As the rumors picked up steam, Hoover not only spearheaded an attack on gay men to deflect questions about his sexuality but also wrote several articles that fueled the public's hatred and fear of them. The most damaging was "War on the Sex Criminal," which appeared in newspapers across the United States on Sunday, September 26, 1937.

"The sex fiend, the most loathsome of the vast army of crime," Hoover's article began, "has become a sinister threat to the safety of American childhood and womanhood," and extending from "one end of the United States to the other, women and little girls have been murdered by this beast. No parent can feel secure that his children are safe from attack. The sex fiend may strike anywhere, at any time. In one large eastern city alone, an arrest for sex crime is made every six hours, on the average, night and day." How the epidemic of perverted crimes came about was clear, at least to Hoover. Americans had ignored, accepted, or supported the pansy during the 1920s, and the pansy became the sex fiend of the 1930s. The "sex criminal," Hoover declared, "isn't some fabled monster; he isn't some demon, born full-blown, that suddenly descends upon women and little girls; he isn't a 'product of our modern age,' he is a definite and serious result of the apathy and indifference in the handling of *out-of-the-ordinary* offenders" (italics added) who "have been repeatedly dealt with as petty offenders when, in truth, their every action was a blazing signpost to a future to torture, rape, mutilation and murder."

Hoover even outlined the evolution of the pansy into the sex fiend. "He often begins with annoyances," Hoover imagined, then "progresses to the sending of obscene letters" through correspondence clubs "or exhibitionism.... For all these things, he often is merely fined, or given 'orders to leave town,' or punished by short jail sentences—none of which deters him in the slightest degree from other and more serious offenses. And every sex criminal is a potential murderer." Hoover's use of *exhibitionism* was ambiguous at best. It may have been that he meant men who expose their genitals in public, but it's more likely that he was using the word to refer to homosexuals who were obviously effeminate. In their article "Social Factors in the Case Histories of One Hundred Underprivileged Homosexuals," sexologists George W. Henry and Alfred A. Gross described three types of gay men: the "orderly homosexual, the exhibitionist fairy, and the hoodlum." The "exhibitionist fairy," or pansy, didn't try to hide his effeminacy but proudly displayed it.

Then, in a last-ditch effort to stigmatize the homosexual as a butcher and to point a finger at those responsible for his crime, Hoover linked the killer's evolution to Americans' culpability. The "present apathy of the public toward known perverts, generally regarded as 'harmless,'" he claimed, "should be changed to one of suspicious scrutiny. The 'harmless' pervert of today can be and often is the loathsome mutilator and murderer of tomorrow." Hoover never referred explicitly to homosexuals, but the words and phrases he used to refer this new enemy of the public—*pervert, deviant, sex fiend, sex criminal—* had already been applied to them time and time again in the popular media, and his readers readily associated those terms with them. By 1937 Henry and other homosexuals had to contend with the panic that Hoover had done much to incite. As historian James Polchin has pointed out, Hoover's "war" against them "made homosexuality a national policing concern. . . . In such fevered moments, queer men were often the target of police surveillance and vigilante violence," and historian Charles E. Morris III has labeled the period begun by Hoover's rabid crusade against them the "post-pansy panic."

To ensure that gay men never escaped the FBI's surveillance, Hoover devised a sex deviant file on index cards the same year that "War on the Sex Criminal" appeared. The cards contained information about the sexual habits of prominent citizens as well as ordinary homosexuals and listed the individual's name, occupation, and specific details of the FBI report with a reference number indicating where the full report on the individual could be found in the FBI's files.* Once identified by his agents, gay men were never free of their surveillance.

New York mayor Fiorello La Guardia joined forces with Hoover in his crusade. La Guardia's clean-up nabbed "500 . . . sex offenders . . . , of which 175 had been charged with various offenses involving homosexuality," who were convicted in New York's courts, and the number exploded the following year: "Twice as many men were charged with sex offenses from August 1 through September 1937 as were during the same period in 1936." The clean-up got worse. As historian Jennifer Terry has observed, "In preparation for the 1939 World's Fair," which opened on April 30 in New York, La Guardia directed his "police force" to ratchet up their crackdown "on men assumed to be homosexual, especially in Times Square and other tourist attractions . . . to make New York vice-free for both its residents and its visitors."

Then the "highly publicized murders" of three little girls—nine-year-old Einer Sporrer, eight-year-old Paula Magagna, and four-year-old Joan Kuleba—in Queens during the spring and summer of 1937 turned the post-pansy panic into hysteria. Although the three girls were sexually abused and murdered by heterosexual men, the news media and the police used words such as *pervert* and *deviant* that had long been associated with homosexuals to describe the killers, which directed the public's wrath toward them.

New York's sodomy laws made it a crime for men "to frequent or loiter in any public place," which included cabarets and theaters, as well as out-of-the-way places, such as parks, public restrooms, and alleys, or to solicit other "men for the purpose of committing a crime against nature or other lewdness."

---

* The file grew to over three hundred thousand names by 1977, forty years after its conception, when FBI staff destroyed it.

If convicted, they faced a six-month jail sentence, a fifty-dollar fine, or a two-year probation. The police applied the law so freely that they arrested any gay man they happened to spot.

During Henry's ten-year tenure with Contacts, at least one of its members had problems with the law. The member was in the military and was shocked and terrified when authorities questioned him about lewd materials another member of Contacts had mailed him. Henry also fell under the authorities' scrutiny. Authorities questioned him about several Contacts members who made sexual innuendoes to other male members. He could have been arrested and charged with obscenity, but he had covered his tracks well enough that the authorities didn't press charges against him. Still, the experience was serious enough to worry him.

It's no wonder, then, that by 1939, after a decade of shepherding Contacts, Henry announced to his members that he was ready to call it quits. He gave them several reasons why. To many, he claimed he didn't have time for the club. After all, Merlin Wand stepped down from Contacts after running it for only a little more than a year because of the extra workload. However, the truth was that, after his little chat with the authorities, Henry realized how threatened his position in the army and his livelihood were, something the married and father Wand hadn't had to consider. "As long as I am in the ARMY," Henry was convinced, "this is entirely too risky." He also had other, more personal and complex, reasons.

Despite his telling Fred Frisbie, Manuel boyFrank, and others that he wanted no part in organizing gay men, he had thought a great deal about what had gone wrong with the Society for Human Rights and how he might have done things differently. He hoped that Contacts would, ultimately, be a substitute for the earlier organization, but he felt he had failed with Contacts in one important, personal way. He hoped to find "romance and love" through it, but to his regret, none of the men in Contacts were attractive to him. It was chock-full of "intellectual riff-raff and screwballs," among them "the matrimonials, tramps expecting to marry a rich widow, and the ugly old spinsters dreaming to find a Prince Charming; the smut dealers which always bring to your door the post office inspectors; the Don Juans, many married, who like a little variety from cunt diet, etc. ad nauseam" and not a fitting mate for him. Others succeeded in finding someone attractive even if just for a quick tryst, and because of their successes and his failures, he couldn't help but feel as if he were being "used as a pimp for others to get their meat." It was time for him to call it quits.

8 | "FAVORED BY NATURE WITH IMMUNITY TO FEMALE 'CHARMS'"

WHEN HENRY ANNOUNCED THAT he was shutting down Contacts, some members were saddened and others were a little resentful, but none were as shocked or felt as abandoned as Manuel, who had moved from Staten Island to Manhattan. He was so anxious over the end of Contacts that he wrote to another correspondence club, the American Service, in New York. He hoped its director, Grace Bowes, might be able to give him some information about Henry. After pretending to want information about her club, he claimed that the way her ad for the American Service began reminded him of how Contacts' ads had, which couldn't have been further from the truth. Then he got down to the real reason he was writing. He wondered if the American Service had "any connexion with Contacts, the service operated by Mr. Henry Gerber. I subscribed to that service a few years ago and made some interesting contacts. Can you tell me where Mr. Gerber is and how he is doing?" Bowes never bothered to answer.

By New Year's 1940 Manuel had settled into his new home and wrote Henry at Contacts' PO box to tell him how disheartened he was over the news that Henry had dismantled Contacts and to ask if they might get together. He promised, "I'll try not to be a pest. Any chance?"

During the Thanksgiving holiday, Henry had moved into his new place at 1568 York Avenue. At the end of January, he responded to Manuel's letter, offering him some consolation over disbanding the club. "Contacts," Henry assured him, was "not really discontinued." He just wasn't in the "mood . . . to put it back into active service," but he had "some half-baked plan" that

106

he might "continue with the creme de la creme" of its membership someday, meaning those whom he had identified as homosexual. Not sure if that was enough to put Manuel's mind at ease, and wondering if Manuel might be a suitable bedmate, Henry agreed to meet him. "Am home every evening except Wednesday after 5.30 PM," he explained, "and all day Saturday and Sunday— except Saturday from 5 to 10 PM and Sunday from 5 to 8" and asked Manuel to call him at work ahead of time to let him know when he might show up and to speak loudly when he did because he had become "hard of hearing." He didn't have a phone at home.

Within a few days, Manuel had written to several members whom he knew only by their ID numbers, hoping that one of them would take Contact's reigns in hand until Henry was ready to or, at least, to recommend someone who might. His letters went to nos. 1744 and 10, whose identities he didn't know. As it turned out, no. 1744 was William Frank McCourt and no. 10 was Henry.

William Frank McCourt, circa 1944, was a friend of both Gerber and Manuel boyFrank. Known as "Frank" to his friends, McCourt was born on May 22, 1887, and died on April 22, 1955. *Courtesy of ONE Archives at the USC Libraries*

Manuel read both men's self-descriptions in the previous September's *Commentary*, the last issue Henry published. Frank's was short, within the fifty-word limit, and full of sexual innuendo: "NYC Male, secretary, bachelor. Anxious to hear from and to meet Contactors—male only—productively interested in photography, more particularly physique work, my hobby. Always glad to develop, print, exchange, suggest, advise along that line. Glad to have Contactors come in for a talk and a few drinks." Words and phrases like *bachelor*, "male only" and "physique work" identified him as gay, and with "Glad to have Contactors come in for a talk and a few drinks," he invited men to visit for a possible sexual encounter.

By comparison, Henry's listing, at over a thousand words, was full of cynicism and stippled with wisecracks:

> NYC Male, 44, proofreader, single. Favored by nature with immunity to female "charms." Atheist, amused by screwey [*sic*] antics of Homo Sapiens. Introvert, enjoying a quiet evening with classical music or non-fiction book. Looking around in life I can understand why monkeys protested over Darwin's thesis.
>
> Of Bavarian descent. Brought up in Catholic faith, but am now an avowed atheist. (God loves atheists because they do not molest him with silly prayers.) Believe in brotherhood of man, but think there is no hope for mankind to free itself from exploitation of the entrencht [*sic*] vested money changers. Religion is a racket and once one believes in a god or other supernatural powers, one is ready to swallow anything else, including Jonas and his whale. Believe in French sex morality, i.e., that it is not the business of the Government to interfere in the sexual enjoyment of adults as long as the rights of others are not violated.
>
> Immune to the alleged charms of the female sex, but do not "hate" women; consider them necessary in the scheme of nature. But if I had made this world, I would have designed a less messy and filthy modus operandi for procreation than "sex" and birth. Children could have been born by sneezing, or rubbing one's coccyx vigorously.

He continued in a similar vein for another 794 words. Like Frank, Henry made his sexual orientation clear with his first sentence, and just in case his readers hadn't caught on, he added, "Immune to the alleged charms of the female sex" a few lines later.

The first half or so of the letters that Manuel sent to nos. 10 and 1744 were identical and mentioned he regretted the end of Contacts and was surveying former members to see if they wanted it to be revived or another club organized to take its place. He admitted how difficult it was for him to figure out if a member was gay or not and then turned his quandary into a flirtatious joke: "In studying a man's listing and doping out his classification," he reminded nos. 10 and 1744, "you have to use your imagination and read between the legs—beg pardon, I mean between the lines. It takes us a couple of letters to feel each other up—excuse me all to hell, I mean to feel each other out." In the rest of the letters, he addressed both men individually, addressing specifics in their self-descriptions.

In his, Henry had mentioned he was "fond of reading nonfiction books" and "classical music," liked to hike and preferred "foreign, especially French films" over Hollywood's "goody-goody" movies, which depicted "all men honest and all women 'pure,'" and considered himself "truly civilized and self-sufficient," but welcomed Contacts members "of like minds" to write him. Nevertheless, the tone of a large portion of Henry's self-description was so cantankerous that there wasn't much for Manuel to respond to, but he did offer Henry some advice, telling him that he "ought to read some fiction" and lay off the nonfiction because "too much serious non-fiction puts a man in the mood of exasperation in which you seem, from your September salvo, to be in." Then returning to his playful humor, Manuel asked no. 10, "Can I come up and see you some time?"—using Mae West's famous invitation to sexual liaison. He ended the letter, "Yours all the way."

Manuel's letter to Frank McCourt was longer than the one he sent Henry by a full page. Frank was "interested in photography," specifically "physique work," and was "glad to develop, print, exchange, suggest, advise" beginning physique photographers, and that attracted Manuel. He thought Frank's collection of over a "thousand ... negatives and innumerable prints" of naked men was a gold mine and wondered if Frank would be interested in starting up a mail-order business with him to produce and distribute them along with "hard-to-get"—that is, sexually explicit—"literature." He even proposed that they could package the items in a special file box that he had invented and patented three years earlier. Getting it mass produced and making him wealthy was something of an obsession with him, but it wasn't his only invention. He had patented a contraption that clipped sheets of paper together five years earlier. He hadn't made a dime from either.

Frank had taken many of the nude photos in his collection himself, and he bought others from photographers who advertised their wares in physique journals. He used them to lure men to his home. Some bought the photos and left, others were willing to shuck off their clothes and pose for him, and a few slipped into bed with him. During the previous Christmas and New Year's holiday, for instance, Frank and Chuck, who had an open relationship, invited scores of mostly gay men to their home at 516 West 140th Street, and

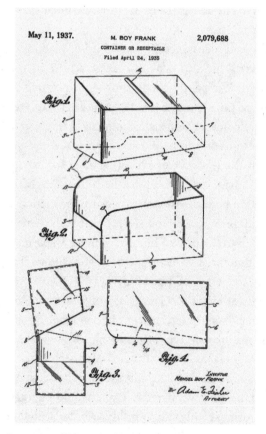

Manuel boyFrank patented several of his inventions, including this file box (patent application 2,079,688), one of his get-rich schemes that he unsuccessfully tried to get manufactured. *Author's collection*

he sold most of his stash of photographs to the soldiers, sailors, and civilians who visited.

A few days later, Frank replied to Manuel with a short, succinct note. He described himself briefly ("I'm 45, and look it"), mentioned his job experience ("Been a sailor, thank God; but a clerical worker for too, too many years"), and ended, "As to politics and religion, I haven't any that I know of, being at least as fed up with conventional radicalism as with tradition-worship. And my morals are quite elastic." Then he invited Manuel to visit him at his home for drinks and to examine his photograph collection. To make sure that Manuel knew what he was getting himself into, Frank added that his collection was "limited in scope—no women," and just in case Manuel thought his flirting had fallen on deaf ears, Frank signed off with "I am intensely interested." What exactly he was interested in he left up to Manuel's imagination.

During Manuel and Frank's exchange of letters, Manuel learned that Frank and Chuck rented rooms in their brownstone to gay men, and he considered moving into one of them. He asked Frank how much rent was and, hoping for a discount, offered to procure men for him: "As I meet a man who would be interested in resorting to the premises I will bring him around and have you look him over." He also wondered if he could bring one of his regular sex mates to Frank's home, a "colored young man" from Boston. Unlike Henry, Frank was racially prejudiced and told Manuel, "As to the negro, I don't think it would work—that is one convention we have not broken, and would not dare to, or want to. It might make for very awkward situations; and I know those of our friends who have tried to defy the taboo, have been made to regret it. I can meet them on their own grounds, so to speak,—but not on the home grounds."

Manuel wasn't able to meet up with Frank for a few weeks, but he did get together with Henry at Henry's place on York Avenue the last week of January 1940. They talked for hours. Manuel had been obsessing about Contacts, and he did his best to try to talk Henry into resurrecting it, this time just for men, and even resorted to stroking Henry's ego unabashedly. "Everybody regrets the passing of Contacts," he said, "and I am trying to get our men to agree to become sustaining members, paying perhaps twice the regular subscription just to keep the service in existence." Henry couldn't be persuaded. "Let me tell you from experience," he began, "it does not pay to do anything for them"—gay men. Then realizing Manuel might misunderstand his rancor, he explained, "I once lost a good job in trying to bring them together. Most men of that type are too scared to give their names or to join any association trying to help them; the other half are only interested in physical contacts and have not the slightest interest to help their cause. I found that out to my own sorrow." Manuel wouldn't take no for an answer, however, and finally, Henry had to put his foot down. "I would like to see such a service going," he said, "but you are more independent than I am, and will not risk my job again. Once is enough."

Henry suggested that *he* should revive it and gave him some advice. "You would not last long," he told Manuel, "trying to run a Contacts for men only, for homosexuals always get themselves in trouble. Ninety percent of all men are heterosexual and would not join your club; the other 10 percent probably do not read the one or two magazines which would take your ad . . . and so your income would be about three or four dollars a month from new members."

Despite butting heads over Contacts, Henry and Manuel's discussion turned to sex. Henry was always guarded when it came to his "private affairs" and was careful not to divulge them "to gossips." He must have felt comfortable enough with Manuel to let down his hair and explain what he was looking for in a sexual partner. "Personally," he admitted, "I am only interested in young boys around twenty who are willing to do all the 'dirty' work for a small fee, say a dollar," which was a bargain for the pinchpenny Henry.* Manuel was astonished that Henry resorted to male prostitutes and asked him why, when he was surrounded by so many handsome, young soldiers on Governors Island. Many of his friends had asked him the same thing, and he always told them that there weren't as many gay men in the military as they assumed and those who were sold their favors on Forty-Second Street, not on the base. Besides, he had had his share of them over the years, and most of the time, they disappointed. Of the "hundred soldiers" he had "tried out," he explained, "only two or three" reciprocated. Then he remembered a joke to distract Manuel from his failure: "Of course if I were a fairy and glory in a big stiff prick I would be like the queer" who, "when asked by a recruiting officer of the navy if he (the recruit) had ever been in the navy, answered quite literally. 'No, sir, quite on the contrary.'"

---

* Henry, and most of the gay men he knew, used *boy* and *boys* loosely, referring to children, adolescents, teenagers, young adults, and young men.

"I like young meat," Henry admitted to Manuel and crowed, "I have never yet run out" of them. When he moved to 1568 York Avenue, he continued, "I did *not* give my new address to a half dozen who were running me ragged at the old place" and scheduled those to whom he gave his new address to appear on his doorstep "on certain days of the week." He reserved the weekends "for replenishing the larder and variety." He ended up apologizing to Manuel, not for bragging but because he wasn't sexually interested in the forty-five-year-old: "Sorry you are not 20 years younger!"

Frank was still toying with Manuel's idea about the two of them beginning a physique photograph business together when, a few weeks later, Manuel contacted Frank and told him he and Henry had met. He had discussed their thoughts about going into the physique photograph business together with him, and Frank guessed correctly that "Henry Gerber didn't have anything very encouraging to say about" their "merchandising idea." Manuel badgered Frank about Contacts as he had with Henry. "I don't know of anyone who would seriously want to start anything like Contacts," he told Manuel, "but of course I would like to see it done, particularly if it were to be for men only; and would be glad to cooperate,—from the side lines."

Following up on Frank's earlier invitation, Manuel knocked on Frank and Chuck's door the evening of February 6, a Tuesday. As it turned out, their get-together wasn't entirely pleasant. Chuck had been ill for quite some time, and the couple was going through a tough time financially. To Manuel's discomfort, Frank and Chuck spent much of the time quarreling. Some of their money problems were caused by the difficulties they had in getting lodgers, especially gay men, whose rent would help defray their living costs. Frank let Manuel in on an idea he had come up with, hoping it would solve their problem. He told friends who told others that, if any of them sent him someone who rented one of their rooms, he would give them a finder's fee. He explained to a friend named Al what a potential lodger could expect at the McCourt-Ufford household:

> There is good food and plenty of it, cocktails before dinner, and if a fellow wants a highball later, there is no restriction on the frigidaire, or the liquor. . . . And if [he] wants to have a friend in for dinner—or for breakfast,—that's all right; in fact, "free and complete use of the

house" means just that; nothing is locked up. (There's a sun lamp, too, and if he's athletically inclined, the 5-in-1 set.) Plus a liberal attitude.*

Despite the arguments with Chuck, Frank enjoyed finally meeting Manuel face-to-face in large part thanks to their discussion of Manuel's fantasy of a community of men he christened the "Abbey of Thelema," which was similar to the commune that he and Maki had hoped to start. Thelema wasn't something Manuel invented but a movement already in existence founded on a "complicated set of magical, mystical and religious beliefs formed in the 20th century by Aleister Crowley," whose adherents followed one rule: "'Do what thou wilt. . . .' And 'Thou wilt' here means to live by one's own True Will.'" Manuel was especially attracted to Thelema because its sole commandment opened membership up to homosexuals.

Manuel had other schemes up his sleeves and relayed them all to Frank. "You have so MANY ideas and angles," Frank told Manuel, just as happy as Manuel was to find someone willing to imagine a better future, but he also realized that Manuel liked to dream big but wasn't interested in doing the work it took to make the dream a reality. He warned Manuel to "concentrate on one at a time" and shared his own plans for a men-only organization. All he would need, Frank explained, was a few men to help him run it, but he didn't go into any more detail than that. Until he could get his group up and running, he offered his house as a meeting place for Manuel's abbey, "preferably after eight o'clock, when the decks will be cleared and it will be possible to get right down to the business in hand."

Within a few days, Manuel came up with two other schemes.

He was tired of reading antihomosexual articles, editorials, and letters to the editors in magazines and newspapers and wanted to do something about it. He hoped to band some like-minded men together who, when they read homophobic items, would let the others in the group know. In turn, they would start a letter-writing campaign to offset the homophobe's ideas. Henry had already agreed to join but warned Manuel that any organization that set out to defend homosexuality needed money as well as the support of prominent physicians and attorneys on call if they were arrested. All three were beyond their reach.

---

* Frank's "5-in-1 set" referred to an in-home workout device.

Manuel called his second scheme a "Santa Claus service." A man would find a sex mate for those men who subscribed to the service for "about $10 or $20 a piece (of ass)" and deliver him, like a Christmas gift, to the member. Henry called it "fantastic" and told Manuel that it "could be arranged," but as frugal as he tended to be, he also advised Manuel that "it would be much cheaper to go to Times Square to pick up the things on display there and pay them the regular small fee of $1 to $2. Then you are always sure you have a ringer and not a dud."

Henry couldn't help but poke fun at the pimp-as-Santa-Claus arrangement by coming up with a scheme of his own. Members would "pass around" a "list of their cast-off lovers" to one another every week. "What you might not like," he told Manuel, "may be just my ideal, and vice versa." He even devised a "weekly schedule: Henry's Paul to see Erling on Monday. Erling's John to see Henry on Tuesday; Frank's boy Nick to see Erling on Wednesday and Henry on Thursday and Henry's Ray to see Frank on Tuesday, until we have run through the list of 3,569,695 punks in New York City." Manuel finally admitted that the service wasn't his idea at all but that Frank had once "told" him of one "run by a hospital orderly in West 57th Street."*

Henry and Manuel's correspondence tapered off for a little while, but Manuel and Frank's persisted, fueled by their shared interest in nude male photographs. Frank sent many of the pictures that he had taken to Manuel who was more than a little perplexed by Frank's ability to find "so many interesting young men" and completely dumbfounded over how Frank was able to convince them to pose for him. Frank never let Manuel in on his secret.

Frank did mention he had run into a problem. He was no good at printing the film and was forced to hire others to do the job for him. One was Antonni O'Brien, who was very good at his job but charged so much that it ate up Frank's profits. O'Brien got himself into a little trouble, perhaps with the postal authorities, and vanished. A short time later, Frank hired another man named Le Gere to print his negatives, but after working for Frank for a few months, Le Gere quit because several wealthy men agreed to buy all the pictures he could produce regularly for a hefty price and he didn't need the extra income he got from Frank anymore. As an apology for not being able

* One of Frank and Chuck's lodgers, Luke Raviella, worked as an attendant in a hospital on West Fifty-Seventh Street, but whether he ran the service or not is unknown.

to send Manuel any new photographs, Frank invited Manuel to a party that would include "half-a-dozen fine men." What went on during the party is unknown, but by mid-March, Manuel and Frank had slept together, and in one of his letters to Frank, Manuel became flirtatious. "As you know, I give and take both, myself," Manuel reminded Frank and added, "how I wish you and I could get together again for a little give and take!"

Not to be stymied in his quest for physique photos, Manuel set out to find other sources. He ordered some from Ermitage Studio's catalog, and at Frank's urging, he contacted Lee Birger, editor of *Physical Fitness*. At the time, Birger was having financial difficulties and had posted an appeal for help from its readers: "We are working in a field that is intensely interesting to us and we know it is for you. We again ask for your help which we need so badly. Do your part to help us increase our circulation. Tell all your friends about *Physical Fitness*." A fan of the magazine's photographs of nearly naked bodybuilders, Frank had gotten acquainted with Birger when he read Birger's call for help and "advised Birger to consider establishing some sort of an association that would include a magazine subscription with the membership dues."

Birger sent Manuel a sample copy, hoping he might subscribe. Although he was "stony broke" and promised to subscribe when he was "flush again," Manuel rose to the occasion and sent Birger a list of the names and addresses of thirteen men he knew who might be interested in subscribing and suggested that Birger should also send them a sample issue to entice them to subscribe. Among the group was Erling Stenberg and Walter Schafer. Manuel must have known Henry enjoyed photographs of naked young men as much as the other men in their circle. He put Henry's name at the top of the list. Manuel even suggested that Birger advertise in the Guiana Hobby Club, a pen pal group that was "full of old Contacts members, all homosexuals."

Six months later, Frank invited Manuel to a "'surprise' (and stag)" birthday party for Chuck on Saturday afternoon, September 28. He wanted to hold it in the evening, but because of Chuck's ill health, he had to retire early. Manuel had a great time with the young men he met there. His favorites were Dick Stuart, Antonni O'Brien (who had unexpectedly reappeared), George Tupper, and Paul Delfino.

On October 10 Manuel told Frank he was moving to Culver City, west of Los Angeles, where he would stay with his elderly parents at 3346 McManus Avenue. The city fathers had dubbed it the "Heart of Screenland" because of the many movies filmed there. *Citizen Kane* was in production in Culver City that year; that (and a note from a friend) set Manuel off on another get-rich-quick scheme. When Walter Schafer, a "grand guy" whom Manuel had met at one of Frank's parties, learned that Manuel had moved near L.A., he promised Manuel to send him contact information for a film writer he knew, probably Roger Q. Denny. Schafer hoped that Manuel might be able to "do something in the way of amateur motion pictures," a reference to producing films with male-male sexual activities, a sure-fire way to make money, or so Manuel hoped.

Schafer lived in Hartford, Connecticut, and was married but had sexual contact with other men. Henry had also met Schafer through Frank but wasn't at all impressed. Schafer told Henry that he liked "to have homosexual intercourse, passively" but claimed he wasn't homosexual. "That of course is so much horseshit," Henry told Manuel, convinced that "any man who lets another man have intercourse with him is just as much a bitch" as those who admitted they were gay. Henry assumed Schafer was just another so-called bisexual, in denial of his homosexuality, and reminded him of Al Meininger and how Meininger's lie caused so many problems for him. Henry told Manuel, "I hate such hypocrisy. It is very widespread among married men."

Although films with male-male sexual activities were difficult to come by in the early 1940s, they were hardly unheard of. Historian Thomas Waugh has identified a "rare group of about fifteen interwar films" in which the "male same-sex activity ranged from a peripheral gesture scarcely disrupting the continuum of the plot to a major episode." With one exception, "all presented male homosexual behavior in the context of heterosexual hegemony," and that exception was "an American film produced between 1929 and 1930, *The Surprise of a Knight*" that focused "exclusively on same-sex activity." Others, such as *A Stiff Game* (1930) and *Piccolo Pete* (1935) presented a scene or two of sexual activity among men as a sideline to a heterosexual film. Other films Manuel and his circle might have seen included *Mixed Relations* (1921), *The Aviator* (1932), *Broadway Interlude* (1931–1933), *The Bellhop* (1936), *Dr. Hardon's Injections* (1936), and *Grocery Boy* (1944). "In such films," Waugh discovered, "men share women, men get off watching men with women, men help men with women, men supplant men with women, men procure women for men, etc."

Manuel's dreams of becoming a producer of blue films for a homosexual audience was short-lived. Denny wasn't interested in Manuel's new scheme and made himself "hard to catch free of his work and social obligations." A successful screenwriter in Hollywood with credits that included *Citizen Kane*, Denny wouldn't have jeopardized his career by working on a pornographic (and illegal) film.

Manuel hadn't bothered to let Henry know that he had moved to California until he was unpacked and settled into his parents' place, over four months after the fact. When he did finally contact Henry, Manuel reminded him that, when they met in Henry's York Street rooms, he had agreed to send Manuel his Contacts membership lists, including the members' self-descriptions. Manuel wanted to look through them to find men in his area who might be suitable bedmates, but to protect himself, Henry had destroyed them. He wasn't about to let them get into the hands of the police as the Society for Human Rights files had.

Henry, Manuel boyFrank, and Frank McCourt only met physically a few times during what would become a two-decade-long friendship, but they kept in contact with one another through letter writing, a three-man correspondence club of sorts. Through it, their friendship developed, despite occasional differences in opinion about politics and religion. Here and there, one or the other of them fell silent for weeks or months or even years, angry at something one of the others had said or simply too busy with work or life to write. Much of their correspondence focused on gossip—who was living where, who was bedding whom, who had been arrested, where to get physique photographs—but almost as much was focused on how they might support one another through the many struggles they, and the rest of the queer community, faced daily. Other men occasionally contributed to the network of letters. They came and went, passing on or asking for information, but none lasted for more than a few letters. Indeed, even Frank's contributions were far fewer than either Manuel's or Henry's and were always much shorter than those of the other two. With tongue in cheek, Manuel dubbed the exchange "Henry's epistles to the perverts."

9 | "I NEARLY FELL OUT OF MY CHAIR!"

NAZIS INVADED POLAND IN SEPTEMBER 1939, but the United States clung to its isolationist stance. Americans had been overwhelmed by the bloodshed and deaths during World War I and weren't eager for a repeat of the carnage, but by September of the following year, Congress took note of the writing on the wall and "passed the nation's first peacetime conscription act," aiming to draft nine hundred thousand men into "active duty" in preparation for the inevitable.

During peacetime, the military felt it had a surplus of potential soldiers, and the "armed forces decided to exclude certain groups of Americans, including women, blacks, . . . and . . . homosexuals" because, military leaders rationalized, those groups "made poor combat soldiers, their presence in units" threatened "morale and discipline, and their integration" turned "the military into a testing ground for radical social experimentation rather than a strong fighting force." However, the military couldn't afford to exclude them if it wanted to win an eventual war. In October 1941, instead of making do with the nine hundred thousand it had already conscripted, the military herded into its ranks "more than 16 million citizens and residents, 10 million of whom were draftees," most "unmarried white young men," of whom, as historian Allan Bérubé estimated, "at least 650,000 and as many as 1.6 million . . . were homosexual."

Because of the draft, young men began to disappear from their circles of friends. Manuel complained from California that the "draft has played hell with our ranks," conscripting many "and making it hard to attract new fellows. Some of the soldiers and sailors have been warned . . . not to make contacts freely with civilian men whom they don't know, lest they give information to enemy spies." Nevertheless, gay men who weren't drafted continued to hold the parties they had often hosted during peacetime, and gay servicemen told their friends on leave in New York and other major cities where to go and whom to see for a good time. The decimated groups began to attract new faces.

Earlier that year, Henry had begun the process that would pave his way for retirement from the army. He hoped to receive "disability with a 3/4 pay pension," but his application was held up because of a bill that had been passed by the House of Representatives and was then with the Senate. Approved on June 30, it provided an "enlisted man of the Regular Army ... who has had less than twenty years of service in the military forces of the United States and who had become permanently incapacitated for active service" with "75 per centum of the average pay he was receiving for six months prior to his retirement plus a money allowance of $9.50 ... in lieu of rations and clothing and $6.25 per month in lieu of quarters, fuel, and light." Henry was waiting to hear if he was approved for retirement with benefits. If so, he swore that he would stay in New York, the "only civilized city in the United States."

At the same time, the staff of the Recruiting Publicity Bureau, where Henry was still working, went into overdrive, producing of all sorts of brochures and booklets, as well as *Recruiting News*, but the Bureau's publications that were most visible to US citizens were its scores of propaganda posters. One pressed young men: BECOME A PARATROOPER. JUMP INTO THE FIGHT. Another urged women to join the US Army Nurse Corps: NURSES ARE NEEDED NOW! By autumn, the bureau's production slowed down, and suddenly Henry's office was at a standstill. Then on December 7, 1941, the Imperial Japanese Army Air Service bombed Pearl Harbor, and the United States declared war on Japan, which led it into war with Germany and Italy. Americans had crossed the threshold into World War II, and out of the blue, Henry took a vacation, his first.

Henry hadn't been out of New York since he moved there from Chicago fifteen years earlier, and except for holidays like Thanksgiving and Christmas, he hadn't had any real time off for that entire time, either. His weekends weren't even his own. He had spent too many Saturdays and Sundays working on Contacts, mailing lapsed membership notices, answering requests for information, typing the stencils for issues of *Commentary* and *Chanticleer*, and submitting ads to popular magazines. The time he spent on the correspondence club was so time-consuming that he called it a "mill-stone-around-my-neck," and he was eager to have some time off and hoped to meet someone who might "excite" his "jaded appetite."

Always frugal to a fault, Henry took advantage of the cost reduction in roundtrip tickets that many railroad companies were offering servicemen and made reservations. He planned to spend a few days in Miami and Key West and then sail to Havana for Christmas. In late December, he got on a train at Penn Station in frigid New York and traveled a day and a half south to balmy Miami. No sooner had he stepped off the train at Miami Central than he ran into an "old soldier friend" who satisfied his "jaded appetite." Once in Key West, which had "long been popular with queer people even before Tennessee Williams first called the city home in the 1940s," Henry picked up another serviceman, but he wouldn't be so lucky in Havana.

Cuba's capital had developed a sizable queer community, and male prostitutes congregated along the Paseo del Prado, a main street of Havana, and in the Parque Central that adjoined it. Henry knew about the Prado and the park, but he "had little time to do any cruising" during his stay. Besides, the language barrier kept him on the straight and narrow, but he got an eyeful, watching the scores of attractive men on the make as they strolled along the Passeo. As tempting as Havana was, Henry missed New York and the men who visited him on schedule. He hadn't bothered to let Manuel know he had been out of the country, but "b.i.o.n."—believe it or not—he sent Frank "*three* postcards." Virulent atheist Henry's sudden friendliness toward Frank, a devout Roman Catholic, surprised him.

From the beginning of their relationship, Henry had been as friendly toward Frank as he was with everyone, but he was also dubious. Like so many other gay men Henry knew, Frank was fixated on sex, not just engaging in it but also in photographing nude men, swapping and selling the photographs, and hosting men-only parties in his home, which often ended up as sexual romps. Historian David K. Johnson discovered that, during the war years, hosts for similar parties often hired men to mingle in posing straps or nude among the attendees, but Frank's financial straits would have kept him from hiring anyone. Instead, he relied on men's sexual impulses and peer pressure to liberate his guests' libidos. Frank and Chuck's home quickly became the hub of a homosexual network of military men and civilians alike.

Some of the sex parties Frank held were impromptu. One Saturday evening in October, for example, "Dick S." dropped by Frank and Chuck's place for a spur-of-the-moment visit, and another man, a "fellow from Connellsville," Pennsylvania, showed up unexpectedly the same night. After introductions and small talk, Dick and the other man stripped, and Frank photographed them. Dick's penis was about "8½" but the "fellow from Connellsville" was "most phenomenal—somewhere around 10, 11 and 12" inches, and "Dick's," Frank gushed, "looked real puny beside it."

Typically, Frank planned most of the sex parties he held and steeped them in ritual. The men who arrived had to

> remove their nether garments on entering the house [for] the "Kiss of Peace" . . . , which consists of sitting around in a circle; one kneels before the man next [to] him and at least presses his lips on the Object of Desire, or thereabouts; when the first has reached his third, the man who had been sitting next [to] him rises and kneels, and so on—and as each completes the circle he returns to his seat for the attentions of all the others. Some adhere strictly to the rules, others of course hold up the line and have to be pried loose from each inturn [sic]—and if there should be those who "don't do anything themselves," or are entirely Greek about it, they stay in their seats and receive ministrations.

Once the round-robin of fellatio was completed, the men paired off, often adding a third or a fourth man.

Even Henry had experienced the ritual at Frank's one evening with "8 or 9 old bitches and two younger ones, one about 25 and the other 30. They were down on their knees praying—or is it playing—all during the evening. Only the younger was attractive enough to me to be tackled but there was no chance. The idea that I would have to kiss these old bitches" was "preposterous to me." Henry was just as disappointed at another party that included a "dozen elderly men and the only two young and handsome men" who "immediately fell around each others' [sic] necks and carried on" until they disappeared "into one of the siderooms for the rest of the evening. I left disgusted although one of the older ones slubbered over me. You are fortunate not to be handicapped by a predilection for youth as I am."

Manuel had experienced a less-ritualized but similar sexual bash. "In San Diego, years ago," Manuel enthusiastically recalled, men would shove two big, double beds together, rope the adjacent legs together to keep the beds from getting pushed apart, and spread the bedding out to make one big wrestling mat. Half a dozen men could wallow on it.

All of them took off their shoes, and most of them would strip to the waist, while the elder brethren would go it raw. Not all of them always got on the bed right away. Some wanted to look at some post cards, of which a good collection was on hand. But sooner or later they would all lie down or crawl around on the beds, as suited their purpose.

In the beginning the fellows would take things gradual. With a good proportion of young men, there were thick chests and muscular arms to admire, as well as other things to investigate. The expert and experienced would set good examples for the bashful, and seeing how another couple did it was bound to warm up even the cold or cowardly.

Frank had first experienced the fellatio ceremony during his World War I stint in the navy as a pay clerk. He didn't mean for it to be simply foreplay but to ensure that every man who showed up at his door for the party was gay. Frank reasoned that, if authorities planted a cop in their midst, he would balk at being expected to strip, and even if he were willing to, he would refuse to perform fellatio, revealing his real reason for attending the party. To memorialize the parties, Frank snapped pictures of the activities. He sent some to Manuel to add to his collection.

Frank also distributed information about where his friends could order written erotica or male-on-male movies, although he never made any himself. The source was usually someone with whom he corresponded. One of his more unique suppliers of both was a "Forest Ranger" who wrote fictional "case histories" and took photographs of the "strange and unusual, hermaphroditism and such." Although Frank wasn't at all attracted to the ranger's more esoteric prints, the ranger had other photographs that were more to his liking.

Along with everything else, Frank often sent Manuel and others the addresses of men who lived in cities and towns near them and who might become friends and bedmates. Manuel wrote to many of them, and while most didn't respond to his overtures, a few did. One was Roger Q. Denny, the screenwriter whom Schafer had hoped to introduce to boyFrank months earlier. The two finally met, and Frank told Manuel that he had "made quite an impression on Denny." Manuel's involvement with Ed Adams, another man he met through Frank, wasn't as successful initially. He was "good," Manuel recalled, "but inhibited" and "particular as to what he takes in his mouth."

Frank became the hub in a network of homosexuals, and his role was solidified at one of his get-togethers. "We've been having some exciting parties, now and again," Frank bragged to Manuel, "to Kiss the Boys Goodby [sic] when they came to town on furlough, expecting to be sent overseas. Sometimes they were, but mainly" they were sent "to the Great American Desert, for further toughening." At one of the parties, six of the men talked Frank into forming a club and publishing a bulletin along the lines of Contacts' *Commentary*, through which they would keep in touch during the war. They and Frank had seen ads in magazines like *Popular Science* for a group called the United States Rocket Society and were thinking along the lines of a group like it.

The United States Rocket Society "numbered 4,000" members, "four-fifths of whom were in the military." One of its ads soliciting membership began, "Rocket to the Moon? Soon!" then described the Society as a "nation-wide organization of service men and technicians of all kinds who are determined to see that our Country wins the RACE TO CONQUER SPACE!" Undoubtedly, the mention of military men had caught not only Frank's eye but the attention of others in the group, and they charged him with writing to Robert L. Farnsworth, its director, in Glen Ellyn, Illinois, for information on how to form a chapter in Manhattan. Neither Frank nor the others were interested in conquering space, but the rocket society would afford the club decorum and decency, camouflaging its gay membership.

The unsuspecting Farnsworth was all too happy to give Frank the go-ahead. Farnsworth sent Frank two lists, one with the names and addresses of the club members who lived in New York City and the other with the contact information of those who had requested information about the group but hadn't joined. Frank invited the men on the lists to his chapter's meetings. He wasn't "indulging" himself with "any extravagant amount of hope" that he would attract a large number of gay men to his group, he promised Manuel, but he believed that the Manhattan chapter "*should* eventually furnish a recruit or three for nudity and other things."

Among those interested in joining Frank's rocketeers, the name given to members, was his lodger, fifty-two-year-old Aubrey A. Levenseller, who was unemployed; Frank's teenage nephew from Yonkers, whom he hoped wouldn't attend any of the meetings because the youngster would put a damper on the sexual activities; and John A. Pyle, thirty-four years old, who lived in Brooklyn and worked for Robins Dry Dock & Repair Company, which built and repaired ships for the war effort. Frank scheduled the first meeting of the chapter for Tuesday, January 27, 1942, at his and Chuck's home. He fell ill and couldn't hold the meeting as scheduled but rescheduled it six months later. Thereafter, the chapter would meet on the last Tuesday of each month from eight to ten o'clock. Frank even promised refreshments as an incentive to attendance.

In keeping with the initial group's interest in keeping in touch with one another, Frank published *Equinox Errant*. Each issue was "2 legal-size hectographed pages" and included lists of the "addressees and names of the various rocketeer members, news concerning them and relevant information." Kepner described it as "very closety, with a sprinkling of het jokes in the midst of a lot of army-buddy stuff." The newsletter's title echoed the title of a popular, homoerotic travel book, *Canoe Errant*, by Roland Raven-Hart, one of Frank's friends who became a rocketeer.

At least a third of Frank's rocketeers were in one or another branch of the military. He listed them in the *Equinox Errant* as they joined, following Henry's practice with *Commentary*, and he added notes to some addresses. Many simply warned, "Letters censored," while others were longer: "Insists letters *to* the base are not censored, hope he's right." Frank was warning his members to be circumspect in what they said in letters and what they sent to servicemen, especially physique photographs.

The rocketeers didn't always heed Frank's warning. After his induction, the military sent Cpl. Paul Delfino, a rocketeer, to Camp Swift, Texas, where he helped to guard the group of nearly four thousand German prisoners of war confined there. He supplemented his army pay by selling photographs of nude women to the German POWs and asked rocketeer Roger Denny to supply them to him. Denny sent what he could gather to Delfino. The FBI found out about the exchange, and an agent questioned Delfino. Luckily, because the nudes were of women and not men, Delfino got away with a slap on the wrist.

To keep the mood of *Equinox Errant* light and, in the process, to help throw any postal inspector who opened rocketeers' mail off track, Frank liked to conclude the bulletin with a joke or two. For instance, he added a "Christmas story" at the end of one:

A little boy wrote God instead of Santa Claus, asking for $100. The letter was passed on until it reached the Postmaster General in Washington, who sent the boy $5 "from God."

In thanking God, the boy ended his letter. "It is too bad you sent the money by way of Washington, for, as you might have known, those bastards down there kept 95% of it!"

With his usual biting humor, Henry belittled the rocketeers: "It seems to me it would be more appropriate to affiliate with the National Society of Morticians, you know, bury the stiff, etc." Frank knew what he was doing, using the rocketeers to hide the club's real nature. The national group gave his chapter a veneer of decency and, because so many servicemen were members of the national group, it deflected any suspicion about the chapter members' sexuality. Regardless of his criticism, Henry not only joined the rocketeers—as did Manuel—but also the Exclusive Hobby Club, which had been advertised on the "Leaguers' Page" of *Strength and Health*. That suggests he browsed copies of the bodybuilder magazine at least occasionally.

Henry was as interested in sex as much as any of the men whom he knew despite his occasional bouts of prudery, but he was very practical and forthcoming about it. "I am only interested in getting my own satisfaction," he told Manuel, "and look at others only as a sex *object*, a means to gratification of myself" while, in the same breath, he admitted his desire for more: "There is nothing more beautiful than mutual love, naked in bed, with kissing and embracing the other person. With me it does not matter 'how one goes off,' the main thing is the embrace and kiss." Frank was the only other person with whom he let down his hair, confessing that "romance and love" had been his "ideal" all of his life, but that he had come to realize that it "hardly exists," at least for him, and that "one must adjust oneself to reality if one cannot adjust reality to own's [sic] own ideas."

Bob Hoffman founded *Strength and Health*, one of the most highly respected physical culture magazines, in 1932, shortly after Henry took charge of Contacts the second and last time. Photographs of scantily clad musclemen accompanied its articles much to the delight of its burgeoning homosexual readership. If the articles' photographs weren't satisfying enough, they could find advertisements for physique photographers' wares in the back pages of the magazine where they were sure to find something that struck their fancy.

Another aspect of *Strength and Health* that attracted them was the League, a pen pal club sponsored by Hoffman.

Hoffman invited adolescents and young men to join the League. He asked his young readers:

> What could be a nicer hobby than to exchange and fill an album with snap shots? Think of the interesting pleasurable hours you can spend bringing back memories of your friends and your past experiences. . . . Obtain as many physique photos as you can from your friends and through actual trades. . . . You'll obtain pleasure from the hobby of making a photograph album, and will interest others when they see the fine collection of photos you have.

Gay men saw Hoffman's notice as an open door beyond which they would definitely find physique photos but, perhaps, also a bedmate.

The revenue the League brought in was substantial. Leaguers, as Hoffman dubbed the club's members, had to subscribe to the magazine before they could join the club, and they made up a "substantial portion" of its subscription base and "kept the magazine financially solid during the Great Depression with "monthly sales of 4,800 in June 1934" that sky-rocketed to "51,333 copies in October 1936." Single-issue purchases were also hefty, thanks to newsstand sales to homosexuals and heterosexuals alike.

Hoffman claimed his reason for running the club was to create a space where young men and teenagers could air their problems and make contact with a pal. That space was a special section of the magazine dedicated to club members, the "S & H Leaguers' Page," and made airing problems or finding friends easy. Like other pen pal clubs, the Leaguers' Page included brief self-descriptions, but unlike typical correspondence clubs, the self-descriptions included members' names and addresses. One member could write another directly without Hoffman serving as a middleman. This kept him out of the loop and safe from prosecution by the postal authorities, but it attracted others, specifically gay men, who didn't need to belong to the club to obtain the contact information. All they needed was the cost of an issue, fifteen cents in its earliest days.

Some of the leaguers used the page to brag about their accomplishments. Ivanhoe Pierce of 23 Logan Street in Denver announced that he had won a "bronze medal for touching the palms of his hands to the floor 150 times without bending his knees" during an exercise he didn't identify, while George McComber who lived at 320 East Third Street in Oklahoma City wanted other leaguers to know that he had won a "silver medal for performing 20 floor dips with 32½ pounds on his back" and a "gold medal for chinning 10 repetitions with 28 pounds of weight on his feet." Harold W. Schmidt received mail at PO Box 173, Terminal Island, California, and reported that he had been hired at the "Department of Justice through physical fitness he secured by the used of bar bells," while at the same time, Raye Peterson used the page to ask for leads for a job. He wanted "employment in a gymnasium" and gave his address as 529 Asylum Street, Flint, Michigan.

Within the Leaguers Page was a special subsection for those who were specifically "Interested in Photographic Studies," another phrase for physique photographs. Neither Edward Hurcomb, who was "interested in photographic studies" and wanted "to exchange photos" with other leaguers, nor Harrison B. Fahn, who wanted to meet other leaguers "who enjoy" photography, had to be ambiguous at all, unlike Henry's Contacts members. Whether he knew it, Hoffman could not have been more solicitous of his homosexual readership.

More than a few of the leaguers weren't at all interested in teaming up with training buddies or jobs in their area but in photographs of well-built men. Because the club was hosted by a physical culture magazine, League members could be confident that the pictures or photography referred to would be of young, muscular, scantily clad or naked men. For example, Andrew A. Jutt of 627 Gray Street, Louisville, Kentucky, who was "interested in writing music, sound motion pictures and the stage," enjoyed "collecting pictures of those who practice the S. & H. life"—i.e., bodybuilding—and wanted "to receive letters and photos from all" with a similar "hobby." Harry C. Sackoff, 58 South Ann Street, Mobile, Alabama, was "interested in French and photography," but it's unclear if he knew that, in gay slang, *French* was a synonym for "oral sex."

It didn't take members of the club, or those who subscribed or bought copies at newsstands, much effort to shift the seemingly innocent show-and-tell aspect that Hoffman supported into an outright show-me-yours-and-I'll-show-you-mine proposition. One of the leaguers, Philip Miller, wrote to Hoffman to complain that he had "only received twelve replies" from his request for photos from other subscribers, "and most of these were from fellows who wanted to trade pictures of a questionable nature. You know what I mean, unadorned."*

Hoffman replied to Miller's complaint, "It takes all sorts of people to make a world they say, but too many of the wrong kind, those with queer tendencies took advantage of the league notes and it came very close to putting us out of business." Hoffman was referring to his trial in a federal court for violating the Comstock Act, and although not convicted, he remembered the "U.S. district attorney shouting and ranting about that 'Slimy Salacious *Strength and Health* magazine, that spawning ground, that breeding ground for unnatural sex practices. Why they even operate a department, in which they encourage readers to write to each other and exchange unnatural sex letters and pictures.'" Hoffman disbanded the S & H League at the end of 1944.

No sooner had Henry returned from Cuba than he found himself in hot water—again.

In February Henry heard a knock on his door. His Liggett Hall roommate, a gay soldier who may have been Drexel, was away, and when Henry answered it, G-2 agents from the Military Intelligence Division of the US Army were standing there. Since moving to New York, he had been beaten up "four or five times" while cruising, "but with the exception of a few black eyes and the loss of not more than a few dollars," he "escaped serious injury." The men in his office at the Publicity Recruiting Bureau and on base would have noticed Henry's injuries, rumors would have circulated, suspicions raised, and the military authorities got wind of Henry's sexuality.

But Henry was far from passive in his response to such violence. A few years earlier, before Henry moved into Liggett Hall, a "punk" whom he had propositioned on the street mugged him. Henry tracked the robber down and alerted the cop on the beat, who arrested him, but the process of getting justice frustrated him. He was the only witness to the crime and had to appear in court to make sure the complaint wasn't dismissed, but the young man's lawyer was able to get continuances for the hearing five times, hoping to wear Henry down until he simply stopped coming to court. Instead, Henry became more steadfast in his resolve to get justice. He also wanted to show

---

* In the mid-1940s, the Leaguers' Page caught the attention of twenty-three-year-old Bob Mizer, and in April 1945 he placed a notice there asking for pen pals. He received hundreds of replies. He would later be one of the most influential publishers of physique photographs with his monthly *Physique Pictorial* and through his mail-order business, Athletic Model Guild.

the mugger and his lawyer that being homosexual didn't mean he was weak and that, as one, he deserved the same protection under law as anyone else. Eventually, the young man was convicted and imprisoned in Elmira Reformatory in upstate New York.

The G-2 agents searched Henry's room for photographs of male nudes, letters from men proposing him or mentioning their sexual exploits, documents that revealed he was a member of a suspicious correspondence club, anything that they might use as evidence of his homosexuality. They found nothing among Henry's things, but they did find a photograph of a young man performing fellatio that his roommate had hidden in his bureau. The photo was obviously not Henry's, but they arrested him anyway. He was confined to a cell in Castle Williams, the lockup on Governors Island, for seven months while he awaited trial.

In August Henry went before a Section VIII hearing, which was typically held to investigate suspected homosexuals who, if found guilty, were dishonorably discharged. The G-2 "tried to get me out of the army" on a charge of "sodomy," Henry recalled, but he wasn't concerned because there were no witnesses and no proof. "No partner in sex," he understood, "will condemn himself by squawking about his partner and co-sinner," which would be an admission of his own guilt and opening himself up to prosecution. As Henry bluntly put it, "It takes a cocksucker to catch a cocksucker." The prosecution even tried to convict Henry under the Comstock Act but couldn't because there was no proof that the photograph had been sent through the mail.

Henry made it a practice to know the sodomy laws in many states, and especially those in which he lived, and so was aware of New York's statues against homosexual acts. At one point during the proceedings, he tossed a wrench into the procedures to see what would happen by telling the court that he limited his sexual activity to "mutual masturbation with men over 21." In New York, men couldn't be arrested for that, and his admission couldn't be used to convict him. Given Henry's testimony, the prosecution's medical expert, a psychiatrist, could only conclude, to Henry's shock, that he was "*not a homosexual.*" The psychiatrist believed that, to be a homosexual, a man had to engage in fellatio or anal intercourse, a commonly held misconception among so-called experts and the public alike.

"I nearly fell out of my chair!" Henry recalled, delighting in the irony, and quipped, "Imagine me fighting all my life for our cause and then be told I was not a homosexual!"

The military authorities had no choice but to abandon their attempt to convict Henry. At the same time, and perhaps simply to get rid of him, they offered to give him the retirement that he had been after for so long. He gladly accepted. He hoped to receive a pension *and* disability pay, but after a quick examination by the army's physicians, they concluded that his "disability existed prior to [his] enlistment" but wouldn't decide about his pension until later. The army dismissed fifty-year-old Henry without a cent of "retirement pay" on August 24 and with scant possibility, at his age, of finding work. He also lost his home in Liggett Hall. Fortunately, the frugal Henry had thoughtfully saved a few thousand dollars over the years, so he wasn't destitute. He contacted Frank, who, Henry knew, was constantly on the lookout for lodgers and learned he had a vacancy. Henry moved into 516 West 140th Street almost immediately and deliberated on what he might do next.

Living at Frank and Chuck's home was no picnic. Henry got along well enough with the two men, but Frank's collection of physique photographs and their men-only parties quickly became a thorn in Henry's side. He described Frank as a "dopey old fellow, half dead and not interested in anything but his picture gallery," but he didn't want to be too harsh on his landlord and admitted that maybe "he had the right attitude" by holding sex parties, collecting photographs of naked men, and forgetting about trying to change laws that criminalized homosexuals.

Yet, while living there, Henry's disdain over Frank's sex parties grew more intense. He was jealous. "I never saw anyone there but a bunch of old queans,"* he told Manuel, "and whenever anyone under the age of 69 would drop in the others would gang up on him," leaving him out in the cold. "When one of my friends came up to see me," he continued, "the McC's"—Frank or Chuck—"would invariably date him up." Henry was unclear on whether the men who visited him were actual buddies or male prostitutes, but his jealousy comes through loud and clear.

---

* Although *quean* initially denoted a female or male prostitute, many gay men, including Henry, used it to denote an effeminate gay man.

On April 27, 1943, the federal government passed an act addressed to older men. Popularly referred to as the Old Man's Draft, it required forty-five- to sixty-four-year-old men to register at their draft board, not to draft them but to discover what sort of skills they had that might help the country in its war effort. On October 2 Henry registered at 250 West 90th Street, cited Frank and Chuck's brownstone as his permanent address, and listed Frank as the person who would always know his whereabouts. Henry gave the clerk on duty his real name, Josef H. Dittmar, and the clerk added two notes on Henry's registration card. One indicated that he had "served as Henry Gerber" and the other, "Red Cross c/o Mrs. Wakefield," referred to Henry's contact at the Red Cross, which had agreed to help him get disability payments along with his pension.

Henry lived at Frank and Chuck's until the end of the year, and despite his discomfort over the sexual goings-on there, he and Frank grew close. Henry realized he had misjudged him. Despite his interests in sex, Frank had thought a great deal about organizing homosexuals to work toward their liberation and not just the men-only club he had proposed to Manuel. Henry was the perfect sounding board for his ideas, and they spent hours planning how, fifteen years after the demise of the Society for Human Rights, they might organize successfully. Henry ended up respecting Frank, something he had never imagined possible, and began to think of Frank as "my dear old friend." Regardless, Henry packed up his few belongings and moved out of Frank and Chuck's in mid-January 1943, the last move he would ever have to make.

PART III

WASHINGTON, DC

10 | "WHAT HOMOSEXUAL IN HIS RIGHT MIND WANTS TO MARRY OR TO BE 'CURED'?"

AS THE NEW YEAR BEGAN, Henry opened a new chapter in his life. Suddenly, he was on what seemed to be a winning streak.

New York's weather was mild that January. The temperature had climbed to thirty-nine degrees, and the sky was clear. He boarded a train at Penn Station, bound for Union Station in Washington, DC, and from there, he took a taxi to the US Soldiers' Home, just three miles from the White House. DC's weather was even better than New York's. Meteorologists predicted the temperature would reach fifty-one with clear skies.

A few days earlier, Henry had been given the go-ahead to retire and permission to move into a veterans' residence in DC. To live there, he needed to have served in the army for at least twenty years or to have been disabled or developed a disease or condition during his enlistment. He met the requirements, thought that he would get disability benefits, and moved into the Sheridan Building. The redbrick building stood three stories high and held nearly five hundred rooms. He had four roommates.

The accommodations were spartan—each man got a bed, nightstand, and lamp—and nearly identical to what he had been used to. Henry immediately deemed it a "haven of refuge; meals free, no rent to pay, and what is most valuable, perfect freedom to do what I please all day. A few of us here have an office set aside where we can write all we please." He wanted to write a few books and thought himself lucky because the home boasted a substantial library, and he had access to the public library and the Library of Congress.

Unfortunately, he wasn't as happy about his fellow residents, a bunch of "old boozehounds and semi-insane wards of Uncle Sam," and he hated the regimen forced on the residents. "They don't let you forget . . . that you are a soldier," he complained, "and we even have guard houses, inspections, buglers and all the rotten idiocies" of military life. But like it or not, he fell into the home's routine quickly: "They turn on the lights at 6 a.m. and I get up at 6.30 and to breakfast at 7. From 7.15 on I am at my 'office' a large room set apart for those who have 'hobbies,' typing, watch making, research (my alibi), clipping papers, etc. I have three lockers here to put my books and papers, typewriter, etc. I am absolutely able to do as I please and no one cares what I write." For years, he had worked on books, making notes here, writing a page or two there, but all too sporadically. He was able to return to them in earnest almost as soon as he moved in. Luckily, when Henry retired for the evening, his roommates were usually at a nearby bar, leaving him alone to enjoy the classical music on his radio.

Unable to shake his lifelong work in publishing, Henry created a "Recreational Bulletin" for the home's residents, the fourth publication on which he worked. He continued it for two years, until the job became too much for him and he closed it down. He also helped residents fill out tax forms and wrote letters for those who were illiterate or physically incapacitated, among them his old army buddy Alva McDonald. McDonald was left physically impaired by a stroke and, because his wife was unable to care for him, had moved into the home a few years earlier.

Manuel was busy, too. He approached Henry with a plan for a new organization that would combine the Society for Human Rights and Contacts. It had two distinct operations. One, which he called the Society of Human Rights, honoring Henry's group of 1924–1925, would focus on homosexual rights, while the other was a correspondence club he called Contact. He even worked on a mock-up for Contact letterhead. Henry didn't reject Manuel's new plan outright, but he reminded him they needed money to get the organization off the ground and then to maintain it. Manuel proposed that they develop a network of men interested in physique photographs, something he and Frank had been discussing, and it would finance the organization.

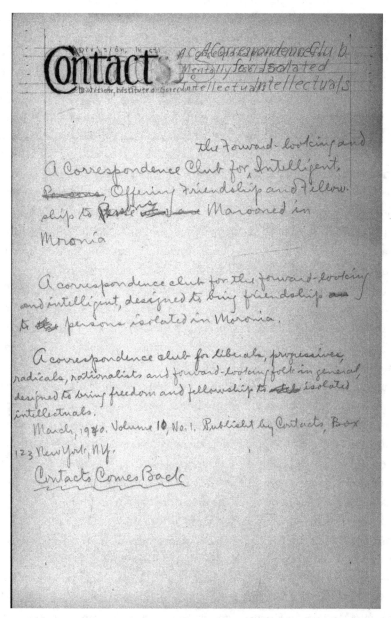

Contacts

Revision, 1951
A co A Correspondence Club b
Mentally ~~foo~~ Isolated
Distribute, distribute a General Intellectual Intellectuals

the forward-looking and
A Correspondence Club for Intelligent,
~~Persons~~, Offering friendship and Fellow-
ship to ~~Persons who are~~ Marooned in
Moronia

A correspondence club for the forward-looking
and intelligent, designed to bring friendship ~~and~~
to ~~the~~ persons isolated in Moronia.

A correspondence club for liberals, progressives,
radicals, rationalists and forward-looking folk in general,
designed to bring freedom and fellowship to ~~the~~ isolated
intellectuals.
March, 1940. Volume 10, No. 1. Published by Contacts, Box
123 New York, N.Y.
Contacts Comes Back

boyFrank was so serious about organizing a new correspondence club to take the place of Contacts, that he gave it a name, Contact, and created this mock-up for the organization's letterhead. *Courtesy of ONE Archives at the USC Libraries*

Manuel and Frank had kept in touch, passing gossip back and forth. Roger Denny's name popped up often, as did mentions of Ed Adams, Walter Schafer, John Ashenhurst, Bill Seidcheck, and Antonni O'Brien. One of Frank's chief topics of discussion was his and his Chuck's health. Frank was fifty-eight years old and Chuck sixty-four. Chuck's health teetered. He could be at death's door one day but fine the next. Frank's health, too, left much to be desired. Two bouts with flu had laid him up badly, but he was nonetheless able to print *Equinox* and send copies of the few photographs he had recently taken to Manuel.

More than anything else, their relationship was based on procuring and sharing physique photographs. Out of the blue, physique photographer Arthur Thornhill had sent Manuel a catalog of his prints. Manuel considered buying some, but a tinge of understandable paranoia made him reconsider. He wondered where Thornhill had gotten his name. Frank told him that he had bought a few photos from Thornhill but was disappointed by them. The models weren't as young or as sexy as his ads led him to believe. He was impressed, however, that Thornhill had shot whites and African Americans together, a rarity in the 1940s. He wasn't supporting civil rights, per se, but being entirely aesthetic.

In his unending quest for satisfactory photographs of nude young men, Manuel contacted Barton Horvath, a bodybuilder who photographed himself and other men in the nude and sold them through the mail-order business he ran out of his apartment and advertised in physique magazines. By then a widely known presence on the bodybuilding scene, he painted posing straps on the prints before mailing them to his customers. One of his ads appeared in the debut issue of *Your Physique*, which also included one of his self-portraits on its cover. The ad read, "Barton R. Horvath wishes to announce that copies of this month's cover pose can be obtained for 75¢ each in the 8x10 size. Barton has also for sale photographs of the best-developed men in the world." Interested men could contact him at his New York apartment, 245 East 87th Street.

In late December 1943 Manuel ordered several of Horvath's photographs and included a letter in which he discussed some thoughts he had about male nude photography. Horvath wrote back, telling Manuel that he was no longer in business, a lie. He was suspicious because of Manuel's overtures. After all, he was a total stranger to Horvath, and as far as the photographer knew, Manuel could have been a postal inspector on his trail. Instead of putting himself in danger of arrest, he told Manuel thanks, but no thanks. The "very puritanical influences, both of us detest," he wrote, have brought pressure to play & I cannot furnish photos any longer. This is a disgusting state of affairs, but must be abided with.

Therefore, your ideas & my own too, must be forgotten, so far as I am concerned at least, & in the future I will confine myself exclusively to courses on physical exercise.

Manuel wouldn't take no for an answer, however, and two and a half months later, he approached Horvath again, this time with a scheme for safely distributing male nudes. Manuel began his proposal innocuously enough. "I am dissatisfied with the amount of money I spend on physique pictures, but I am at a loss to remedy the condition," he told Horvath, adding, "it is hard or impossible to get pictures enough, exciting enough, and cheap enough." His proposal came next, rather offhandedly. He wished Horvath would begin a club, charge members a fee, and in return, they would receive all the photographs Horvath took during that year via "express or by courier." Postal authorities could only tamper with mail sent through the post office.

Intrigued by Manuel's proposal, Horvath ignored his suspicions about Manuel and sent him a free copy of his booklet, *Art in Photography*, that gave any budding physique photographer hints on how to shoot the "most artistic and photographically perfect studies" and sold for fifty cents (about eight dollars in today's currency). He included Catalog H.

In the letter accompanying the gifts, Horvath told Manuel that he thought his scheme was innovative and agreed, in theory, that the club idea might work and offered his take on the idea. They should wait until after the war because so many of the men whom they might interest in becoming members were in the military and constantly moving as the military stationed them in the United States and Europe only to be reassigned to a new place within weeks. Keeping track of their whereabouts would be a nightmare. He proposed an annual membership fee of twenty-five dollars (about $400 in today's currency), which the photographer would pocket and for which members would receive as many as one hundred photographs each year. They needed to select a photographer—Horvath nominated himself—who would travel across the United States during the year to photograph men.

After returning to his home base, the photographer would print the pictures and then set out on another trip to deliver the photographs to each member by hand, bypassing the post office authorities. To make the club financially viable for the photographer, they would need a few hundred members, and he would have to be guaranteed that amount if Horvath were to become the club's photographer. He bragged that his current business brought him $10,000 annually (more than $166,000 in today's currency). If that plan didn't suit Manuel, Horvath suggested an alternative. Instead of hiring a photographer, the club would purchase all the photographs taken by the well-known physique photographers of the day: Gebbé (a.k.a. Robert Gebhardt), Lon (a.k.a. Alonzo Hanagan), and Earle Forbes.

Manuel got cold feet and decided he needed Henry's take on his and Horvath's plan, and out of the blue he wrote Henry for his advice. Their correspondence had taken a nosedive, but Manuel's need for Henry's approval—or, at least, his realistic evaluation of the prospect—jump-started a new wave of letter-writing among him, Henry, and Frank. Always wanting to stay out of the line of fire, Henry warned Manuel not to get involved in running the club and to keep operations simple. He suggested that all Manuel had to do was to figure out who took the best and cheapest photographs, give members their names and addresses, and let each order whatever he wanted on his own. He liked Horvath's idea of buying up a photographer's complete stock because it was simple and practical, and yet, he didn't "know a single" man "who would spend $25 a year" on physique photographs. Stepping onto his soap box, he added what other men did with their hard-earned cash was their business, but he had "daily intercourse" with actual men. Photographs were a poor substitute. They "may be all right for . . . members in Eskimo land who can never get warm enough to enjoy themselves," he told Manuel, "but for me, I get no more joy at looking at pictures than does a squirrel from looking on an advertisement of Planter's (pea) Nuts."

Henry contacted Frank immediately to get his take on Horvath and Manuel's scheme and especially to feel him out on the fee Horvath wanted. Henry's take on the scheme exasperated Frank. "Damn it all, Henry," Frank said, "of course there are plenty of people with 'perverse' tastes, who have money, and who are willing to spend it" on physique photographs. What bothered Frank was how Horvath and Manuel were to contact potential members and introduce them to the idea of the club. He had known Horvath a few years earlier and let Henry in on a little gossip. "Judging by the way he lived over on East 87th Street, Barton Horvath never made $10,000 a year, though he was manager for a liquor importing company, and sold quite a few of his pictures. He's now . . .

selling a book on lighting and posing, for I think 50¢. Married, bisexual, exhibitionist, magnificently built—glad to strip on any excuse or none."

Manuel ignored Horvath's proposal for nine months, then wrote him in December, oddly offering as *his* plan what Horvath had already outlined as his own idea. He was also duly impressed by Horvath's salary. "Hearing about your $10,000-a-year income took my breath away," Manuel gushed, as Horvath had undoubtedly intended, and then, during the next dozen pages, took off on several tangents that included how important Contacts had been for him.

In the meantime, Manuel had also contacted Frank to get his reaction to the club idea. Frank was just as blunt with Manuel as he had been with Henry. "I . . . think you waste your time with Horvath," whom he described as "small-time and small-minded; although BH is, or was, manager for a wholesale liquor store, I rather doubt his 10,000 a year assertion,—certainly he has never lived up to or acted up to it." He asked Manuel not to mention his name to Horvath. There was bad blood between them.

Years earlier, Frank had heard that Horvath was considering "going into business with Melan" (a.k.a. Louis Melancon). Known for his photographs of the stars of the New York Metropolitan Opera, Melancon also took physique photos on the side and "distributed action pictures," or films, "expensively, extensively but underhandedly." Horvath was considering expanding his operations and wanted to team up with Melan. When Horvath mentioned his possible new enterprise to him, Frank asked Horvath "if he intended to participate" in the movies and have sex with other men on film. Miffed by the insinuation, Horvath, who was "careful of his 'manly reputation,'" cut off all contact with him. Instead of Horvath, Frank suggested Manuel ask Antonni O'Brien to be the club photographer. Frank had always appreciated O'Brien's photographs and his ability to print film, and because Manuel knew him through Frank's parties, he could trust O'Brien.

Horvath didn't bother to respond to Manuel's December letter—not because he had lost interest in the club, but because he had been arrested on obscenity charges.

In late October 1944 Horvath answered a knock on the door of his home. He was now living at 1055 Boulevard East, Weehawken, New Jersey. When he answered it, he found "Post Office Insp. L.A. Miller" there with a search warrant. It took Miller no time at all to find Horvath's equipment, prints, negatives, and related items, and he arrested Horvath for sending "obscene, lewd and lascivious pictures" through the mail. In his defense, Horvath claimed he sold the photographs to artists who couldn't afford live models, but he, and all the other photographers who sold physique photographs, knew that his principal customers were homosexuals. He was convicted on November 2.

Horvath claimed to have dissolved his mail-order business, but he didn't quit taking physique photographs. He simply included them in the several different bodybuilding magazines that he published and had gained a large gay following. It had grown so large that, in 1957, the editor of *Strength & Health*, one of Horvath's chief competitors, attacked his publications:

> Barton Horvath . . . is putting out his own homo-pornographic booklet, *Muscle Sculpture*. This bird was hauled in some years ago on a rap of selling nude photos. His new classic, featuring pretty boys in and out of G-strings, is made to order for the *swish* trade. We gently warn unwary bodybuilders about sending photos to such publications, because you, too, may wind up in court . . . and you will be barred from competing in any sanctioned AAU physique contest, such as the Mr. America competition. *You have nothing to gain and everything to lose.*

While Henry, Manuel, and Frank debated one another over photographs and Manuel's plans with Horvath, they seldom mentioned the war, although it was raging, and newspaper headlines across the country constantly reminded readers of that fact daily. Frank had become "numbed by this endless, senseless war," and except for mentioning those who had once been guests in his home and were now in uniform, such as the "healthy young Rocketeers, Lester Winters, HA 1/c, and Rutledge Keith, RM 3/c" who had appeared at Frank's doorstep one night to his delight, he ignored it.

Henry, who had declared himself a conscientious objector in 1917, became more and more angry over the government's hypocrisy as the war intensified. "Most homosexuals," he observed, were "willing to fight for their country . . . even though their country treats them like outlaws," and he was all too happy to identify those who treated homosexuals as "outlaws": "religious fanatics who suffer under the Christian delusion that sex pleasure is sinful, imperialistic politicians who want a big turnover in population for the warmongering, extortionists and blackmailers who take advantage of futile sex laws," and "psychiatrists who wish to earn easy money 'curing' them."

Many homosexuals fell victim to "extortionists and blackmailers," but Henry wasn't overly concerned about them. "As long as there are laws and public opinion against homosexuals," he said, "there will be blackmailers" who use the laws and attitudes as leverage to exhort money from them, but Henry came up with a solution: "I have decided that professional prostitutes are the safest in the long run." Because they were breaking the same law at the same time, they were just as criminal as their clients and wouldn't incriminate themselves by testifying against them.

However, men who sought a cure for their homosexuality confounded him. Marriage had long been held by psychiatrists and laymen alike as a surefire way for a homosexual to become heterosexual, and it was, they believed, quicker than therapy, but Henry saw that neither changed a man's sexual orientation. In utter dismay, Henry threw his hands up and asked rhetorically, "What homosexual in his right mind wants to marry or to be 'cured'?" While the blackmailer and the psychiatrist might be thorns in a gay man's side, his real enemies, as far as Henry was concerned, were the "imperialistic politicians" and the "religious fanatics."

The United States declared war on the Axis powers to defend the rights of foreigners and to defend itself against fascism, but at the same time it was prosecuting its own citizens for their sexual expression. On more than one occasion, Henry pointed out to Manuel that because homosexuals enjoyed sex without any concern over procreation, they threw a wrench in the government's "imperialistic" machinery. The "Hitlers, the Mussolinis and the Stalins and Roosevelts" wanted their citizens to have as many children as possible, specifically boys, to become servicemen who would fight the wars governments waged.

The "religious fanatics" were just as threatening to gay men. The Church taught the *natural* purpose of sex was procreation, not pleasure, and any sexual act that wasn't intended to produce babies was unnatural. Homosexual acts, by definition, were unnatural, perverting and degenerating nature. At the same time, many heterosexuals used condoms, coitus interruptus, oral sex, and perhaps even anal intercourse to enjoy sex without the threat of pregnancy, but only homosexuals were persecuted for engaging in those same acts. The Catholic Church, as Henry concluded, "put her foot" on "our constitution" by supporting laws against homosexuals but ignoring hetero-sexuals who committed the same crimes, "and it is a sorry spectacle to see Americans prostitute themselves to the great whore in Rome and betray American freedom." Despite his bitterness toward the government and its collusion with the Church against homosexuals, Henry joked about the situation: "Now with the rubber shortage [caused by the war], it is even patriotic to be a homosexual. At least we do not deplete the dwindling rubber supply," unlike heterosexuals who used condoms.

Because Henry saw religion as such a monolith in contemporary society and such an adversary to queer people, the fact that many of the men he knew were religious both dumbfounded and angered him. He was so incensed that he needed an outlet for it and wrote a letter to the editor of the *Truth Seeker*, a liberal, progressive, pro-atheism magazine. Entitled "Excerpts from After-Thoughts," Henry aimed the short, satirical piece at Christianity, beginning with an observation: "Many errors occur in the translation of books from for-eign tongues," one of the few restrained comments he made in it. He offered the reader several examples, including the passage in the Christian Bible in which the crucified Jesus tells the "repentant thief" that he will "see him in paradise," which Henry preferred to render, "Verily I say unto you, this very day you will be with me in the—cemetery." He saved the sharpest barb for the end: "Remember, when you read [the word *god*], it spells D-O-G" backward.

"Quite a lot of 'bitches' are very religious. Religion has never made any homosexual 'normal,' or any heterosexual 'pure,'" Henry believed, and he often called religious homosexuals on the carpet, Frank McCourt among them. Henry was convinced that Frank, the devout Catholic, was angry with him because of a comment he made. Frank had asked readers of *Equinox* to say a prayer for the men whom they knew who were either headed to, or who were already in the throes of, the war. "Unless he meant it as a joke—which I doubt as he really is religious—it is about the biggest horseshit I ever heard," Henry told Manuel, and complained about "the poor saps rounded up to die for our brand of fascism and doomed to die in front of Hitler's machine guns waiting for the invasion. And Frank *asks them to pray.*" Henry's actual remark to Frank was more barbed than he let on to Manuel:

> I do not quite agree with your Pollyana [*sic*] philosophy, telling those
> poor saps *to be cheerful!* Smile like Mrs. Roosevelt, eh! And the habit

of prayer. Why if god—if there be such an animal—gave a good god-
dam about us, why doesn't he stop the war. Why give birth to Hitler?
I think most of the people who get your letter are not bright enough
to guess what you mean by "praying." It might be a typographical
error for "playing (with their dicks)." Try it, if you need it, it can be
a marvelous relief . . . ! After 2000 years of Christianity, we all have
become hypocrits [sic]!

Admitting that "we all have become hypocrits" surely didn't appease Frank
after Henry's insult.

Others fell victim to Henry's antireligious ire too. A man whom Henry
met through a correspondence club responded to one of Henry's letters and

started in on religion right away. When I told him that his talk about
10 inch pricks and 69 parties did not sound very 'spiritual' he stopped
writing.

I hate those hypocrits, talking about god all the time but being just
as swinish as others.

Men babble bout spiritual values, but follow their physical instincts.

I told him the only difference between an atheist and a godite
is that the atheist enjoys fucking and forgets it, while the Christian
feels remorse, gets down on his knees and prays to god to forgive
him his "sin."

Nor did Henry reserve his polemics for the Catholic Church. He was
also apt to poke fun at Jesus himself: "I am a pessimist and would not spend
a nickel to see Jesus Christ on roller skates. I think he would be a flop in a
circus, too."

During his diatribe against politicians and Christians, Henry unexpectedly
became melancholic and forthcoming about his past relationships, a rarity
for him. "I was once married to a young tenor,"* he said, "that is he did my
cooking and the usual duties of a wife." Then one day, he continued, "I came
home unexpectedly and found" him "in *my* bed" with another man. Henry
told his lover that, if he wanted to have sex with other men, do it elsewhere.

---

* In earlier eras, gay men who formed romantic and sexual relationships and lived together often
considered themselves married. Gerber used "tenor" as a synonym for young man.

Henry wasn't monogamous and didn't expect it from his young lover, but the relationship soon ended.

Other relationships ended as badly:

> I once was in love with a handsome young tenor and he was very zealous and was around me all the time. One day I got fed up with his close attentions and told him that next day I planned to go to a nearby town to visit an aunt(ie). I met an Indian boy friend and he took me to a hotel where an Indian "princess" lived whom he knew. The gab was rather monotonous but nothing [sexual] took place and when we left the hotel lobby my friend stood there; he had been following me. Of course he concluded that we had had a party and from then on he never spoke to me again. How silly!*

Henry also lived with a third lover. After he and Henry had been together for some time, the boyfriend revealed that he was a "first degree Baptist," and Henry broke off that relationship too. Interestingly, Henry began the two earlier memories with the stock fairy-tale phrase "Once upon a time"—but none ended happily ever after.

---

* *Party* was homosexual slang for any sort of sexual activity between men.

11 | "NOTORIOUS AS A HOMOSEXUAL PARADISE"

HENRY CONTINUED TO WRITE essays after he and the other staff members shut down *Chanticleer*. One of the first was about sex—"keeping a boy," cruising, and hiring male prostitutes—but his creativity blossomed once he moved into the Soldiers' Home.

The office he worked in was a godsend. It wasn't a private room, but a large one he shared with other residents. For the first time in his life, he had a space devoted to writing and not just a corner in one of his rented rooms. He spent almost every day there, and within his first year and a half in the home, he finished substantial drafts of four books. In *Moral Delusions*, he traced the development of the laws against homosexuality from their beginnings in the Old Testament and revealed how different they were from one state to another. In his other books, he focused on Christianity and advocated atheism; explored ethics, as applied to politics; and surveyed his lifelong "struggle to do something for the cause."

Henry was also revising a fifth book, two thematically related novellas that he had written in German years earlier and then translated into English. *Boy Meets Boy* was the story of a young bisexual Parisian, and the other, *Angels in Sodom*, explored the experiences that a young Berliner, who was arrested and convicted for same-sex sexual activities, faced in prison. He called the collected novellas *Angels in Sodom* as well. Despite his years as a proofreader, Henry was unsure about his ability to write well in English and asked Harry Seguin, with whom he had kept in contact since his *Chanticleer* days, to proofread the manuscripts for him.

Manuel was also busy with a book. He had begun *Boys, Men and Love* shortly after he enlisted in the army in 1917 and circulated the manuscript "samizdat fashion" among his buddies in all branches of the military, asking for their input—what to include or delete, what to change—and inviting them to add paragraphs or even whole chapters if they were moved to do so. The manuscript had grown to over six hundred pages, and Kepner called it an "extensive account of Male love throughout history" that also included sections with "practical tips on how to stretch skimpy military pay, how to avoid VD, how to keep up one's uniform and weapons, and essays on whatever took his fancy. They [*sic*] 'juicy' parts were especially popular, and many servicemen came to read and stayed for more personal entertainments." Pedophilia was front and center in some of the erotic pieces.

Manuel sent *Boys, Men and Love* to Henry in installments of up to twenty pages for his feedback. Henry was diplomatic in his responses, telling his friend that, all in all, he liked the book, but its "repetitious . . . personal accounts" of sexual escapades left him cold. Sex should be experienced, Henry told him, "not read about. Just like reading of a chicken dinner. Test of the pudding is eating it." Henry kept the installments of Manuel's book under lock and key, and yet he felt threatened with it in his possession. "I am surrounded by a bunch of dirty, filthy little" men, all heterosexual," he told Manuel, and if they discovered the manuscript, they would "throw me out on my fanny."

Henry had known Manuel for nearly seven years before he felt comfortable enough to send any of his work to Manuel for feedback, but once he did, he mailed his friend *Moral Delusions, Angels in Sodom,* and even his autobiography. He must have also asked Frank for his reaction to *Angels in Sodom* because Frank retuned the "translations" and some of his "pictures," probably physique photographs, to Henry by express mail to ensure the package wouldn't be opened by postal inspectors. Manuel's response to *Moral Delusions* was wishy-washy at best. It was, he told Henry, the "nucleus of a valuable work," complimenting him on the book's basic ideas but hinting that there was more work to be done. However, Manuel was bedazzled by Henry's autobiography.

He liked the manuscript so much that he told Henry to get it published as soon as possible because, he was sure, it would sell vigorously and earn him a great deal of money. Henry dismissed the idea. "I never intended it for publication," he told Manuel and belittled the book, calling it just an "informal memorandum of my life. Autobiographies in order to be published must be of famous or notorious people and I am neither." Then he made an antisemitic remark: "You must have Jewish blood in your veins to think of everything in terms of money!" Similar bigoted comments crept up here and there in Henry's comments.

He once told Manuel, the "Jew and all profit-minded people are simply free of the Christian spirit of submission and do not believe that it is harder for a rich man to enter heaven than an elephant or Camel can enter a needles' eye. Give me the money and you can have your heaven. That is exactly what the Jewish religion means." A few months later, Manuel posted a personal ad in *Writer's Digest*, hoping to interest someone in collaborating with him on another book he was writing, *Defending the Sex Offender*, aimed at lawyers who defended gay men in court. Henry asked if he had received any replies but answered his own question before Manuel could: a "bunch of Jews no doubt who try to get money out of you."

Then, once, to illustrate his "philosophy of life," he told an antisemitic joke:

[An elderly] Jew had a young son who had all the faults of modern youth; he went wild. He bought a new roadster and burned up the roads in the neighborhood. This was before gasoline rationing, of course. The father bewailed the errancy of his son but seeing that no paternal advice would help, he cautioned the boy. "Abe, my boy, if you must run into something, run into something cheap."

At the same time, Henry deplored the Nazi takeover of Germany, their invasion of other countries, and their extermination or sterilization of the countries' marginalized populations.

Manuel realized that lawyers defending gay men needed a guide to help and that some of the nonfiction material he had included in *Boys, Men and Love*, all of which he thought was publishable, could. He decided to remove that material and publish it separately as *Defending the Sex Offender*, which he often referred to as the "'pervert's-defense' book" and which, unlike *Boys, Men and Love*, he planned to publish under his own name.

He believed other parts should be published as *Job for a Boy* but under a pseudonym. Central to that book, Manuel claimed, was the "candid advice a boy needs about his taking charge of himself and making himself over between the ages of 12 and 25.... Transforming himself from a boy, with a boy's limitations, to a man, with a man's tremendous possibilities." Regardless of how he described *Job for a Boy*, Manuel could not disguise its strong hints of pedophilia. It began and ended with Manuel's veneration of the "ancient Greeks" who "spent all the time they could spare teaching boys and watching their progress. They had mastered the secret of living." Manuel rationalized,

> Thinkers have often wondered why it was that a certain period in time there developed in Greece a civilization superior to that of neighbor-ing countries and far superior to the civilizations that succeeded it. Paiderastia may be the key to the riddle. It spared a man the burden of supporting the enormous families that play hell with most people's efforts to better their condition. . . . Moreover, alliance between the elder and the younger of a pair of Greek lovers made it possible for the one to pass on to the other all the accumulated knowledge of a lifetime.

In many ways, Manuel was a better writer when it came to his essays and stories than Henry. For one thing, he was able to keep on track and, as important, be brief. He also had a unique style. Henry's writings wandered, went on for page after page, repeating key ideas (and sometimes specific words and phrases), and were stylistically ho-hum if not downright stodgy. Bertha Klausner, a New York literary agent who represented some of the most famous writers and actors of the first half of the twentieth century, among them Upton Sinclair, Anthony Burgess, Lionel Barrymore, Theda Bara, and Marcel Marceau, saw value in Manuel's writing and added him to her stable of talent. Unfor-tunately, she was never able to place any of Manuel's pieces in a journal, and because he never finished any of his books they were never published.

Henry had other things on his mind besides his books, not the least of which was his sex life—or lack of it. He complained to Manuel that, although he had been living in DC for thirteen months and had been writing to his various pen pals who lived in the area, he hadn't heard from any of them. On one of Frank's rocketeer member lists, the address of a sailor in the DC area caught his eye. The sailor may have been Ross W. Ketchum, a yeoman first class in the navy reserves. The sailor didn't respond to Henry's letter, and to hide his disappointment, Henry wisecracked that he hadn't replied because he was "probably in Guadalcanal" and had "been eaten by the cannibals there." Henry asked Manuel if he "knew anyone in or near Washington" who was "not too old" whom he might recommend to Henry.

His second preoccupation was the riddle of homosexuality: Why were some men homosexual and others not? That question had dogged him all his life. Now, having retired, Henry had time to reconsider his view of homosexuality and to read what current sexologists had to report. "Since writing that article for the Modern Thinker, 'In Defense of Homosexuality,'" he told Manuel, "I have changed my point of view about the inborn nature of homophily. After all, it is a mental matter. No homophile is *physically* unable to have intercourse with a woman. It is his mind that stops him from doing so, his sex *association*, not his penis." He was sure that homosexuality wasn't *inborn*, by which he meant biologically inherited or genetic, but *acquired*, by which he meant influenced by the individual's experiences. For centuries, the debate, which was usually framed as nature versus nurture, had addressed the larger issue of human nature in general, but by the 1940s it had narrowed to focus on homosexuality.

Henry had kept up with the debate. He had put his trips to the New York Public Library during his furlough and the Library of Congress while he was in DC to good use, keeping up with the recent research by medical and psychological experts on whether people were born or were somehow turned into homosexuals. Nevertheless, he had his own experiences to draw on, and it was difficult for him not to stand with those who believed homosexuality was somehow learned or developed. After all, he had engaged in sex with other boys during his childhood, and now, as an adult, he was only sexually attracted to men.

Henry reasoned that homosexuality couldn't be inherited because "only physical things can be inherited. A man can be born blind and no matter of seduction can make him see. But a man can also turn blind from too much reading or a disease in which case his blindness is *acquired*." He refined his view by admitting, the "sex *instinct* is inherited, but not its final *direction*, any more than a man is born to be a Catholic or a Protestant. *Belief* is inborn but what form this belief takes is a matter of later *environment*. But *race* is inborn: a negro will necessarily have to have negro parents."

Supporting his stand was his belief that a "normal bisexuality underlies all sex, just as an ability to eat anything is true in the matter of food," and applying it to homosexuality, he concluded:

> Homosexuals are boys who have become sex conscious at an early age and have formed the habit of associating sex pleasure with boys at an early age, before they get to be 16 or 18 when society wants

boys to get interested in girls. Then it is too late to change for the homosexual and he rejects heterocrapaganda. But if the boy is not sexually very strong and has retarded his sex development and has not associated his sex pleasure with boys before 16, he can be pushed into the heterosexual field and made to believe that marriage is as desirable as the belief that there are three persons in the trinity or any similar crap.

While considering the origins of homosexuality, Henry couldn't ignore the concepts of heterosexuality and marriage, but he hadn't changed his mind in the least about either of them:

After all, the whole business of sex is so much eyewash and a very clumsy device to make the suckers marry and furnish cannon fodder for the politicians' wars. There are no homosexuals. There is only sex pleasure and the various forms of acquiring it. Since everyone practices birth control, what difference does it make HOW to cheat Nature? It is all a matter of individual taste.

Marriage is a profitable institution where the morons are tied down and can easily be kept at work supporting the home and exploited in every possible way.

Why should anyone take upon himself a thousand responsibilities just for a little pleasure for a half hour or less? Why rear children and spend one's income in getting them educated and then see them dragged over to Europe to fight Churchill's wars and be killed?

I am afraid dull humankind will never wake up. That is why it is so necessary to have religion to keep them doped up metaphysically. Only in this light can we understand the furor with which the politicians look at homosexuals and those who ignore the "blessings" of marriage and parenthood.

Henry didn't dislike heterosexuals but felt

pity for the poor suckers being unable to see the light. Everytime [sic] I see in the movies an alleged happening of a cheap dame making a damn fool out of a nutshot nuts-hot, not shot—pretty boy, my heart aches. It is a pity to see so many men make their lives miserable by getting tangled up with some dizzy dames. . . . But I do not hate these suckers. But are we not justify [sic] in hating those who do us dirt? I should say so. Dirt for dirt and ass for ass. That's my slow-gain.

"Some people are still able to see the racket," marriage and procreation, "behind it all and keep their heads out of the sling," he decided. "Whether homosexuals are born that way or whether homosexuality is acquired is . . . a moot question." He told Manuel that it was an "academic matter and it does not matter to you or me whether we are born that way; the most important thing is make use of it while we last," and Henry did his best to "make use of it" as often as he could.

Henry's health was another concern. He was already dealing with hearing loss and pain in his arms and shoulders, but shortly after he arrived at the Soldiers' Home, he underwent surgery to remove his prostate and had a vasectomy at the same time. He was quick to reassure Manuel that the surgery had "not extinguished" his sex drive one bit and bragged that he still "managed to have a little fun at least once or twice a week." The only difference, he quipped, was now he couldn't be a "father!" but didn't care because he was only interested in "sons."

Because of the war, the darkened balconies of movie theaters in which men cruised—the National, the Strand, and RKO Keith's—began attracting servicemen who would have sex with other men for a price. The fifty-two-year-old Henry occasionally made "contact with some young and handsome fellows" who were willing to let him feel them up or fellate them but weren't interested in any mutual sexual experience. Only older men were, and he wasn't attracted to them. Henry's unsatisfactory hunt for sexual release was only one irritation facing him. With the help of the Red Cross and the Veterans Bureau, he was still fighting for his full pension from the army but felt he was at a dead end.

Then, in a very rare moment of sentimentality, Henry glued a stamp-sized photo of himself to the upper left-hand corner of a letter he had written to Manuel. The fifty-one-year-old is dressed in a dark suit, a white shirt, and dark tie with light-colored speckles in it. His hair is thinning, his face full, what some night call chubby. His eyes stare into the viewer. There is a hint of a smile on his lips. Nothing betrays the exasperation he was facing at every turn.

Gerber sent this photo of himself in a letter to boyFrank without comment in 1944. Gerber (né Josef Henrik Dittmar) was born on June 29, 1892 and died December 31, 1972. *Courtesy of ONE Archives at the USC Libraries*

Manuel added to Henry's frustration by continuing to hound him to resurrect Contacts. When his objective, rational reasons for revitalizing it didn't work, Manuel set out on a sortie of flattery. "I think 'Contacts' did more good in the few years you ran it than anything else I recall that has existed in this generation," he told Henry, but always on the offense when it came to revitalizing Contacts, Henry turned the tables on Manuel and shot back, "Why don't you take up Contacts?" Henry couldn't be bothered because he had dreamed up another organization, one that he was sure would succeed where the Society for Human Rights had failed.

In mid-March 1944 Henry wrote to both Frank and Manuel with his idea for a new organization. He was tired of the way society perceived homosexuals and had made up his mind to do something about it. He introduced his plan with a brief description of the homosexual's life:

> The homosexual knows that although his condition is of course not a "freak of nature," a disease or "degeneration," but the most effective and cheapest form of birth control, he is for that very reason persecuted by the politicians and priests who profit by the mass production of morons.
>
> But since homosexuality is not an inborn defect like color-blindness or left-handedness, it cannot be detected and he can safely pretend to be "normal" and get by in his every day pursuit of earning his bread and butter.
>
> Society forces the homosexual to be a "schizophrenic," living a normal life at night with his homosexual paramours, and at day time [sic] pretending to be a heterosexual, but that game is not very difficult because many heterosexuals are misogynists realizing what a trap a woman is. No one ever hears of a homosexual "manhater."
>
> So the hilarious comedy of pretence [sic] goes on and many of us have learned to play it so well that even our mothers and fathers do not recognize us for what we are. . . . And that after all is our salvation.

Next, he formalized his ideas in a one-page précis for the Society Scouting Sex Superstition:

> That it is nobody's business what two adults (at the age of 16) decide to do to enjoy themselves sexually, as long as they act in mutual agreement, without violating the rights of others. That every person has a right to decide whether he wants to marry or not, whether he wants to have children or not, and how to practice birth control, either artificially, by the use of instruments or devices, or naturally, by masturbation or other manual or onanistic (nonprocreative) means.

The new society would fight antihomosexual sentiment wherever they found it and serve as a clearing house, exchanging information on dangerous cruising areas, arrests and convictions, new sodomy laws that had sprung up, and other topics important to keep them safe and out of harm's way.

Henry envisioned three levels of membership in the group: "founders," "contributing members" who supported the society financially, and "active members who detected persecution of homosexuals" in magazines and newspapers and reported it to the founders. The founders would then take action, writing letters to the publications' editors and enlightening them about homosexuality. Henry had already been writing letters to editors for years, and Manuel had come up with the idea about the same time as he devised his Santa Claus scheme. After reading the précis, Manuel dubbed the letter writers the "committee of correspondence" after the groups that promoted support for independence during the American Revolution. As safety measures, they would never hold meetings, never collect dues, never have membership lists, and never create anything that could be used to identify members.

Henry checked the lists of Frank's rocketeers to consider who might be a good letter writer, and among the candidates were Luke Raviella, who had roomed at Frank's; A. A. Levenseller, another of Frank's lodgers; Don Shattuk; Paul Delfino; the married bisexual Walter Schafer; and even Henry's army buddy and former roommate Erling Stenberg. While trying to decide, his distrust of gay men got the better of him, and he couldn't make up his mind which to ask. In the end, he decided that he and Manuel could handle the job, at least for the time being. Then, in a rare moment of hopefulness, Henry proclaimed, "All great causes start from small nuclea [sic]," and "we have the nuclea of some 10 million homophiles in the U.S. and although most of them do not cooperate, and some of them even make our work harder by their antisocial deeds, we are, nevertheless on the way."

Henry had softened his view of homosexual men a little, but only a little. He still believed that they preferred to socialize than work for their rights, but he now understood that they were mostly driven by how afraid they were. "FEAR," he explained to Manuel, "is the driving motive that keeps people from being free to do as they pleased, as free as our fellow-animals."

They had a good reason to be afraid. The authorities revved up their war against homosexuals as the European theater of World War II was winding down. One of their first targets in Washington, DC, was the Riggs Turkish Baths at Fifteenth and G Streets, in the basement of Keith's Theatre, where men had met one another for decades. The only bathhouse in DC, Riggs boasted of its "Superb Steam and Hot Rooms," "Special rubs by experts," and "Delightful Swimming Pool" in its ads in local newspapers. All would have caught

March 19, 1944

Society Scouting* Sex Superstition
An International Underground Movement ~~fxxxt~~ Fighting Fascism in Sex
Slogan: Truth, Liberty, Humanity.

* The proper word of course would be SUPPRESSION, but since we are fighting all
suppressions, it would be inconsistent. Other words that could be used:
Scorning, spurning, squashing, stalling, stopping, and sanitation.

The main idea of course would be to protect homosexuals against persecution.
This could be done in two ways:
1) fighting persecuting in law, in the press, personally. *
2) keep homosexuals in touch with each other and thus protect them from outsiders.
The three enemies of homosexuals are recognized as:
1) religious fanatics who spread the dogma that sexual intercourse is sinful.
2) imperialist and fascist politicians who want a big population for cannon fodder.
3) extortionists who take advantage of laws against homosexual acts. *
* above: 3) collaborating with organizations who fight fascism in other fields.
(such as the Truth Seeker, fighting religious fascism.)
Philosophy: That it is nobody's business what two adults (at the age of 16)
decide to do to enjoy themselves sexually, as long as they act in mutual
agreement, without violating the rights of others. That every person has a
right to decide whether he wants to marry or not, whether he wants to have
children or not, and how to practice birth control, either artificially, by
the use of instruments or devices, or naturally, by masturbation or other
manual or onanistic (nonprocreative) means.
This society would be a secret underground but perfectly legal as it would
use only weapons of propaganda and education. There would be a nucleus of
about 3 - 7 directors, men who could absolutely rely upon each other who would
conduct the society without being known to the members at large. They would
devise the literature to be sent to those who oppose liberty and democracy
and try to force people to obey certain religious dogmas in matters of sex,
i.e. fascist suppression of sex freedom. Pamphlets, such as "what is
homosexuality," "Who are the perverts?" etc. pointing out the facts about
sex, would be printed by the society and sent directly to offenders, judges,
legislators and authors writing against homosexuals, and would be distributed
among the members to distribute discretly where it is most needed.
Membership would be strictly selective.
There would be three types of members:
1) the founders.
2) contributing members who want to contribute to the society for the expense
   of printing, etc.
3) active members who would serve as scouts detecting persecution of homosexuals
   and reporting these cases to the founders who would then act.
There would be no meetings and no dues to pay, no membership cards or anything
identifying the members with the society.
It would be interesting to see some hypocrit who himself practices birth control
get a letter from England or Canada, or California or Washington, pointing out
to him that he is as much of a pervert as those whom he attacks and that he
ought to be ashamed of his hypocrisy and mend his way or else...since it is
no longer possible to attack a minority as the witches of old, since they now
are organized and know how to defend themselves against fascists.....

*The word homosexual would nowhere appear, we fight any kind of sex superstition

In 1944 Gerber created a précis for the Society Scouting Sex Superstition, the
second organization that he established to fight for the rights of homosexuals.
Courtesy of ONE Archives at the USC Libraries

homosexuals' attention, but if they didn't, the ads offered another incentive. Customers could even "spend the night" in the bathhouse's "excellent sleeping accommodations."

Henry mentioned a raid on a "Turkish bath" to Frank, but he didn't give any details. Weeks before the raid, "special investigators and military police" had gone to the bath pretending to be customers to investigate rumors of sexual trysts between servicemen and servicemen with civilians. Then in the early hours of Sunday, March 25, 1945, thirty police officers stormed the bath and took fifty men into custody, crowded them into four patrol wagons, and hauled them to the police station. Authorities were taking actions against bathhouses in other cities too. In Chicago, for example, Henry's friend Franz Spirk told him that so "many service men frequented" the "baths" that the military made them "off limit. They always spoil a good thing."

Gerber couldn't shake his disdain for homosexuals who claimed to support homosexual rights but weren't willing to do the work required for liberation. One of his correspondents, Bill Tullos of Imboden, Arkansas, who ran the Atheneum Club, had the "old-fashioned idea that homosexuals should be 'pitied,'" but Henry put him straight. "Homophiles want no pity," he told Tullos in no uncertain terms, "but the equal right to enjoy" sex "according to their own methods."

As far as Henry was concerned, the Society Scouting Sex Superstition would become an equal to the "efforts of other great liberators who in times past have worked against slavery and the abolition of [the] punishment of 'witches.'" His reference to "slavery" echoed his involvement with the Society for Human Rights when, twenty years earlier, he believed that, if the society was successful, he would be "known to history as deliverer of the downtrodden, even as Lincoln."

Manuel couldn't hide his excitement over Henry's précis. "Our movement," he gushed, "is probably the most useful endeavor with which a man can identify himself." With *movement*, Manuel had suddenly stamped Henry's dream with political activism, a label Henry hadn't used before, and to put his money where his mouth was, he pledged to "put up a hundred dollars within the measurable future, and perhaps more, to further the cause." Manuel admitted, "That would be only a drop in the bucket, but it might be the means of starting the flow of other drops." Henry appreciated Manuel's support. "That is the main thing," Henry told him, "to know that I can count on your full support, morally and 'spiritually,'" but not to be outdone by Manuel, Henry vowed his financial support too: "I just collected $200 mustering-out-pay and that would be a nice contribution of Uncle Sam to our cause!"

Although Frank was initially "enthusiastic about the plan," he quickly "cooled off." He had come to the same conclusion that Henry had after the fiasco with the Society for Human Rights. Any attempt "to help those who don't, and won't, help themselves let alone others" was doomed to utter failure.

Manuel had only one reservation about Henry's new organization. He hated its name because it had "eight sibilants," the sound of the letter s, in it. He preferred Band of Brothers but suggested seven other possibilities, including Children of Light, Committee on Education, and Fraternity of Greek Love. Henry wasn't at all upset about Manuel's reaction to the name and told him that "it does not . . . matter much what we call it. We all must in the last resort make personal concessions. To argue over trifles would be silly. But I think we ought to have a name first to express the purpose of our work, but that could be made as wide as to include any type of person who values his sex liberty." Nevertheless, Henry couldn't help but mock Manuel: "Band of brothers is inappropriate though the implication of playing an instrument—flutes?—is not so bad. But band of sisters would be better. Then again this includes two sibilants which you do not like. Do you lisp? Perhaps we could compromise on band of queans." Henry countersuggested naming it the Society for Human Rights,* after his Chicago group.

Henry's arrest and trial in 1925 still loomed large in his memory, and he couldn't help but fear facing the same experiences, perhaps even worse ones, a second time. At the top of his précis, he added a directive, that Manuel and Frank should destroy their copies after reading it. He also told them they needed to use a code when they wrote to one another, and to that end he devised two.

The first, and the one used more often than the other, borrowed from the vocabulary of the Church. They wouldn't use their real names. "I can call you

---

* After Henry left Chicago in 1925, the Society for Human Rights had a life all its own. The secretary of state's office sent a notice to Henry on November 6, 1936, to his Crilly Court address, the last known address the state had for him. He was living in New York by then, and no one at the Crilly Court address knew where to forward it. Consequently, between 1936 and 1956, Henry failed to pay the society's taxes and to submit annual reports, both required by law. The state officially dissolved the Society for Human Rights at 3:09 on December 3, 1964, twenty-one days short of its fortieth anniversary.

Doris," Henry told Manuel, "and I can sign my name as Saint Simon." Henry chose Simon, referring to St. Peter's name before being called by Jesus, to underscore his role as the group's leader just as St. Peter had become the leader of the early Christian Church. By calling Manuel Doris, Henry wasn't just being campy by feminizing him. Doris was an area of ancient Greece, and gay men had long associated Greece with homosexuality. It also echoed Oscar Wilde's Dorian Gray. He christened Frank, an animal lover, St. Francis, patron saint of animals. "Instead of" calling the new group a "society," he explained, "we call it the Church and the homosexuals are the saints or the members of the church."

Henry created a glossary for Manuel and Frank to illustrate how church-related words could refer to homosexuality and sex between men:

> God—homosexuality.
> Church—underground cell, apartments where homos meet.
> Priest—one who performs a sex act.
> Communion—fellatio, to give to take communion, active and passive.
> Baptism—browning,* to give—to baptize, to be baptized.
> Last unction—cunnilingus.
> Prayer—solitary masturbation.
> Family prayer—mutual masturbation.
> Celibates—Platonic homosexual affair, necking.
> Chapel—a movie for groping.
> Cathedral—a public comfort station.

Perhaps joking, perhaps not, Henry told Manuel that he "left out Jesus for penis" because he didn't want to stir up trouble with the Christians in the movement, an obvious jab at Frank. He was infuriated at Henry for appropriating Church vocabulary and concepts and refused to use the code. He told Manuel that he shared one of Henry's letters composed in the code to two men he knew, a Methodist and a Roman Catholic, and it shocked both. He didn't complain to Henry face-to-face, however. He got Manuel to do it for him.

Manuel, caught in the middle of his two friends, was being diplomatic when he told Henry, "I have studied your code scheme for a long time, and I

---

* *Browning* was gay slang for anal intercourse.

like it a lot. I have heard only the objection to it that many an emancipated former Christian has a surviving affection for some of the old expressions—only a personal and sentimental association, you see. If that be worth regarding, it is easy to substitute words that are used in connection with foreign religions," Buddhism or Hinduism, instead of Christianity. Henry thought that by not using *Jesus* as a code for *penis* he was already bending over backward for Frank.

Henry began using the code immediately. In one instance, he used it to discuss the nude male photographs that Manuel sought and that Frank produced and sold. "Very interesting to know about your effort to get good pictures of the lord," he told Manuel, "but it seems strange that you ask me to tell Bishop Frank of Brooklyn about this interchange since he himself has an art gallery of all the saints of the church and deals with those holy images. Did you not know it?"

It took Manuel several months to begin using the code because, as he told Frank, he was unsure if using it was even worthwhile:

> Henry would be mortified to hear it, but his piece belongs in the same epistolary category . . . as the Revelation of John the Divine: it is an attempt to devise a means of writing something which shall have one meaning to the uninitiated reader and another meaning to the person who knows how to interpret it. Henry's idea has utility, I am sure; but exactly how much utility, and how available that utility is, I am not yet prepared to say. I have given it a good deal of study, and presently I shall give it more.

After considering the code further, he began using it, which "delighted" Henry, who assumed that Manuel hadn't used it in solidarity with Frank.

Despite his refusal to compromise the Church-based code, Henry devised a second one. For it, he used music-related terms to refer to sex and queer men, as in this description of his time in a bathhouse:

> When I was at the concert . . . they had all sorts of music there. I saw one gorgeous bass drummer who also played the piano and the piano sure must have been made of solid brass to stand all this heavy pounding. But most of the musicians there—most of them tenors, of course,—went in for fiddle playing and most of it was in duet form. But it is always the

> case that the younger set flock together and as there were only two or three under 30, the older ones of course grabbed them up as soon as they came in, and there were not enough to go around for all. There were some old musicians there, most of them just for curiosity who pestered me to play their violins but I did not like this at all.

Both Manuel and Frank ignored the second code, and Henry quickly abandoned it too. The Church-related code eventually fell by the wayside as well.

In the meantime, Henry dove into his role in the committee of correspondence. His first letter was addressed to the editor of *Time* and responded to its article "The Lonergan Case." Standing over six feet tall, the twenty-four-year-old Wayne Lonergan was a head-turner. While working at the 1939 New York World's Fair pushing sightseers in wheeled chairs through the exhibitions, he met wealthy, forty-three-year-old William Oliver Burton who "had several homes, a wife, a daughter Patricia, and . . . a penchant for husky good-looking" young men on the make. Lonergan became a fixture in Burton's retinue. Burton died a year later, and used to the high life that the older man's fortune had afforded him, Lonergan eloped with Patricia to Las Vegas where they were married. The following year, their son was born. They were divorced in August 1943, and on October 22, 1943, police arrested him for bludgeoning her to death during an argument over visitation rights.

During the trial, headlines about the Lonergan case were splashed across newspapers in most major cities, and statements about his many homosexual liaisons, which crept into the articles, stirred up even more antihomosexual animosity than was already brewing. The jury didn't believe his alibi, that he had spent the night of Patricia's murder with an American serviceman, and found him guilty. He was sentenced to thirty years in Sing Sing.

Published on the eve of Lonergan's trial, *Time*'s piece was, Henry thought, fair to homosexuals despite some mistakes in it. He wrote to correct the errors. One of his first steps was to dare *Time* to print his letter, exactly as he had with the *Chicago Daily Tribune* nearly thirty years earlier:

> Since suppression of all "non-procreative sex acts," such as birth control, artificial and natural (of which homosexuality is one method), is a public policy in these united states [sic], I doubt if you could print this letter. Although you would not, perhaps, be dragged to a

concentration camp as in other fascist countries, the least they would do to you is cancelling your mailing privileges.

Then Henry got down to business. Among the twelve points Henry addressed, several concerned definitions. Lonergan was "*not a homosexual*," Henry declared, but "a bisexual—half homosexual and half heterosexual." Henry's definition of *bisexual* had expanded to include persons attracted sexually to both genders. He also advised the editor that he shouldn't use *perversion* to refer to homosexual acts exclusively. Heterosexual men also engaged in oral sex and anal intercourse, the difference being their sexual focus was women. He also wondered, tongue in cheek, if Lonergan's sexual relationship with this father-in-law should be considered "sodomy or incest."

In response to the *Time* piece's suggestion that homosexuality could be inherited, Henry schooled the editor on the origin of homosexuality. He announced that it was "not 'inborn' but . . . acquired." He agreed that it was appropriate for the law to step in "when the rights" of someone "are being violated" as in "the case of rape" or the "seduction of children," but he noted that "society should stop wasting time trying to 'cure' or 'save' homosexuals" because in a "civilized country . . . people do not make it their business to interfere with the private sex lives of their neighbors."

Henry didn't sign the letter with his name. Concerned about the backlash his letter might provoke, the same fear that he had seen in other homosexuals and, time after time, had denounced, signed it with the pseudonym Pro Domo, Latin for "to speak for one's own benefit." As he told Manuel, "Having arrived at the age of discretion—being now 52—I have few delusions left. I no longer believe in martyrdom for the sake of others."

The letter was never published, but that didn't dampen Henry belief that he and Manuel had a mission:

We are in possession of a priceless truth, and that we should be disposed if ever we be given a good opportunity to give that truth to anyone else who wants it, is about the best definition we could adopt for our cause. I use every opportunity in writing to others or speaking to them to divulge this truth. Even if it falls upon dry ground, it still will give them food for thought, and once doubt of their heterosexual dogma is injected, it will bring food for thought. And at least these people will no longer see any reason why certain types disagreeing with conventions should be persecuted."

Fighting bouts of ill-health, his own and Chuck's, Frank never joined Henry and Manuel's letter-writing campaign.

Four days after mailing his letter to *Time*, Henry wrote another, to the editor of the *American Mercury*. The magazine had published an article by a physician, J. H. H. Upham, who supported birth control and then, two issues later, a lengthy rebuttal by a Catholic priest, John A. Ryan, who supported the Catholic Church's ban. Upham advocated giving birth control information to married Catholics. He called the Church's actions a shameful violation of the separation of church and state and argued for the individuals' right to choose whether to use birth control. Ryan countered Upham by stating that the Catholic Church couldn't be anti-American because it followed current laws enacted through American legislatures and by asserting that the Church hadn't trampled on anyone's rights.

Henry enjoyed the melee between the scientist and the priest and denounced the priest's argument as "one of gross stupidity, hypocrisy and futility." He included statistics to illustrate the physician's stance and clarified the situation that people supporting birth control found themselves in. He castigated the priest and others like him who didn't understand the realities of parenthood and drew the editor's attention to the laws against homosexuals, suggesting that the government "remove restrictions on *natural* forms of birth control," which he identified as "homosexuality, onany,* etc." He ended his three-page ramble with a challenge to the editor. "You are, of course, free to publish this letter if you care," he said, "but I doubt if you can, for regimentation in sex matters is just as strong over here as it is in Germany, Russia and other fascist countries. What we really need, is a fifth freedom. Freedom of Love!" As with his letter to *Time*, he didn't sign off with his name, but called himself Voluntary Nonparent. Numerous letters reacting to the physician's and the priest's views appeared in the June, July, and August issues of the magazine, but not Henry's.

---

* *Onany* was a term once used for "masturbation."

12 | "THIS FASCIST WORLD"

TRY AS HE MIGHT, Henry couldn't devote his full attention to the committee of correspondence. In early 1944 the army's retirement board called him to appear on January 5, present his case, and, he hoped, end his frustration. He had been working to get the tangle of his retirement straightened out since March 1941, and he was so exasperated that he regretted beginning the process in the first place. Nevertheless, he clung to the hope that, if he won his case, he would be given an extra seventy-five dollars a month (more than $1,200 in today's currency). Almost immediately, the glimmer of hope faded. Getting the army to recognize his disability was going to be far more complicated than he had imagined.

To get his case reassessed, fifty-two-year-old Henry had to reenlist. The news flummoxed him, but if that was what it would take, he was willing. He reenlisted on August 10, 1944, his third swearing-in, hoping that all would go well. It didn't. Within a few days, another glitch compounded his frustration. He had to undergo a series of tests that would ascertain if he had a disability that was caused by, or developed during, his previous enlistments.

The army sent him to the military hospital at Fort Meade, near Baltimore. The physicians there would ascertain if he was disabled, what his disability was, and more important to the military, when and how it came to be. When he arrived at the hospital, the beds were full, and he had nothing to do but cool his heels until one was available, but the army wasn't about to let a soldier remain idle for long. It gave him the rank of staff sergeant and a job of escorting thirty-six recruits to Denver by train. On August 15 they left from Union Station in DC amid intermittent showers and a temperature that topped ninety degrees Fahrenheit. The train had luxurious accommodations, with roomettes and double bedrooms, a lounge where meals were served, and a dome car. The troops had a car to themselves, and as Henry later told Manuel with a wink, a "nice time was had by all," hinting at sexual trysts among the men. He was just teasing his friend.

The train laid over in Chicago nearly twenty hours after it left DC, and Henry took advantage of the stop to visit his sisters and a friend for a few hours. Anna had immigrated to the United States with him, but Maria, who was twelve years younger than he, had immigrated in mid-December 1927. The friend whom he visited was undoubtedly Franz Spirk. He and Henry had corresponded off and on since Henry moved to New York. Chicago's weather was only slightly better than the DC's—hot and humid with rain in the forecast. He visited them again on the return trip.

When Henry arrived at Fort Meade on August 19, a bed was available in a ward with over a dozen other men. On August 23 preliminary examinations began. Initially, the doctors suspected he didn't have a disability and considered reassigning him to active duty. Henry was more than a little elated over the prospect. Germany hadn't yet surrendered to the United States and wouldn't for another eight months, but its eventual defeat was expected. Henry had enjoyed his time in Coblenz and especially Berlin in the 1920s and looked forward to returning.

The physicians put Henry through a battery of checkups. These included a series of X-rays and examinations of his circulatory system. The tests suggested that Henry had developed heart disease, but the doctors weren't sure and sent him to Walter Reed General Hospital in Bethesda for yet another series of physical examinations and more weeks of frustration.

When not being prodded by the physicians at Walter Reed, Henry began making plans for his future. If he received his disability pension, he wanted to return to the Soldiers' Home until the war ended. After that, he might move to Chicago or to New York and rent a small apartment and, maybe, even take another vacation, this time to Europe. He even thought that he just might settle down there, perhaps "in France or Switzerland where they do not have such silly sex laws as in this country and where people are really civilized and free from religious superstitions." He was still hoping to meet his ideal mate.

Henry, an introvert, was unnerved by being in the hospital with his fate in the hands of strangers who might discover he had a life-threating condition.

His introspection was getting the better of him, and he complained to Manuel about it. He needed someone to talk to, at least occasionally. Manuel was quick with advice. He explained that all Henry had to do was to take the first step. When he met someone who attracted him, he should say hello first and show interest in him. Henry took Manuel's advice to heart and was delighted by the results. "Everytime I talk to one of the soldiers," he told Manuel, "they are so friendly and willing to enter into conversation. Formerly my reserve and their reserve made an acquaintance impossible." Thanks to Manuel's advice, he ended up doing more than just passing the time "reading, writing and going to the movies," as he had planned, but meeting a few men.

One was a young man with whom Henry was a little smitten. "One day," he told Manuel, "a very handsome boy" named Richard, whom he "suspected" was gay,

> came into my net by what you call circumstances. At 3 p.m. I went to music school and as no one was there yet I sat alone in the dining room where classes are held. In comes Richard and I started a friendly conversation explaining about the music classes and he was from then on always looking for me. We went to school together having the same classes and I was always near him. When lights went out in the movies he did not object to my putting my hands on his lap. He seemed rather innocent but seemed a misogynic and said he did not want to marry. However I did not approach him in any way sexually. But I got a great kick out of going around with him all week. Tried to get him to go downtown with me or swimming in the pool but he was too bashful and probably broke. He could not go in swimming as he had a breast injury—shrapnel in his chest. . . . Of course no one wears clothes in the pool and one can sample the wares.

For decades, public swimming pools, such as those in YMCAs and high schools, required men and boys to swim in the nude, and to Henry's delight, it was no different at Walter Reed. But sexual flirtation and physical examinations weren't Henry's only pastime at Walter Reed. He attended lectures given by the base psychiatrist who was very liberal about homosexuality. Henry became guardedly optimistic about the future because of the psychiatrist's statements, although he knew any sort of change would take many years.

Then after nearly five months of testing, Henry got word that the physicians were going to decide Henry's case. He hoped it would ensure a raise in his pension and his permanent admission into the Soldiers' Home. He got unofficial word that the physicians would be deciding in his favor, and much to his surprise, the army also awarded him a "112-day furlough." Henry left Walter Reed by train on Wednesday, February 7, 1945, under cloudy skies and cool temperatures and headed for Penn Station in Manhattan. He arrived the next day to clearer, but much colder, weather. He immediately sent Manuel his New York address: the Men's Residence Club at 317 West Fifty-Sixth Street. He was excited about his disability pension and his future. He told Manuel, "Retirement means just that. . . . From now on it is only relaxation and finding ways and means of finding enjoyment in love, reading, shows, walks, travel, and writing."

For the next three and a half months, Henry lived at the Men's Residence Club for a dollar a night. A former YMCA, it was a "less expensive and shabbier version of the YMCA," was "packed with gay servicemen and civilians," and was "notorious as a homosexual paradise." Besides rooms to rent, it had a "steam room, massage rooms, showers, and a pool," where men swam naked, and had earned the reputation of being a "combination old men's home and whorehouse." Tennessee Williams stayed there around the same time that Henry did.

Despite the club's potential for sexual contact, Henry stuck to his recurring claim that he wasn't interested in sexual encounters with strangers, but the truth was that, now in his fifties, Henry was having a difficult time picking up men to whom he was attracted. He resented the position he found himself in, and he lashed out at those younger and more attractive than he. Those "brazen bitches," as he called them, were enjoying themselves sexually "while the decent homosexuals" suffered their rejection "in loneliness."

Otherwise, Henry's routine while at the Men's Residence Club was simple and satisfying. He spent "2 days a week in the library," the main branch of the public library at Forty-Second Street and Fifth Avenue, "2 days . . . writing letters," and the rest of the time going to "operas and concerts and . . . shows." All in all, he was happy to be back in New York and swore that "there is nothing like a big city to live your life according to your individual ideas and not as ordered to live by hypocritical priests and crooked politicians." He planned on visiting Frank, but whether he did is unknown. Nevertheless, he found time to take several side trips.

His first was a jaunt to Philadelphia, where he made the tourist rounds, including stops at the Liberty Bell and Independence Hall. The weather was too cold that February for him to cruise Rittenhouse Square, a popular haunt, so one night shortly before returning to New York, he visited another gay hot spot, the Camac Baths, where Henry encountered "positively the most bacchanalian orgy" he had ever "imagined . . . possible," but no one invited him to join in. The few younger men who appeared were quickly preoccupied with other younger men. Plenty of effeminate men showed up that night, too, but they weren't to Henry's liking either, and again, he felt left out in the cold.

In late March or very early April Henry slipped away from the hustle and bustle of New York and took another short trip, this time to the Catskills, where he hoped to spend the last few days of his furlough hiking in the mountains. Unfortunately, the weather there was blistering, and hiking was out of the question. Back in New York, he packed up and took the train to Walter Reed on May 28. Three days later, he learned that the physicians finally and officially agreed to grant him retirement with disability, and he wasted no time in moving back into the Soldiers' Home.

Henry had several projects in mind that he wanted to begin immediately. The principal one was to revise the four books he had written earlier, but he wasn't about to give up on "romance and love." He met a few men who gave him hope, but only briefly. They turned out to be "self-centered" and only interested in a "purely physical" experience with him. He felt defeated, and during his setback, he went through a period of self-examination. He came to realize, "I have always haughtily disdained to avail myself of the vulgar meat markets in shows and parks where meat is always prominently on display, but recently with the dire meat shortage, I have come to realize that when in Washington one better do as the Washingtonions [sic] do, and therefore I have swallowed my pride and lots of other things (!!!) and everything is lovely."

Many of the DC's queer men congregated "around public toilets and the notorious Lafayette Park where the conspicuous fairies do not seem to be bothered by anyone." One person related to Henry that "as long as one does not bother young boys, no one seems to care what one might do." Henry met one of his pen pals in Lafayette Park on Sunday, June 17, but he was disappointed when the man turned out to be too old for Henry, bald, and a drunk.

The experience finally made it painfully obvious to him that his age was an obstacle in his love life.

At the end of the month, Henry turned fifty-three and, to celebrate, decided to set out on a little excursion. He took a bus to Annapolis, Maryland, the last Friday of June and sent Manuel a picture postcard with a photo of the entrance to the US Naval Academy. While the photo didn't include a single sailor, Henry meant to tease Manuel with it. He hoped that, with thousands of young sailors there, the possibility that he just might get lucky and pick up one or two of them would make Manuel a tad jealous.

A few months after he returned from Annapolis, he placed an "ad in the Writers' Digest" for a correspondent "and had 13 letters" in reply. They were from a

1. chap in Chicago who wanted exciting letters. He did not reply to my letter telling him I had no hymn books, etc.
2. A boy, 29, in Virginia, 40 miles from here, who has been in bed 5 years with TB. Wrote nice letters first but then said he was only interested in someone playing his fiddle although he himself was not interested in tenors.
3. A fellow in Louisville Ky, sounded rather curious. Answered his letter a month ago and just had a reply. Works in a hotel as clerk and wants to come to Washington where the hotel has a branch. (Gilbert system hotels). Doubtful.
4. A newspaper reporter in North Carolina, 30, ex-officer, rather romantic and afraid to have a real party. He is nice though but rather religious and you cannot do anything with taboo-ridden people. Never will have fun in life.
5. A young radio announcer, 27, ex-Los Angeles boy, who tells me he masturbates a lot. Just the opposite of #4, too excessively interested in sex and its physical side, but may tone down a bit later. He is in Arizona.
6. A Washington civil service man, 49, did not answer my letter. Too old anyhow.
7. A fellow in Pennsylvania who seems to be a prostitute says he is interested in Lesbians, homos, etc. Says he is 35, very healthy!
8. A fellow in Pennsylvania who was in Contacts and the National Friendship service but never answered my letters before.
9. A snooty NY fellow who wants me to tell him all what others wrote to me. Told him I was no information clerk.

10. A fellow in Montreal, 55, did not answer my letter.

11. An old handyman in a roominghouse in Baltimore, a *"mystic"* who says he thinks this world of the senses is not real. Too idiotic to enjoy such corresp.

12. A plain ad from a music publishing house (this time not in code!)

13. A fellow in upper NYS who had been writing to me in Contacts and is a stupid and fanatical Catholic and we had a falling out. My ad was in box number style and my name not given.

He "got about three nice correspondents out of the bunch which might last," he thought. They didn't.

Another of his correspondents, a man who lived in Louisiana, whom Henry referred to as the "Louisiana bitch," sent him the address of a serviceman he knew and urged Henry to write him. Henry undoubtedly thought the GI was young and desirable and was eager to get to know him. The GI wrote Henry twice before disappearing, but in one letter, he described a group of gay servicemen and civilians in France who had organized and called themselves Queers, Incorporated. After Henry hadn't heard from the serviceman in quite some time, he wondered if the group had been arrested, if the GI had been transferred, or if he was simply on his way back to the States.

The GI had told Henry he wanted out of the military and would take a dishonorable discharge without a second thought if it meant he would be sent home, but Henry advised him about the consequences of that sort of release. The GI argued with Henry about it, and exasperated, Henry declared, "You cannot talk to these young whippersnappers. Let him dig his own grave if he wants to, what do I care." Henry was too distracted by the lies he had told about himself over the years and their consequences to worry about the GI anymore.

Henry knew about the long tradition in the United States of automatically naturalizing immigrants after they had served in the US military. It dated as far back as the Revolutionary War. During both world wars, a huge number of naturalizations of military personnel took place, a "total of 244,300 individuals naturalized through military service from 1918 to 1920; and 109,392 from 1943 to 1945." Henry planned on becoming a citizen through his military service, but he never got around to applying for it until March 23, 1944, and then only with the encouragement of the Office of Immigration. Two men from the Soldiers' Home, Jack Hasel and Alva McDonald, served as his witnesses.

As part of the process, officials dug into Henry's past and discovered that, because he had been confined in an asylum, he had forfeited any chance of citizenship unless he was able to get the court order that had institutionalized him revoked. Henry wrote to the Circuit Court of Cook County, explained his situation, and asked for help. The circuit court transferred his letter to the Veterans Bureau. Its solution was to send Henry a form attesting to his sanity that needed to be signed by two psychiatrists. He followed instructions, but the process opened up another can of worms.

First, because Henry was declared insane, he had committed a crime by reenlisting in the military. But according to the law, he had to enlist as a condition of his release, a catch-22 that left him facing arrest and imprisonment. Second, he falsified several official documents, claiming to have been born in Chicago, a lie. Third, since 1919, he had been living under an assumed name, Henry Joseph Gerber, without having changed it legally. Last, he had faced a Section VIII hearing in 1942. Although he was cleared of the charge of being a homosexual, the hearing was on his record. The disclosures about his past threw a very dark shadow over Henry's citizenship proceedings and threatened not only to destroy his chance at becoming one but, because of the growing crackdown on homosexuals in DC, to expose him to possible arrest and a prison sentence.

There was nothing more that Henry could do to fix the jam he had gotten himself into but wait. Other issues began to vex him. His old friend Franz Spirk had dropped out of sight, and Henry was concerned. As it turned out, Spirk had moved to Los Angeles and discovered that he liked the "angels" in Pershing Square "very much," and they had taken up so much of his time that he hadn't written. Spirk began pressuring Henry to move to L.A., dangling the mild climate and cruising Pershing Square before him as enticements. Henry was "fed up with Washington" and his "sex-starvation" and "would like to live and love a bit more *now* before" he got "too old," but Franz's inviting descriptions of easy sex weren't attractive enough to lure Henry away from his cushy life at the Soldiers' Home.

Spirk had only one trait that bothered Henry. He was a "romantic fool" with a habit of going "nuts over" any "pretty face" that crossed his path. He had fallen for one of the young men he picked up in Pershing Square, who turned out to be a "fanatical Jesus-lover" who teased him with the promise of sex but never acquiesced to the older man's advances. Henry thought the young man was out to drain Spirk's bank account, not Spirk, and advised him to break it off. Spirk ignored him.

Spirk's young man wasn't the end of his troubles. Six months later, the police arrested him in the park. Henry had warned him about the dangers in cruising there and assumed Spirk would be fired from his job, learn nothing from the experience, and continue in his risky cruising habits. Henry had some sober advice when it came to cruising: "Whenever I see a handsome thing I usually shy away and say: That is not for you to monkey with. Plain faces and even ugly people often are honest and appreciate attention. . . . I am glad that I am much more practical in such matters."

Perhaps because he had so many other problems on his mind, Henry had done nothing to expand the society's membership. Manuel and Henry were its only members—but Henry's troubles didn't dampen Manuel's enthusiasm for organizing. He began to plan another society, the Dorian Brotherhood, and hoped for Henry's support. Manuel admitted,

> To a practical man it may seem senseless to go on making plans which so seldom work out; but I think that planning and preparation are worth doing. A time will come when it will be possible to accomplish something; and if we keep on the lookout for the opportunity, and have definite plans formulated ahead of time, we shall find our preliminary work and worry bearing good fruit.

Henry ignored his new scheme. Frank enthusiastically supported it, but after a few months Manuel lost interest in the Dorian Brotherhood and let it drop.

Nevertheless, Frank was glad that Manuel hadn't let "Henry discourage" him. Henry's negative attitude toward gay men and the superior attitude he often took toward Frank and others soured him on Henry. "Within his limitations," Frank confided to Manuel, "he has done great work, but he fails, I think, in his lack of humor and of the ability to dream."

Henry was mistaken about Frank's involvement in the Society Scouting Sex Superstition. He wasn't "25%" interested in being involved with it. He had no interest in Henry's new organization at all. As he told Manuel,

> I have not only no ambition, but also no intention of being known as the head of whatever "movement" stems from our activities. My

entire aim, its limit, is to as far as may be possible reassemble the original kin souls who used to meet at the house, with a few very carefully chosen additions. . . .

I have little or no missionary spirit, save as it applies to those with whom I am in personal contact. And too, I nowadays feel peculiarly vulnerable—an apartment offers so slight facility for secreting the thousand and more negatives and innumerable prints, and none for the destruction.

Frank was feeling "vulnerable" not only because of his and Chuck's recent move but, more important, because he had just gotten some worrisome news from a friend of his, Roland Raven-Hart, an English travel writer and a major in the British military. The major had been arrested for mailing "some pictures" of nude men to Frank, and "it had cost him some $250 in fines and law fees" to get himself off the hook. Frank was sure that Raven-Hart's arrest had drawn the authorities' attention to him, that he was now in the crosshairs of the "P.O. Gestapo," who were about to raid his and Chuck's apartment any day.

Raven-Hart had already published several books about his "canoeing marathons" down "the world's major rivers" in his inflatable "two-seater" canoe when he and Henry met, probably through Frank. A member of Contacts and then one of Frank's rocketeers, Raven-Hart had stopped in New York City in 1930 for a short visit with friends and to find a companion for his next canoe trip, planned for the Mississippi River. He always reserved the second seat of his canoe for a teenager. In the subsequent book aptly entitled *Down the Mississippi*, Raven-Hart explained how he found his new companion. A "friend of a friend"—Frank's friend Henry—had introduced him to a "boy" named Phil. Henry told Manuel that Raven-Hart was fond of "boys 10–12" years old, but the photos of Phil in *Down the Mississippi* reveal someone in his late teens and perhaps several years older.

To take his mind off the problem that Raven-Hart might have laid at his door, Frank began planning his own organization, something he had "nursed along for some time" and had roots in ancient Greece. He had none of Henry's altruistic motives. His were sexual, pure and simple. He was convinced that he could reorganize the young men he had known before the war, before they were drafted or enlisted and were scattered across the globe. The club's "philosophy" would emphasize "this life, rather than an afterlife;" its membership would be restricted "to men" with an "emphasis on physical beauty;" and its

Gerber introduced a young man known as "Phil" to Major Roland Raven-Hart (right), who hired him as his companion during the first half of a canoe trip. Raven-Hart recounted the trip in his book *Down the Mississippi*. *Author's collection*

activities would focus on the "phallic (specifically the worship of the phallus)." He even came up with an ad that he fantasized placing in the *New York Times*: "THE RELIGION OF BEAUTY. Shall the Hedonic Association be revived? Former members, anyone interested, urged to write the Archon, P.O. Box so and so." Manuel though he was "on exactly the right track" and gushed, "Your Religion of Beauty advertisement would pack 'em in, in Los Angeles."

Frank asked Manuel to keep the idea of the new organization from Henry because "it would but upset him." Henry became volatile whenever *religion* was mentioned. Manuel promised and admitted the idea was "hardly Henry's dish. Fortunately there are other lines of endeavor he can profitably pursue." Manuel was sure Frank was on to something important. "Actually, the thing we are doing," he told Frank, "is breath-taking in its probable results—whether we live to see the full fruits or not."

Frank contacted his friends, told them his idea, invited them to join his group, and suggested that they pay a small fee to cover costs, such as refreshments, during their get-togethers. The results discouraged him. "There is plenty of enthusiasm for the ideas," he told Manuel, "but they duck suggestions that they might contribute financially or otherwise."

In the meantime, Manuel asked Frank to read and comment on *Boys, Men and Love*. "Two healthy young Rocketeers"—Lester Winters, a hospital apprentice first class, and Rutledge Keith, a radioman third class—happened to be visiting Frank when the manuscript arrived. He shared it with them, and all three agreed that it was an "encyclopedia, or perhaps better a symposium (a true feast)." Frank thought it was valuable and suggested that they should print the most important chapters separately as booklets. They could either sell them to members of his hedonic group to pay for the printing or pay for the printing out of membership dues. To help Manuel, Frank asked some of his other friends whose interests, he thought, would help him revise the book, including John Ashenhurst and Walter Schafer. Ashenhurst was a rocketeer and former reporter for the Chicago *Daily Times*, a tabloid. According to Frank, Ashenhurst was "interested in extreme youth" sexually, and as such, Frank thought he could "contribute valuable critique" to the chapters focused on the "boylover's standpoint."

As a favor to Frank, Walter Schafer agreed to read the manuscript and sent Frank some suggestions to share with Manuel. In short, he was supportive of Manuel's efforts and offered advice to strengthen the manuscript, but his final comment, meant as a compliment, was lukewarm at best: "It is an interesting attempt . . . to compose such a discussion. It must have taken a lot of time on BF's part." At the same time, Schafer wrote a second letter that was more critical, for Frank's eyes only. It was short and sharp. He was "fed up on a lot of this 'apologia for sin.'"

Manuel told Henry that he was sending his book to friends for their feedback, but he didn't tell him to whom. Henry warned him not to send his "opus to Stenberg or Frank. . . . The one [Stenberg] is entirely non-intellectual and too scared to cooperate," and "the other [Frank] is too far gone in deterioration to even elicit comment." Henry had been getting reports about Frank's poor health from Drexel and Stenberg. Drexel "said that the two, Frank and Chuck, looked and acted like decrepit undertakers," and Stenberg thought their apartment had "a gloomy atmosphere." Henry's take on Frank was simple. "Frank is going to the dogs slowly" because he had been beaten down by "this fascist world."

Henry had a point. The previous summer the postal inspectors had called Frank into their offices, but Raven-Hart's trouble with the law hadn't brought them to his door. He described the meeting succinctly to Frank: "Had the heat turned on yesterday afternoon, in an hourlong 'interview' with a Postal Inspector downtown, because of a few sample prints I had sent a man named Reed in Hollis, who had advertised for nudes in Science & Mechanics, somewhat over a year ago." Near the end of the interrogation, the inspector brought up Manuel's name. Frank was shocked that the inspectors knew about his friend. He only told the inspector that Manuel had been his lodger and was now a "retired Coastguardsman," and then, "thinking a little rank wouldn't hurt" and might even deflect the inspector's attention from Manuel, he told him that Manuel "was a Captain in the Coast Guard." Luckily for Frank, the photographs he mailed to Reed "were plain poses and not obscene," and he wasn't "locked up" or fired from his job. Nevertheless, the meeting left Frank shaken.

Compounding his stress, Frank had had a stroke and was trying to decide whether he should retire from his job as an office clerk with the New York Central Railroad. Henry was concerned about him. "The way Frank and Chuck

Gerber (left) with Erling Stenberg, one of his oldest friends, circa 1940s. *Courtesy of ONE Archives at the USC Libraries*

have been living, on booze and poor food—they spend everything they have on showing off to parasitical 'friends' and mourning over past splendour," he told Manuel, "he will probably not enjoy his retirement very long." Henry wasn't surprised that post office authorities had knocked on Frank's door. "When I lived with him," Henry recalled, Frank often left photographs of nude men lying around, and anyone who visited him or Chuck could have turned him in to the police.

Manuel didn't have to keep his promise to Frank about not mentioning his Hedonic Association to Henry. Facing so many overwhelming problems, Frank abandoned the idea.

Frank wasn't the only man Manuel and Henry knew who had recently drawn the attention of post office investigators. Authorities interrogated Erling Stenberg about some pictures he ordered from a photographer. The harassment of his friends—and his concern that that were drawing a bead on him—infuriated Henry. "That taxpayers' money is used to trip up citizens, and agents provocateurs used to snare people," he railed, "is something few people know, but is an old trick of the Catholics they used during the Inquisition."

13 | "SO MUCH POPPYCOCK"

THE EUROPEAN THEATER OF THE WAR ENDED on May 7, 1945, but the fighting continued in Asia until August. Neither Manuel, Frank, nor Henry had much to say about the war's end. As pragmatic as ever, Henry's attitude about the destruction war brought to Europe was unequivocal. "In such a cosmic holocaust as the war," he declared, "one must take on quite an unsentimental philosophy and say. 'All is lost, what of it? Let us not spill tears over what cannot be changed but start from the bottom again.' Pity for the victims of war is waste of time. After all, *we* did not start the war. In a way it will teach the Germans a lesson to think twice before starting a new war." Nevertheless, he felt a tinge of nostalgia and began to consider taking a trip home. "Perhaps in a year or so when the European entanglement has straightened itself out," he thought, "I might make a trip to Europe for a few months and I might even live there if the conditions are favorable financially." His parents were long dead, but he hadn't seen his brother, sister-in-law, and nephew since he left Coblenz over twenty years earlier.

In early 1946 Henry received a letter from his brother, his one sibling who had remained in Germany. He had become a lawyer and, although fifty-five years old, was drafted into the German Army to serve as a judge during military hearings. Sent with Hitler's Sixth Army to Stalingrad, where the war's "bloodiest battle" took place, he was captured and imprisoned, along with ninety-one thousand other German soldiers, when the Red Army defeated Germany's forces. He fell ill, probably from typhus, which ran rampant through the POW camps, and once he was released and returned to Germany, he and his family faced starvation. His letter to Henry was a plea for help. Henry's nephew, his brother's son, had eluded

179

being conscripted until March 4 when he was drafted during Germany's last-ditch effort to win the war. American soldiers captured him, and he was imprisoned at Camp Somerset in Westover, Maryland. Henry wanted to check on his nephew and set out from the Soldiers' Home on Saturday March 23 for Camp Somerset.

The morning was chilly when he left, but the temperature rose to sixty-two degrees by the afternoon. He traveled by bus to Annapolis and then crossed the Chesapeake Bay to Salisbury, where he spent Saturday night. When he woke on Sunday, the weather had turned cold and rainy, but he hiked south until he got tired of sloughing through the nasty weather and began to hitchhike. A ride took him to Westover. He hadn't seen his nephew, who was now in his midthirties, since the boy was twelve. The Americans had treated and fed him well and even paid him a small amount of money for the work he did in and around the camp. By June 22 Henry's nephew and other POWs were on their way to England to be repatriated. Eventually, he made his way back to his wife and three children who were living with relatives on a farm. Henry put the few thousands of dollars that he had saved for a rainy day to good use. He began sending money to his brother and sister-in-law as well as to his nephew and his family.

In the meantime, Henry was eager to discover what American servicemen, finding themselves released from military service and now stateside and often jobless, might do for an income, and he concluded that many would turn to prostitution. As it turned out, Henry's libido-driven intuition was prescient. Prostitution by former GIs became common in larger cities, and Henry was ready to support it.

He even made several trips to Baltimore because, with its many naval, coast guard, and army personnel stationed there, it was teaming with men in uniform. He picked up several, perhaps while cruising the City Hall Square. He good-naturedly fibbed to Manuel that "thousands were willing to make a couple of dollars and getting pleasure on top of it too." Then he added, "The law does not bother you as long as you are not caught in flagranti [sic]."

As GIs were beginning to be released from duty and returning to civilian live, a rash of murders in which younger men killed older ones began making the headlines, both locally and nationally. The cases didn't escape Henry's attention:

> One got away with murder, that is the jury exonerated him and the Jewish lawyer wailed that the poor man (punk) was a victim of an abnormal sex degenerate, and the stupid women and men fall for that. The other was apprehended in Niagara Falls and tries to get the same

lawyer but even if he should get off—this case was plain robbery and murder—he has before him a charge of desertion from the Army.

Details of both cases became known to the general public as the cases unfolded in DC newspapers.

On February 26, 1946, police discovered forty-year-old taxi driver Andrew Nault dead in his "swankily furnished apartment," and the next day, eighteen-year-old Robert Pope Lennon, formerly in the navy, phoned a friend of his, Andrew F. Scheible, a police officer, to confess to the crime. After a few drinks, Nault and Lennon had argued about Lennon's girlfriend, and then Nault made an "indecent proposal" to Lennon, who struck the older man on the head with a blunt object, part of an airplane propeller. Lennon claimed he had tried to revive Nault with artificial resuscitation, and once he realized Nault was dead, he "prayed over the body for about 15 minutes." Police charged him with second-degree murder.

Lennon's trial began on June 12. When the young man took the stand in his own defense, his testimony was noticeably different than what he had told the police. The two weren't strangers. Lennon was at Nault's to pick up several radios he had bought from the older man several days earlier, and while he was there he overheard Nault on the phone with a man to whom Nault owed $2,000. Lennon testified that the "man who made the phone call might have come to the apartment and injured Nault," which resulted in the older man's death. Lennon didn't mention the drinks the two shared nor Nault's comments about his girlfriend. However, he left Nault's "improper advances to him" in his new version of the incident.

After nearly four days of trial, the case went to the jury. In his closing remarks, Lennon's lawyer, Bernard Margolius, said the man to whom Nault owed money was the murderer, not Lennon; that Nault, who had been described as "one who bled freely," might "have bled to death" after being wounded by the propeller; and "emphasized that 12 men had keys to Nault's apartment." In case the jury—all men—hadn't caught on, Margolius's remark about the dozen men underscored Nault's homosexuality. After only three hours' deliberation, the jury returned its verdict to the court. Lennon was not guilty and set free.

While Lennon was behind bars awaiting his trail, another forty-year-old man was murdered by a younger one. Neighbors discovered the naked body of Don B. Glendening, a radio repairman, on his "blood-soaked bed," his head bashed in by a "war club" from his collection of Native American artifacts. Nothing but his car was missing, ruling out a robbery gone wrong. The next day a woman reported that she saw a man park what turned out to be Glendening's car in a no-parking zone on her street, and when they investigated, police found fingerprints on the steering wheel and stick shift. She described the man as being of "about 5 feet 8 inches tall" with "long, wavy, blond hair" and "exceptionally broad shoulders."

As the police investigated, hints about Glendening's past became public knowledge. Although never married or a father, he kept photos of women and children in his "elaborately furnished" apartment to support his heterosexual masquerade. He also displayed "some pictures of servicemen" and hosted "frequent parties attended by large numbers" of them. Police uncovered a stash of letters from military men and learned Glendening had given keys to his apartment to many of the soldiers and sailors he knew. They also discovered he had an arrest record. He had been taken into custody twice for "sex offenses."

Police quickly pieced together the events leading up to Glendening's murder. On Monday of the week before his death, Glendening had thrown himself a birthday party, and the next day, his actual birthday, his friend Richard L. Dietz brought a young man, Henry Eisenbarth, who had turned eighteen two days earlier, to Glendening's apartment and introduced the two. Dietz had met Eisenbarth at a bar. "Glendening took a liking to the youth" and invited him to stay in his apartment while he taught the eighteen-year-old how to repair radios.

The next evening, Wednesday, Glendening held another party and invited a married couple, Byron and Mary Preston, Dietz, and Eisenbarth. Everyone spent the night at Glendening's—the Prestons on a spare bed, Dietz on a cot, and Eisenbarth with Glendening in Glendening's bed. The next night, Glendening hosted his friends for another party, but this time, the Prestons went home and Dietz, Eisenbarth, and Glendening slipped into bed together. The chief of detectives, Robert J. Barrett, described the threesome as a "sex affair." The next morning, Dietz left, but Eisenbarth stayed, and a day or two later, killed the older man because he made "improper advances" toward him.

It didn't take police long to identify Glendening's murderer. The barely eighteen-year-old was stationed at Fort Belvoir in nearby Virginia undergoing training to become an engineer, but he had been AWOL since February 16. They described him as "5 feet 6 or 7 inches tall, weighing 150 pounds, having broad shoulders and athletic build, light blond curly hair combed back and a round face with freckles and slightly turned-up nose." He was a "hanger-on in taverns." They refused to name him initially.

Six days later, police tracked Eisenbarth to Niagara Falls, where he went sightseeing. Local police spotted him from a photograph distributed across the East Coast and followed him to his hotel room, where he was holed up with married, eighteen-year-old Ethel Harris. They arrested both but released Harris a few hours later. A photo of Eisenbarth at the Niagara police station, where he was being held, shows Eisenbarth standing between the two arresting officers, patrolmen George Truesdale and Roy Daubney. Baby-faced and smiling broadly, he appears unconcerned about his future.

Once he was back in DC, police charged Eisenbarth with murder in the first degree, and he told police he killed Glendening because the older man had made "improper advances" to him. He posed for photographs a second time, and again he smiled for the camera, still seemingly unfazed by his arrest. He had contacted Robert Lennon's lawyer, Bernard Margolius, thinking that because Margolius got Lennon acquitted, he could do the same for him. Margolius turned Eisenbarth down, and he was assigned a court-appointed attorney, William H. Collins. During Eisenbarth's trial on November 26, the assistant US attorney, his lawyer, and the judge agreed that he should be allowed to plead guilty to manslaughter, a lesser charge than murder in the first degree.

During their investigation, police learned that the Brooklyn-born Eisenbarth's father died when he was six, and he was sent to live at the Masonic Home in Utica, New York, where he remained for the next nine years until he was "expelled on sex charges." Shortly thereafter, authorities took him into custody, and he was jailed for "illegally wearing a naval uniform." He enlisted in the army and in February, four months before killing Glendening, he went AWOL.

Two and a half weeks after Eisenbarth's trial began, Judge Holtzoff sentenced the eighteen-year-old murderer to a "5-to-15 year prison term," the actual penalty "for manslaughter" in DC, but with his next breath, and thanks to Eisenbarth's indecent advance defense, he reduced the minimum from five years to three "to give the youth every opportunity to be considered for early parole."

The indecent advance defense wasn't invented in the 1940s, although its popularity blossomed in that decade. The oldest case of a man using that defense was reported in Massachusetts seventy-eight years earlier:

> A young man named Samuel M. Andrews claimed that he had been driven into "transitory insanity" when the friend pushed him down, tore open his pantaloons, and said, "Now I'm going to have some,

this time." The word *homosexual* wouldn't début in English for almost another two decades, but a fear of homosexuality was already being presented as a justification for murdering them. In the end, a jury did convict Andrews of manslaughter, perhaps because jurors were unable to square his claim that the overture had terrified and enraged him with his admission that his late friend had been making passes at him for the previous nine years, ever since an attempt on a memorable stormy evening that they had spent in bed together.

From its beginnings, the indecent advance defense was not just a rationalization for murder but, in the minds of many young men, a license to kill. Over the next few decades, scores of other young murderers and their attorneys used the same defense successfully. Eisenbarth served only three years for murder. It's unknown if he was ever punished for going AWOL.

What incensed Henry was not the killings per se. After all, the murdered men had taken their fate into their own hands by picking up strangers. What infuriated him was the line of defense that the defendants' lawyers followed, the same that scores of others took to justify their crimes. Simply put, the attorneys argued that their clients acted spontaneously and violently because gay men had propositioned them. The attorneys reasoned that members of the jury would understand that any real man would be incensed by a homosexual's sexual advances and would be justified in reacting violently to protect his manhood from perversion. Historians have called the lawyers' tactic the gay/homosexual panic defense and indecent advance defense. That same summer, another case found its way into the District of Columbia's newspapers. It, too, drew Henry's anger and disdain, and it would affect the lives of homosexuals for decades to come.

On Monday, July 1, Ellen Ridgeway hosted a party for her recently married daughter. Guests included her daughter, Joyce Allen, Joyce's husband Harold, and two teenagers, George T. Alwine, a student at McKinley High School who had just turned sixteen, and seventeen-year-old Thomas Gordon. Around 3:00 AM, after discovering that Alwine was missing, Gordon set out to find him, and grimly succeeded. Alwine had hanged himself, using his necktie as a noose, in the back of the house.

According to his mother, Alwine had run away from home three weeks earlier and was living at Ridgeway's, but earlier that day, Ridgeway had asked him to find someplace else to live. When interviewed by reporters, Alwine's mother told them that her son had been "'restless' ever since the death of his father" six years earlier. Concerned, "she had taken him to two psychiatrists." Alwine's diary, which was examined by the police, revealed that he had been meeting men in an area of Lafayette Park known as Queen's Row and that he counted over two dozen homosexuals, "older youths and men," among his friends. His mother "blamed her son's death on his 'bad companions'" and believed he had been "victimized by perverts."

With the influx of GIs in major cities, and the subsequent rise of male prostitution, the police stepped up their surveillance of areas where men congregated, and "homosexual arrests—including those for sodomy, dancing, kissing, or holding hands"—rose drastically, occurring "at the rate of one every ten minutes, each hour, each day" across the country. In DC the law punished men who engaged in sex with minors with up to one year in prison. George Alwine's suicide intensified the ordinary citizen's disdain for homosexuals, and it became the driving force behind a newly formed crusade that sought to punish "adult perverts convicted of molesting minors" with either a fine of $2,000 or a decadelong prison sentence.

Dr. Edgar D. Griffin of St. Elizabeths Hospital and Dr. Leopold Wexburg, director of the DC Health Department, joined the crusade. Their stance against homosexuals was reported in an article Henry mailed to Manuel. In it, Wexburg responded to Alwine's suicide and stated the population of homosexuals in DC was rapidly growing and children needed to be protected from them. At the same time, Joseph Bryant and Michael Appereti, detectives with the Police Juvenile Bureau, threw their weight behind the movement and spoke in public about the need for stricter laws.

Henry wasn't convinced that teenage boys needed protection from gay men as the physicians and police officers maintained. His experience told him otherwise. One midsummer night, he noticed a group of young men milling around the Lodge, which housed a public men's room, in Lafayette Park:

> They seemed charming and I was sympathetic, but I found out that they are the worst gang of extortionists who would not stop to murder a man for a dollar. They somehow know that homosexuals are afraid to get in with the police and blackmail is very profitable on those who have jobs or are socially prominent. The youngest of the gang was no more than 14. The boys in Christian America are thoroughly corrupted and a nasty bunch of nogoods. It is true one may find some

boys who are homosexual and who are not out for money, but in their association with others they soon learn the game of gimme or else.

Henry was certain "most of these boys" cruising parks and other areas where men congregated were "dangerous extortionists," not simply making themselves available for sex, and concluded that "the concern of these doctors and police for their 'purity' is so much poppycock."

Manuel pointed out the obvious in the article Henry sent him. Alwine's mother and society's attitudes about homosexuality caused the teenager to take his own life, not the gay men the teenager knew. "I can't think of anything the 'perverts' might have done to him that would cause him to kill himself," he told Henry, "though I can imagine his suicide as prompted by the attitude which society—including his mother—might take toward him." He was suggesting that the threat of society's and his mother's contempt and rejection pressured him into hanging himself.

The Lodge in Lafayette Park, Washington, DC, housed the men's room that many men cruised and where many of them were arrested by police decoys. *Courtesy of the Library of Congress, Prints & Photographs Division, Historic American Buildings Survey, HABS DC, WASH, 613–6*

Supported by the police, local psychiatrists, and at least one newspaper, the *Evening Star*, lawmakers rejected what they felt was a long-held view of homosexuals as harmless and caricaturized them as sexual vultures. The "sex pervert, in his more innocuous form," they charged, "is too frequently regarded as merely a 'queer' individual who never hurts anyone but himself. All too often we lose sight of the fact that the homosexual is an inveterate seducer of the young of both sexes and is ever seeking for younger victims," virtually echoing J. Edgar Hoover's claim a decade earlier.

The chief of DC's Police Juvenile Bureau, William T. Murphy, warned the public that the number of cases of homosexuals engaged in sex with children was exploding, and he even went so far as to claim that he had witnessed young heterosexual boys turn homosexual after being seduced by men. Murphy used a story similar to Alwine's to make his point. He "cited the case of a 15-year-old who met an older man at a soft-drink stand. The influence of the pervert on the boy became so pronounced that the youth's mother noticed the change in the boy and brought him to the Juvenile Bureau." That boy ended up hanging himself too. Murphy's example was so vague as to appear invented, but he fueled the public's fear and loathing with it.

With the indecent advance defense and the crusade to raise the penalties for gay men who were caught with boys underway, the DC police joined the movement and, on October 1, 1947, launched their effort to curb the problem, the Pervert Elimination Campaign. Oddly enough, when Officer Robert G. Thompson explained the rationale behind the police's action to the newspapers, men having sex with boys seemed to have nothing to do with the effort: "We've had a lot of robberies in the parks because of these sex offenders," he told the press. But the police's real objective had nothing to with snaring robbers and everything to do with the relentless clamor of the news media, politicians, religious leaders, and the medical profession against homosexuals. During the entire decade of the 1940s, the police didn't arrest a single man for a robbery associated with cruising, and yet during the same decade officers took hundreds of men into custody.

The police targeted five major cruising areas—Meridian Hill, Dupont Circle, Lafayette and Franklin Parks, as well as the Washington Monument grounds—and a few other places for surveillance. Statistics from the Pervert Elimination Campaign's first fifteen months, from October 1, 1947, to December 31, 1948, were kept and put into the official report of a hearing before the

US House of Representatives. The House had legal control over DC, including mandating the laws that governed it. The report revealed that the police arrested only seventy-six men during that period and charged them "with disorderly conduct, loitering, indecency, or some other violation." At the same time, the report revealed, they "warned" 467 others.

The use of the word *warned* is misleading. It suggests that the Park Police approached the men (86 per cent of them in Lafayette Park alone), scolded them, and then sent them on their way. In reality, the police took them into custody and processed them, which meant police questioned, fingerprinted, and photographed the men; recorded their names, addresses, occupations, and places of employment in a "pervert file"; and then released them. The police often leaked the men's names, addresses, and employers to the press. Although not arrested, their lives were ruined.

The largest number of men taken into custody during that fifteen-month period were students, ninety-two of them. Military men made up the second largest group: some fifty-eight soldiers, twenty-eight sailors, and two marines, totaling eighty-eight men. Most of the men who cruised the parks were young, but the police didn't take only adult men into custody. During the same period, they discovered twenty boys cruising for sex partners. The youngest, two of them, were thirteen years old. One, a "ninth-grader from Jefferson Junior High School," hadn't wandered into the park by accident. "Having once fondled a man at a Ninth Street movie house," he told the police, "he had come to Lafayette Park to 'see what would develop.'" The oldest boys, eight of them, were seventeen. DC's age of consent law gave boys as young as sixteen the right to marry, but not the right to choose their own sex partners.

The abusive "warnings" weren't the only instance of police underhandedness. To ensure they detected and warned or arrested as many men and boys as possible, they resorted to employing decoys to entrap their prey. This wasn't the first time DC police had resorted to entrapment. At least as early as the 1920s, authorities assigned a plainclothes police officer to patrol Lafayette Park. His quite unsubtle "obvious surveillance technique" made him well known among the men who cruised there, and Carter Bealer had even given the officer a nickname, the "Sneak."

The police decoys frequented "popular bars, restaurants, and theaters; they clustered along highly trafficked parks, streets, and bus terminals; they loitered in public bathrooms, bathhouses and gyms"—all places where homosexuals congregated—hoping the men there would be attracted and approach them with an invitation for sex. Understandably, the decoys couldn't be just *any* man on the police force, either. They were selected specifically for the job "on the basis of two factors: age and physical attractiveness." If the decoy wasn't young and good looking, he didn't stand a chance of appealing to their victims.

Frank N. Manthos not only fit the bill of desirability to a T but, within a few months of being hired for the vice squad of DC's Metropolitan Police Department, had become so adept at his role as a decoy that the news media christened him a "one-man vice squad," and it stuck with him for years. Although he arrested other lawbreakers, including female prostitutes and their pimps, his notoriety came from his arrests of homosexuals. During one night's work, Manthos arrested seven men in Franklin Park alone, and within his first eight months on the vice squad, he racked up "150 vice convictions."

Homosexuals knew that, if they were arrested, they would lose their cases no matter how good their lawyers were. Most "simply pled guilty" to the charge, "paid the fine," and got out of the police station as quickly as possible, and even those "who swore they made no sexual advances" toward the decoy, historian Anna Lvovsky discovered, "were sometimes so intimidated by the arresting officers that they found it easier to sign a false confession" than to fight the charge.

Despite the well-publicized campaign against homosexuals, none of the proposed new penalties were incorporated into the law. Henry didn't stop cruising the places that the decoys patrolled, either, and he may not have realized how lucky he was when he resolved to ignore any handsome man who crossed his path. His resolve kept him out of the clutches of police decoys like the Adonis Frank Manthos.

14 | "EVERYONE IS AFTER THEIR SCALP"

IN MAY 1947 HENRY TRAVELED through the South, from DC to Atlanta, then southeast to Florida, and from there northward through North Carolina, Tennessee, and Virginia, back to DC. He "had many nice parties" along the way.

A few months later, Manuel wrote Henry after a period of silence between them and asked him how his work on *Angels in Sodom* was going. He also gave him an update on *Defending the Sex Offender* and described a new get-rich-quick scheme that he appears to have based on at least some of the chapters in his *Job for a Boy*. He presented it as an educational program that would give boys a sexual outlet so that they didn't impregnate girls and ruin their lives financially and socially, and again, he couldn't disguise the pedophilia that underpinned the program.

He planned to approach boys' fathers (not their mothers) because they would understand the male's sexual urges. With their fathers' permission, he would train the boys with "boy-boy sexercise" at a secluded spot in the country that he compared to a boarding school. "By that means," Manuel fantasized, "a boy could receive our special indoctrination while studying his schoolbooks and be under our exclusive influence long enough to give him fuller mastery of the sexual plexus than a few brief lessons can impart." All he needed, he believed, was to find a "few hundred men" willing to give him a "few hundred dollars apiece" to teach their sons how to be sex mates for other men.

Manuel understood that he couldn't "come right out and say" to a boy's father, "Look, Mr. DuTell, what you need is for somebody to teach your Johnnie how to suck pricks. I'm the man to do it. I'll wise the kid up and give him an expert breaking-in for seventy-five bucks." Instead, he proposed, a more sophisticated approach:

> "Mr. DuTell," we might lead off, "an informal committee of fathers has been conferring, studying, and investigating with the purpose of inaugurating a program for boys' development. Research indicates that an American boy can be given a short course of training to supplement his regular schooling, the equivalent of that extra benefit derivable from attendance at a famous English boarding-school—at a fraction of the expense of sending the lad to a private school."

In his spiel to convince fathers to enroll their sons in the program, Manuel planned to use a variety of references to the ancient Greeks, rumors and some truths about English boarding schools, fathers' fears about their sons getting girls pregnant and having to marry them, and his own versions of cultural and political history. He even came up with how he could convince the boys that the instruction was somehow reasonable. "[The] man may give his son (and the son's mother if she *must* hear of the errand)," he explained, "the impression that the public-education authorities are trying out a new and extra-helpful course and that he, the father, through 'connections,' has been able to get Johnnie designated to receive the instruction."

Frank's and Henry's reactions to Manuel's boarding school were similar. Frank calmly told Manuel that he was impressed by the amount of thought and planning that he had obviously put into the plans for the school—faint praise at best—but he couldn't possibly get it up and running now because of societal and legal restrictions. He added that he wasn't interested in helping Manuel with it. Henry wasn't as diplomatic as Frank. He saw through Manuel's delusion and was quick to condemn it. "Your [sic] are entirely off your nut if you think that fathers would let their boys become homosexuals!" he shot back at Manuel.

Despite Manuel's crackpot scheme, Henry was happy to hear from his friend again, and he responded quickly. He was pleased with his revisions of *Angels in Sodom* and felt it was in as good a shape as possible. Despite all the time he had spent on it, he wasn't interested in getting it published. He was open about sex in it and knew a publisher would demand he cut the sex scenes. He would rather not let it see the light of day than bow to society's hypocrisy.

Henry had returned to his work with the committee of correspondence. He wrote to the editor of the *American Mercury*, responding to Bergen Evans's editorial "That Homosexuals Are Always Effeminate." Evans showed sympathy toward homosexuals and animosity against the "barbaric laws" that criminalized them, but at the same time he followed the more popular line of thought concerning why certain men were homosexual. He believed that homosexuality was an illness or was caused by a physiological weakness.

Henry's letter appeared in the July 1947 issue, one of the few to be published and, despite the antihomosexual sentiment across the nation, one of the few to bear his name instead of a pseudonym. From the outset, he corrected Evans on the terms he had used and on several of the concepts to which he referred. Evans thought Oscar Wilde was homosexual, but Henry claimed he was bisexual because he had married and fathered children. He humorously countered the widely held belief among physicians and many others that the effeminacy that some homosexuals displayed was caused by some sort of glandular problem. "I do not think that women would like the statement . . . that 'glandular deficiency suggests womanliness.' The ancient Greeks who were notoriously bisexual (women for breeding and boys for pleasure), could not all have had bad glands."

Cordial and apologetic for any misunderstanding, Evans printed his reply following Henry's letter. He apologized for his misunderstanding, but he was happy that Henry, whom he referred to as *Dr. Gerber*, had corrected him. Evans had confused Henry with Dr. Israel J. Gerber, a rabbi and well-known speaker and author, who took a liberal stance concerning homosexuality. Among his books was *Man on a Pendulum: A Case History of an Invert*.

Henry's letter caused a stir—intense, but brief—among the magazine's readers, and their letters began appearing in the October issue. Clinton E. Albertson took umbrage at Henry's comment that the law forced people to marry. Paul Brinkman Jr. thought that Henry contributed sound information to the topic but believed that Henry didn't understand that homosexuals were entrapped in self-love. John D. Lane, a physician, was adamant against Henry's assertion that men such as Julius Caesar or Lord Nelson were homosexual and asserted that homosexuality destroyed society. Only one of the letters fully supported Henry's, a brief accolade from William Hamilton. "Dr. Gerber certainly knows what he is writing about," he wrote, "and I agree with every sentence." For the first time in his life, Henry's work on behalf of gay men had an obvious, measurable result. His letter had created a conversation, and his committee of correspondence had done its job. Henry was heartened.

The *American Mercury*'s managing editor, Charles Angoff, was impressed by Henry's letter especially because Henry had struck a nerve among the magazine's readers. He invited him to submit an article on homosexuality for the magazine. Henry was flattered. He hadn't published anything since the piece about rations in *Recruiting News*, but that was an assignment, not a topic that he chose to explore. Finally, someone he didn't know and who wasn't obligated to compliment his work because of their relationship appreciated his writing. Henry promptly sat down in his desk in the Soldiers' Home and began an essay. He submitted "Is Homosexuality Inborn or Acquired" to Angoff a few weeks later, but Angoff turned it down almost immediately, saying "it was too much definition while he wanted the human side of the question." He invited Henry to try again.

Despite the rejection, Angoff's second invitation gave Henry enough encouragement to go back to his office and begin typing. In the second essay, Henry wrote about "three theoretical psychoanalyses of three inverts and ended up with one 'incurable' case in which" he allowed the homosexual to defend his sexuality, while also "pointing out that the authorities encourage murder of homosexuals by their attitude" toward them. Angoff returned Henry's second essay, too, and asked Henry to rewrite it and to include "statistics of how many homosexuals can be cured" and information on "the complication of homosexuals who marry."

Henry had had it with Angoff, certain that the editor was just giving him the "run-around." Besides, he grumbled, Angoff obviously didn't know anything at all about the adversities homosexuals faced day to day, which occasionally overwhelmed them, or that most weren't at all interested in being cured, even if they could be. Henry didn't need to waste another second with Angoff and moved on.

On the heels of a double rejection from the *American Mercury*, Henry took up the mantle of the committee of correspondence with a vengeance. On September 4, incensed over an editorial that blamed homosexuals for the downward trend in births in the United States, he wrote a letter to the *Times-Herald* of Washington, DC, and directed the editor's attention to the obvious: Catholic priests and nuns weren't procreating, nor were prostitutes, men who masturbated, or women who had abortions. He also reminded the editor that heterosexuals engaged in the same, nonprocreative sexual acts that homo-sexuals did and wondered why they should be persecuted while heterosexual men were ignored. "Your editorial," he wrote, "is indeed the worst form of a kettle calling the pot black." He dared the editor to publish the letter, signed it "Tolerant," and dropped it into a mailbox on his way out of town. He was taking another trip to Baltimore and, from there, to the Blue Ridge Mountains for some hiking. Henry's letter went unpublished.

Although the weather was very warm and humid, Henry kept busy in Bal-timore, cruising its theaters and parks. One hustler whom Henry approached charged $2.50 and told him he "was strictly 'passive.'" Initially, Henry wasn't sure what that meant but wasn't intrigued enough to find out. He also ran into a good-looking former sailor whose charms so excited Henry that he broke one of his cardinal rules and followed him into an alley. As soon as they were far enough in so that they couldn't be seen by passersby on the sidewalk, the ex-sailor turned and asked Henry, "What's up, bud?" Henry lost interest immediately and left him among the alley's shadows. He was unsure of the ex-sailor's motives, anyway. "He was broke," Henry explained, "and wanted me to take him to a hotel but as he said that he would leave town early next morning for New York," Henry "suspected" that the ex-sailor planned to rob and perhaps even murder him.

Back in DC, Henry set his sights on movie theaters as his best option for finding sex partners and met a "16-year-old boy"—the same age as George Alwine—whom he had seen on several occasions hanging around the theaters. He was "100% heterosexual" but had sex with men for a price, "50 cents for masturbating one, and $1.50 for fellatio" (in today's currency, about $6.25 and $19, respectively). Henry never revealed if he and the teenager came to an under-standing. Several days later, two editorials caught his eye—and stoked his wrath.

Newspapers were inundating Henry and other readers with the hysteria surrounding homosexuality, and when Cissy Patterson, owner of the *Times-Herald*, wrote an editorial about homosexuals in DC, he replied with one that raked her across some very hot coals. He began, "Your editorial of September 3 . . . was indeed a sickening, nauseating display of (female?) hysteria and hypocrisy." She had cited a nine-month-old case of an adult male molesting a boy on the West Coast to show her support for new proposals for changes in the law concerning homosexuals, and Henry pointed out that she could have used a case that was reported in her paper on the same day that her editorial appeared. She didn't because the case was the "rape of a 14-year old girl, not by a homosexual, but by a married heterosexual!" in DC. "I suppose you do not read your own crap," he charged and complained about the practice of pointing "to an exceptional* homosexual who seduced a fourteen year old boy" and using it as evidence to condemn "all homosexuals."

In the same piece, Patterson also blamed homosexuals for the recent decline in the birthrate, and Henry was all too happy to hold a mirror up to her hypocrisy. She could have blamed the "thousands of priests, nuns, and monks who . . . 'defy the eternal theme that the race shall continue,'" he pointed out, or the "millions of prostitutes who do not procreate," or the 20 percent of childless marriages in the United States, or even the women who account for "three million estimated abortions per year." Instead, she blamed the dip in the population on homosexuals. Of course, Henry's letter never appeared in the *Times-Herald*.

Another editorial caught his eye the same month. In "Wacs and Waves Can Stop This," the *National Defense* editor John H. Hoeppel complained about the "*moral depravity*" of the servicemen who had engaged in sexual "excesses" with the "women of the conquered nations" during World War II and its aftermath, but what angered Hoeppel even more was the "wave of homosexual offenses" in the military and its reaction to it. He claimed the War Department recruited a "large army of Wacs and Waves to *obviate* increasing homosexual offenses," by which he meant the women served as sexual playmates for the servicemen so that they would not turn to other men for their sexual release. He strongly urged the War Department to castrate any homosexual discovered in the military's ranks.

Henry ridiculed Hoeppel's bizarre opinion. Hoeppel gave no evidence in his editorial that the War Department recruited women to act as little more than prostitutes, and he pointed out that Hoeppel's belief that having sex with women might transform homosexuals into heterosexuals was absurd. He accused Hoeppel of not knowing what a homosexual was and, for the record, set him straight. He also schooled the editor on bisexuals, who, he thought, outnumbered homosexuals and often turned to male prostitutes. The ones whom Henry knew told him that "married men are their best customers."

Unwittingly, in his zeal to show up Hoeppel, Henry revealed his misogyny, which occasionally cropped up in his remarks to Manuel and Frank. Except for his childhood and a few years when he and Anna first arrived in Chicago, he

---

* With *exceptional*, Gerber meant "rare."

served for over thirty years in the military, among men, and had virtually no contact with women except for a lesbian couple whom he considered friends. He acknowledged women's important role in human history as childbearers and neither hated them nor thought they were inferior to men. He simply didn't have much use for them, and he even told Manuel the "normal homosexual does not hate women—he is only indifferent to them."

However, Henry did believe they were his rivals, competing with him for the affections of men and stood in the way of his ability to find "romance and love." He assumed women felt the same about homosexuals. "Women are good psychologists," he admitted, "and it did not take them long to find out that homosexuals are their deadly enemies in the capture of the male." Making matters worse for him, they played the game unfairly, attracting men "by hook and crook," and more than a few men who bragged of "having fucked a woman" discovered, he said, that it was they "who 'got fucked.'" A heterosexual man, he was certain, could enjoy the same pleasures with another man, no strings attached. "Why should anyone take upon himself a thousand responsibilities just for a little pleasure" with a woman? Henry wondered. "Why rear children and spend one's income in getting them educated and then see them dragged over to Europe to fight Churchill's wars and be killed?"

Henry shot his letter off to Hoeppel, but as with so many of the letters he wrote to editors, Hoeppel immediately dropped it into the wastepaper basket. Manuel commiserated with Henry over his repeated rejections and offered him some advice. "Editors want things concise to the point of crampedness," adding that to get a letter to the editor published, the writer needed to be "brief, brief, brief," something that was impossible for Henry.

As Henry was doing what he could to make the best of a bad situation, legal authorities in DC were doing their best to make the lives of gay men hell. As Henry observed, "Everyone is after their scalp." When George Morris Fay became DC's US attorney in 1946, he immediately set off on a crusade against homosexuals, claiming that two men were arrested each day on sex charges, stirring up the antihomosexual sentiment already fermenting. Consequently, the District's Bar Association named a committee of fifteen lawyers, plus representatives from the Women's Bureau and the Juvenile Bureau, from the directors of federal prisons and St. Elizabeths Hospital, and scores of others to help Fay develop a statute to "insure full prosecution of sex offenders, particularly those who endanger children."

As the new proposed law began to take shape, its intent became obvious. It wasn't just aimed at adults who engaged in sex with children, as Fay initially claimed. It greatly increased the punishment for any gay man whom police arrested for any reason. Previously, a homosexual who had been taken into custody could receive a "fine of up to $100 and up to 90 days in jail." The proposed new legislation carried a "penalty of 10 years in prison or $1,000 fine or both for persons guilty of sodomy or any other unnatural sex act" and a "penalty of 20 years in prison or $2,000 fine or both for persons guilty of these offenses against children under 16 years." The law also

> mandated that anyone accused of sodomy (defined as either anal or oral sex) had to be examined by a psychiatric team. . . . If a man were picked up several times by the D.C. police for cruising in Lafayette Park, for instance, the psychiatric team could diagnose him to be a "sexual psychopath," and he could be committed to the criminal ward of the District of Columbia's St. Elizabeth's psychiatric hospital, even before being allowed his day in court.

And "he would remain there until the superintendent of St. Elizabeth's" decided he had "'sufficiently recovered,'"—that is, until he was cured. Henry agreed with the proposed law's stand against adults who abused children sexually but was concerned that the proposal was actually aimed at homosexuals in general, the vast majority of whom never considered children as sex partners. Again, Henry was prescient.

Congressman Arthur Miller sponsored the new legislation that was signed into law by President Truman on June 9, 1948. Officially known as Public Law 615 or the Miller Sexual Psychopath Law, it was popularly called the Miller Act and "provided for the indefinite interment [sic] and treatment for 'sexual psychopaths' in the District." J. Edgar Hoover's concept of the "psychopathic child molester" had taken hold, and gay men across the United States would be labeled "sexual psychopaths" regardless of their mental health for the next several decades.

Ironically, the first person prosecuted under the Miller Act was sixty-three-year-old Amide Landry, who lived at the Soldiers' Home with Henry. He was charged with "improper advances" with an eight-year-old girl in an alley. He had given her money for a sexual act that went unidentified in the local press.

Rumor ran rampant in the home when he was arrested on June 17 and continued through July 20, when he was examined by a psychiatrist, found insane, and committed to St. Elizabeths Hospital. So far, the Miller Act seemed to be accomplishing what Fay and his colleagues believed DC needed, but it didn't take long for it to be used against consenting adult homosexuals. Only two years after President Truman signed it into law, research by Bernard A. Cruvant, Milton Meltzer, and Francis J. Tartaglino* made it clear that the authorities had applied it widely, arresting any homosexual who crossed their paths for any reason.

Shortly after Landry's prosecution, police caught thirty-year-old Bennie Buntone and eighteen-year-old Edward P. Flaherty, a sailor, "on the Mall in an apparently consensual encounter." Under the old law, the two would "would have been charged with disorderly conduct, required to post a twenty-five-dollar bond, and released," but under the Miller Act, the two "were held on a one-thousand-dollar bond." The following Christmas Eve, Buntone, an African American, was sentenced to prison with a two-to-six-year sentence while Floyd, who was white, received a "suspended sentence and was placed on probation for two years." Homophobia and racism had linked arms in the nation's capital.

By the end of the year, the depths to which authorities would sink to entrap homosexuals became apparent, even to the public. On November 10, 1947, a parkgoer discovered that one of the benches in Lafayette Park had been bugged. Wires led from the bench to the Park Police headquarters. The Park Police refused to comment on the situation, but finally, the US Army's Civilian Intelligence Division admitted that it was trailing an officer believed to be homosexual, and the bench in question was the one where he usually sat when he visited Lafayette Park. The police finally removed the wires.

It didn't take long for the bench to achieve a near-legendary status in DC. Scandal mongers Jack Lait and Lee Mortimer wrote about the bench four years later in their *New York Times* bestseller *Washington Confidential*, hinting that the bench was still in use. "One of the benches in Lafayette Square, gathering place of the faggots, across from the White House is wired up. You ought to hear some of the gay conversation. We did. Then we squirted penicillin in our ears," they explained in their typically sensationalist and derogatory fashion.

---

* The research was subsequently published as "An Institutional Program for Committed Sex Deviants," *American Journal of Psychiatry* 107 (September 1950): 190–194.

15 | "AS IF WE DID NOT KNOW!"

ALTHOUGH HENRY OCCASIONALLY MENTIONED his Society for Human Rights to Manuel and Frank and a few other men, such as Fred Frisbie, he was sure his attempt "to ameliorate the plight of homosexuals" had disappeared on the trash heap of time. That wasn't the case. On the other side of the country, in Los Angeles, one man was especially eager to reignite the torch that Henry had once lit and that society had extinguished.

Harold "Harry" Hay was in high school when his classmates warned him to "avoid Pershing Square 'because queers hung out there,'" but already aware of his homosexuality, he took their warning as a green light. In 1929, after exploring the park for a few weeks, the seventeen-year-old Hay "enticed an 'older' gentleman (he must have been at least 33)" to "sleep with him." The man was Champ Simmons. "Poor guy," Hay later recalled, "he was appalled to discover . . . I was both a virgin and jailbait," but that didn't keep the two from getting together a second time.

Their next tryst took place at Simmons's sister's place, and they continued to see one another for months, but their relationship was more than sexual. They discussed the problems homosexuals faced, and Simmons mentioned that he had been a "friend of Henry Gerber in Chicago" and belonged to Henry's Society for Human Rights. "So I first heard about that group only a few years after its sad end," Hay remembered. Simmons gave him the impression that the "society was primarily a social thing," something Henry was either blind to or didn't realize. For Hay, the "idea of gay people getting together at all, in more than a daisy chain, was an eye-opener of an idea. Champ passed it on

199

to me as if it were too dangerous; the failure of the Chicago group should be a direct warning to anybody trying to do anything like that again." Simmons meant to protect the teenager, but the seventeen-year-old didn't take his warning to heart. Instead, it gave him ideas.

Nearly twenty years later, on August 10, 1948, Hay attended a party with twenty or so other gay men. Their talk turned to the forthcoming presidential election, and he and a few others began to fantasize about organizing a group to campaign for the Progressive Party's candidate, Henry A. Wallace. Wallace was running against Democrat Harry S. Truman and Republican Thomas E. Dewey. Hay and the others hoped that, by supporting Wallace, he would, in turn, support reform of the laws governing sexual matters. As the discussion became more and more involved, Hay came up with a name for the group, Bachelors for Wallace. Although his enthusiasm over organizing may have seemed spontaneous to the men at the party, the ideas that Simmons's remarks about Henry had formed in Hay's imagination now seemed vaguely possible.

At home, he worked feverishly all that night, writing down the ideas that he and the others had discussed until had had composed a "five-page organizational outline and manifesto" that he entitled "The Call." The next morning, Hay telephoned the men who had been interested in organizing the night before, expecting them to still be excited. None were. Bachelors for Wallace never came to fruition outside one night's revelry and a manifesto, but the experience and the excitement that it generated in Hay set the wheels in his mind in perpetual motion.

In the meantime, the findings of a decadelong research project by an unknown entomologist, a professor at Indiana University, appeared as a book in January 1948 and took America by storm. Alfred C. Kinsey's *Sexual Behavior in the Human Male* was amazingly popular and reached the number two spot on the *New York Times* bestseller list. It remained on the list for twenty-seven weeks and sold 250,000 copies, an unheard-of achievement for an academic tome. News of its 804 pages of tedious, academic writing swept across the landscape.

In researching *male* sexuality, Kinsey didn't ignore homosexuals, and he found that "10 percent of white males were almost exclusively homosexual for at least three years" and that "18 percent had as much heterosexual as homosexual contact during a similar period." Furthermore, some "thirty-seven percent had had at least one homosexual experience in their adult lives." He summarized his findings by saying, "It is difficult to maintain the view that psychosexual reactions between individuals of the same sex are rare and therefore abnormal or unnatural." Homosexuals suddenly weren't a slim minority of perversity but a large slice of the majority. Having grown up believing—or forced to believe—that heterosexuality was the only natural and acceptable expression of sexuality and that their difference was both perverse, degenerate, and disgusting, they felt as if a huge burden had been lifted off their shoulders, changing their self-image.

Samuel Stewart, a former university professor turned tattoo artist and novelist, called Kinsey's book a "watershed moment" that "simply blasted this damn country wide open." He added, "There wasn't a radio stand-up comic, or a television comic, or a nightclub comic who didn't have a thousand jokes to make of it. His name was a household word. . . . Even the dumbest guy on the street had heard of Kinsey," and as far as the gay community was concerned, the book "represented a transition for homosexuals from invisibility," which had settled on them during the post-pansy panic, "to a central place in the nation's consciousness. 'He was our Stonewall.'" Hay was so excited by the Kinsey report and its revelations about homosexuality that he carried his copy everywhere he went "as though it were a Bible," and with his knowledge of Henry's Society for Human Rights, he had a platform on which to "imagine how powerful homosexuals might be if only they organized."

The Miller Act was signed into law just five months after the appearance of the monumental *Sexual Behavior in the Human Male*, and the book may have played a decisive role in the new legislation because of what it revealed. Legislators for DC and elsewhere were doing everything in their power to counter Kinsey's findings, and not just his statistics about homosexuality. According to historian Holly S. Heatley, "Kinsey reported that 95 percent of American men participated at some point in their lives in sexual activities that were illegal," including cunnilingus and fellatio. Kinsey held a mirror up to the American public and showed that there was a gap the size of the Grand Canyon between society's sex laws and what people did in the privacy of their bedrooms. Much of the American public didn't like what it saw.

Henry was very enthusiastic about Kinsey's revelations and sent Manuel an article that discussed the results of his research. The "article debunks socalled [sic] Christian sex morality," he gushed, happy to have his own ideas supported by Kinsey's research, "and shows that 95% of all men in America indulge in some 'criminal' sexual pursuits. As if we did not know!" Frank was just as excited. Manuel was interested in Kinsey's claims but wasn't sure he would read the book or even how valid the findings could be. He couldn't imagine any homosexual telling a complete stranger about his sexual activities.

While Kinsey's revelation that 37 percent of adult men had engaged in at least one same-sex sexual experience buoyed gay men in their quest for the legitimacy of their sexual orientation, "37 percent" also became a trigger for many conservative heterosexuals. The editor of the *American Journal of Psychiatry* declared, "Kinsey's evidence of a 'gap between cultural mores and private behavior' . . . set off a 'reaction' . . . that led, in turn, to the scapegoating of . . . sexual offenders," particularly homosexuals. More specifically, the victimization zeroed in on DC government workers at first but quickly spread to include homosexual men and women across the United States. The victimization would be dubbed the Lavender Scare.

Park Police decoys continued the surveillance of men's rooms in DC parks, theaters, and the YMCA. The criminalization of gay men intensified, and the Park Police's "pervert file" grew fatter. The media responded with a round of articles in well-respected magazines that fueled sentiment against homosexuals. In his "Murder as a Sex Practice," published a month after *Sexual Behavior in the Human Male*, Frank C. Waldrop claimed that "FBI records" revealed that a "rape or criminal assault" occurred every 43 minutes" and that arrests "for rape" had risen "62 per cent" since 1938. He added, "Arrests of homosexuals and other types of perverts have gone up by 142 per cent," lumping homosexuals into the same group as rapists and other violent criminals.

Newsweek ran "Queer People," an editorial that reviewed *The Sexual Criminal*, a "sensationalized exposé on so-called sexual deviants" written by the founder and former director of the Los Angeles police department's Sex Offense Bureau. The editorial began, the "sex pervert, whether a homosexual, an exhibitionist, or even a dangerous sadist, is too often regarded merely as a 'queer' person who never hurts anyone but himself. Then the mangled form of some victim focuses the public's attention on the degenerate's work." It concluded, a "stern attitude is required if the degenerate is to be properly treated and cured. The sex pervert" should "be rerated not as a coddled patient, but as a particularly virulent type of criminal." *Newsweek* also equated homosexuality with violent crime. Other magazines and newspapers quickly followed suit, swamping readers with homophobic rhetoric, some subtle, but most obvious and lurid.

At the same time, Communist countries across the globe were flexing their muscles. In September 1949 the Soviet Union detonated nuclear weapons for the first time in history, and three months later, Communists took control of China's government. The next month, January 1950, Alger Hiss, an American accused of spying for the Soviets, was convicted of perjury, and on February 3, 1950, Klaus Fuchs, a German physicist who worked in the United States and spied for the Soviet Union, was arrested for espionage. Anxiety over Communism settled into every corner of US society.

Then on Thursday, February 9, 1950, US senator Joseph R. McCarthy delivered a speech to the Republican Women's Club of Wheeling, West Virginia. He claimed to have the names of 205 men who were members of the Communist Party and employed in the State Department, making them risks to national security. He never revealed the alleged spies' names nor gave any evidence that they even existed.

The next day, during a radio interview, McCarthy changed his report. He had the names of only fifty-seven Communists employed in the State Department and again refused to offer any names or any evidence that the men existed. The following Saturday, he sent President Truman a letter in which he claimed that only eighty of some three hundred men identified as security risks had been fired by the State Department and accused Truman of pandering to Communists. For the third time, McCarthy expected others to accept his accusations as truth without any evidential support. By February 13 the undersecretary for security of the State Department, John Peurifoy, challenged McCarthy to put up and reveal the names of the alleged Communists or shut up. McCarthy refused to divulge the identities of the security risks, but he wasn't about to shut up. His accusations sparked a witch hunt that historians have labeled the Red Scare.

Then eleven days after his address to the Republican Women's Club, McCarthy took the floor during a meeting of the Senate and went on a five-hour tirade about security risks, focusing on two men. One, case no. 14, worked as a translator for the State Department. His friends included several ties to the Communist Party. McCarthy didn't believe that case no. 62 had any Communist acquaintances, but because both no. 14 and he were gay, McCarthy was certain that they could be easily blackmailed. In a few breaths, McCarthy linked gay men to the national hysteria over Communism, and the Red Scare and the Lavender Scare were forever linked.

McCarthy's statements specifically affected the District of Columbia, and as its governing body, Congress formed a committee led by senators Kenneth Wherry and J. Lister Hill to investigate McCarthy's accusations. The Wherry-Hill Committee called Lieutenant Roy Blick, head of the DC vice squad, and other law and government officials to testify. Blick estimated that some five thousand homosexuals lived in DC and that that approximately thirty-seven hundred of them worked for the government.

When the Wherry-Hill Committee concluded its work, Congress formed a much larger one to further the investigation. Senator Clyde Hoey, who had begun his career in politics on a "white supremacist" platform, headed the second committee. Among those the Hoey Committee, as it was popularly referred to, called to testify was police officer Lieutenant Edgar Scott. He explained that when a government worker was taken into custody by the police and the interrogators learned he was homosexual, they notified the department in which he worked as well as the FBI. The notification included a simple note "in parentheses 'homosexual' or 'pervert.'"

The Hoey report fueled the nationwide paranoia. Disparaging homosexuals, it concluded that "those who engage in acts of homosexuality and other perverted sex activities are unsuitable for employment in the Federal Government," and to underscore its judgement, it even added its rationale for the verdict: "Persons who indulge in such degraded activity are committing not only illegal and immoral acts, but they also constitute security risks in positions of public trust." From that moment through the next several decades, queer men and women were hunted down by the FBI, accused of being security risks, and fired from their jobs. The FBI added their names to its files, making them easily targets for future persecution.

The "purge," as historian David Johnson called it, didn't just affect government employees but also queer people who held jobs in the private sector and needed security clearances. Their applications for clearances would pass through the FBI and, if their names were in its files, would be rejected. Many other businesses, such as aircraft builders and universities, followed the government's lead and either didn't hire men suspected of being homosexual or fired those whose homosexuality had been discovered.

The rise of the Lavender Scare across the United States motivated Hay. According to Kepner, Hay was "hot to emulate Gerber," and he organized a small group of liberation-minded men in Los Angeles in November 1950.

Eventually dubbed the Mattachine Society, the group drew members from across southern California, and within a few years, chapters had been formed in several major cities.

Neither Henry, Manuel, nor Frank lost jobs or were directly affected by the witch hunt, but they, and queer men and women across the country, were intensely threated by it. One man in Chicago wrote in despair to a friend, "They blame us for everything and incidentally it is more and more in the limelight everyday—why they don't round us all up and kill us I don't know." As Kepner wrote, the "paranoia" that many queer men and women exhibited "was by no means without grounds." Although he followed the development of both committees with increasing disgust, a personal loss distracted Henry for a short time. His war buddy Alva Lee McDonald died that December 8 and was buried in the cemetery associated with the home.

Since the end of the war, Henry had hoped to return to Europe. He wanted to visit his family again and travel. He also wanted to escape the growing sentiment against homosexuals that engulfed DC and much of the rest of the country and hoped for relief in Europe because of its liberal views on sexuality.

On April 24, 1951, Henry took the train from Union Square in Washington, DC. The sun was bright, the weather was warm, and there wasn't a cloud in the sky. He spent the night in a hotel in New York. Overnight, clouds gathered, and the temperature dropped ten degrees, but that didn't dampen his enthusiasm. The next day, he boarded the SS *George Washington*, the same ship that he and Anna had taken from Germany to the United States in 1913 and that he had taken again a decade later when he returned to the States from his stint in Coblenz. This time when he boarded the George Washington, he admitted on the paperwork he had to fill out that he had been born in Germany and even gave his correct age and birth date.

He disembarked in Bremerhaven, Germany, and remained in Europe for over three months. He visited his brother and this brother's extended family and, afterward, did a little sightseeing in Austria, Italy, Luxemburg, Switzerland, and finally France. The SS *Washington* was waiting for him in Le Havre on August 5 for his weeklong voyage back to New York. He hadn't presumed that the politics in the United States had changed in such a short time, but it had—for the worst. The medical profession had joined forces with the legal authorities and legislators. Within five months of his return to the United States, both the American Psychiatric Association and the American Medical

Association branded "homosexuality an illness" and recommended "electro-shock therapy, drugs, lobotomies, and castration" to cure it. Henry took another trip, this time to Mexico City for a month. In the meantime, Harry Hay's Mattachine Society was growing slowly but surely in response to the extreme antihomosexual climate, but in November 1952, its membership split over a dispute. The splinter group called itself ONE Inc., an organization that Henry could throw his support behind.

How Henry learned about ONE is unclear. Its leaders placed membership ads in *Writer's Digest*, and Henry, who scanned that section of the magazine for information on pen pal clubs, may have run across it there, wrote for information about the group, liked what he learned, and joined. ONE encapsuled everything that Henry had wanted to accomplish with the Society for Human Rights and the Society Scouting Sex Superstition but couldn't, and very surprising to him, it had a membership willing to support it financially. Beginning with his experience with the Society of Human Rights in Chicago nearly a quarter of a century earlier, he had been steadfast in declaring that gay men were "too scared to give their names or to join any association trying to help them" and were "only interested in physical contacts and have not the slightest interest to help their cause." The emergence of the Mattachine Society and ONE changed his mind.

By January 1953 Henry was so sure of ONE's importance to queer people that he subscribed to *ONE* magazine, which cost ten dollars (about $100 in today's currency) and included a subscription to *ONE Confidential*, the organization's monthly newsletter. *ONE* magazine's goal was to distribute information about queer people and their repression, and consequently, its first issue included "To Be Accused Is to Be Guilty" and "Report to the California State Legislature." It published "news, book reviews, opinion pieces, fiction" and "letters to the editors." GS, who lived in the District of Columbia, wrote one of the letters it published. It began:

> Dear Friends,
> Received the April issue of your fine magazine, ONE, and liked its make-up very much. It is well edited and has articles interesting to our friends. I am enclosing $10.
> In 1925 I met several inverts in Chicago and conceived a society on the order of that existing in Germany at that time, Society for Human

Rights, and we published a few issues of a paper called *Friendship and Freedom*, and even had a charter from the State of Illinois.

But one of our members turned out to be a married man (bisexual) and his wife complained to a social worker that he carried on his trade in front of his children and the social worker found a copy of our paper and all of us (4) were arrested without a warrant and dragged to jail.

I managed to get out on bail and hired a good lawyer but the first judge was prejudiced and threatened to give us the limit ($200 fine) but I got a better lawyer who was politically connected and we also got a new judge, who was rumored to "be queer himself" and he dismissed the case and find [*sic*] the married member $10 and cost.

I was then a postal clerk and a stupid and mean post-office inspector brought the case before the Federal commissioner with an eye to have us indicted for publishing an "obscene paper," although of course, like your paper, no physical references were made. But the Commissioner turned it down. However, the post office inspector, even in spite of us being acquitted, arranged my dismissal from the post office. The whole thing cost me all my savings of about $800 and no one helped us, not even the homosexuals of Chicago.

Of course, I see now the faults we committed. We should have had prominent doctors on our side and money on hand for defense, and a good lawyer.

I returned to the army in 1925 and am now retired and doing well.

GS was Henry, of course.

Henry was so enthusiastic about what ONE was attempting to do that, despite his frugal nature, he supported it financially. His letter to the editor included a ten-dollar donation, making his contribution to the cause in ONE's first year twenty dollars (about $200 in today's currency). As GS, Henry, who had just turned sixty, ensured that, with his 289-word note, the history of the Society for Human Rights and his experience with the law because of it would be known by the magazine's readers and, he must have hoped, for generations to come. It was the first time an account of his experience appeared in print since the *Chicago Evening American* ran GIRL REVEALS STRANGE CULT RUN BY DAD twenty-eight years earlier.

The fact that Henry didn't sign the letter with his name and not even with his real initials is noteworthy. Obviously, he felt threatened enough by the political climate to keep himself in the shadows—and with good reason. Within two months, on April 27, 1953, President Eisenhower signed Executive Order 10450, "Security Requirements for Government Employment," into law in response to the nationwide fear of government employees being blackmailed by Communists. It mandated the firing of any individual whose actions might be considered "criminal, infamous, dishonest, immoral, or notoriously disgraceful" or who were accused of "habitual use of intoxicants to excess, drug addiction, or sexual perversion." The police force revved up its purge of homosexuals, but at the same time there was no effort to rid the capital of those who used "intoxicants to excess" or even those addicted to drugs. Despite the wholesale attack on queer people as security risks, "There was not a single example of a gay man or a lesbian who ever submitted to blackmail by a foreign agent, not a single one."

Henry didn't simply support ONE financially. He publicized it whenever he was able. In August 1954 he wrote to *Writer's Digest* to thank its editors for publishing ONE's ads. He explained to them that ONE tried "very hard to overcome the stupid attitude people" had about "homosexuality," and because the United States was dealing with the "segregation of colored people," he thought "we might as well do away with the unreasonable and uncivilized attitude towards some sexual variants." He hadn't meant for *Writer's Digest* to publish his letter, but its editor ran it along with his address anyway. Half a dozen people wrote to him for information about ONE, and he replied to all of them with ONE's address, its membership fee, and his strong recommendation to them to join. Without meaning for it to happen, his committee for correspondence had taken on another, unanticipated activity, and his support for the homophile movement quickly became even more substantial. He began donating money to ONE's efforts regularly.

He didn't ignore the Mattachine Society either. In his attempt to further support the cause, he subscribed to its magazine beginning with the first issue, January 1955, for $2.50 a year (about $25.00 today). *Mattachine Review* "included scholarly and philosophical articles on homosexuality, as well as regional reports on censorship and police crack-downs on gay bars and clubs." He wrote to its editors:

Your magazine is as fine as ever and I try to get other people to subscribe, but most of them only want to read it without paying for it. Some are distrustful and believe that it is a racket and that names of the members might be given away for blackmail, etc. . . . how silly! However, I often wish we could be more outspoken in our country which boasts of its freedom of the press.

The editor added his reply immediately following and on the same page as Henry's:

The Review and the Society have been investigated by several police departments, including that of San Francisco. They have found all activities conducted legally and properly. These police departments have asked for names of no one and no names (except of members of the Board of Directors and the Review staff) have been given. None will be. Fears you mentioned are commonplace, we have found, but nevertheless groundless.

The editor didn't mention how revealing it was that Henry signed the letter with his initials, not his name. Henry couldn't be fired from a job, but he was concerned that his retirement and his residency at the Soldiers' Home might be compromised if his homosexuality was uncovered.

The climate for gay men had gotten so fraught with homophobia that the police didn't feel the need to witness same-sex sexual encounters in order to take men into custody. Those whom they "observed in Lafayette Park" or in public restrooms, but not engaged in sexual activity, were hauled into jail. Police even charged two men who had simply been sitting in a parked car because, in the police's estimation, it appeared that an "act of perversion *had* taken place." Another male couple was "arrested for kissing and charged with disorderly conduct."

16 | "BORN 1000 YEARS TOO SOON, OR 1000 YEARS TOO LATE"

BY THE MID-1950S Henry was convinced that the "best thing" that he, Manuel, and Frank could do was "to let the coming generations fight for the things which we could not accomplish."

One of the many young men who was on the forefront of a nationwide response by gay men to the nation's persecution of them was Gonzalo "Tony" Segura Jr. While working as a research chemist in New York, he joined the League, a secret society of homosexuals who met in a loft on the Lower East Side. Segura became active in the group, and through it discovered the Mattachine Society. As the League began to disband, he worked diligently to convert it into a New York chapter of the Mattachine and earned the reputation of being the "sparkplug of the whole organization" in the process. He and Sam Morford officially founded the new chapter in December 1955, but Segura also took a national role by serving on the editorial board of the *Mattachine Review*. His work on the *Review*, to which Henry subscribed, evidently led him and Henry to begin a substantial correspondence undertaken at a "furious pace" with Henry trusting Segura so much that he mailed the younger man "tons of very interesting material."

In late 1955 Segura learned that Buell Dwight Huggins, a clerk typist who worked in a government office in the District of Columbia and was a member of the Mattachine Society, wanted to begin a Mattachine chapter in DC. Segura offered to help and took the train down from New York to meet with him and several others who were interested. Segura wrote Henry to let him know that he would be in town and to invite him to the meeting, and he was surprised when Henry didn't bother to respond or show up.

Unknown to Segura, Henry had developed some health concerns and had been admitted to Walter Reed again for tests and treatments that took eight months to complete. Henry hadn't thought to have his letters forwarded to him and hadn't received Segura's invitation. Physicians diagnosed him with a goiter, but treatment was delayed because of his metabolism. It rose and sank, weakened then strengthened then weakened again, over and over. To combat its irregularity, his physicians put him on a diet usually prescribed to diabetics supplemented by daily shots of insulin. The physicians also found that he had developed bursitis in his arms and shoulders, which made sleep very difficult and getting in and out of his clothes without excruciating pain virtually impossible.

By the end of July 1956, Henry's physicians were able to get his condition under control and released him. Segura's letters were waiting for him at the Soldiers' Home. Huggins had already held the first meeting of the chapter that month in the home of a member who lived in Arlington, Virginia. Four men showed up. They called themselves the Council for Repeal of Unjust Laws and began a fund through which they would hire lawyers, planned strategies for equality, and issued the chapter's first bulletin, the *Washington Newsletter*. Segura made sure that Henry was on Huggins's mailing list.

The first words in the debut issue of the *Washington Newsletter* were "Forward and Foreward," a phrase of hope and safety and an introduction to the Mattachine Society and its goals. *Forward* means, of course, "to move ahead," but *foreward* is a little-used British word for "to guard (something) in front." The Mattachine Society hoped to attract "all homosexuals of good will who are interested in improving their lot and that of others, including homosexuals of future generations."

The society's goals, as Higgins listed them, included the

> education of the heterosexual public concerning sexual deviation; education of the sex deviates themselves in order that they may better understand their deviation from the norm; . . . preventing discrimination against homosexuals in employment; obtaining repeal or modification of existing laws pertaining to homosexuality; . . . and securing the active cooperation and support of legislators and professional people and of medical, scientific, research and other institutions.

He assured readers that the chapter was on the up and up and countered any rumors that potential members might have heard about it. It was not, Huggins was quick to report, "organized to blackmail homosexuals or to compile any blacklist. Nor was it organized to found a mecca for homosexuals. . . . It was not organized to drive the 'gay' bars and Turkish baths . . . out of business. And its members do not indulge in marijuana cigarettes at chapter meetings." He "promised to fight antihomosexual laws and attempted to combat local homosexuals' fears" about joining the group and assured them the "risks that you will assume with us are far less than the risks many take in their daily and nocturnal rounds of the parks, theatres, and bars." Many of the chapter's goals echoed those that Henry thought were important and had set for the two groups he organized.

An item Huggins included in the first issue of the *Washington Newsletter* surprised Henry. Huggins hoped to hear from anyone who might have information about the Society for Human Rights, but he didn't mention Henry by name:

> It seems the first American organization and magazine for homosexual people came into existence during the Twenties (about 1925). The organization was called the *Society for Human Rights* and was located in Chicago. The magazine, *Friendship and Freedom*, seems to have been published in Philadelphia, but by the organization. It will be greatly appreciated if any reader having additional information on this matter will send it in, together with any available copies of the magazine or literature issued by or about the organization.

Huggins must have gotten the information about the society from Henry's letter in the July 1953 issue of *Mattachine Review* and hoped that GS, who lived in DC, might hear about his request for information and contact him.

The prospect of a local chapter of the Mattachine Society excited Henry, and by August, he had joined, paying the ten-dollar membership fee (about $100 in today's currency). It's also likely that he mentioned he was GS to Huggins. The chapter had attracted thirteen members by then, including Henry. By the middle of September, Huggins bragged in the *Newsletter* that membership had risen to nineteen and included two women.

Although his bursitis finally subsided, it left Henry's "arms . . . crippled." Despite the physical limitations he now faced, Henry threw himself into the work of the Mattachine Society, donating money, time, and his advice as an experienced elder activist to the group of younger men. Within weeks, he had gained the reputation of being the "most zealous" of its members, but three months later, Henry was ready to call it quits. He had become disillusioned by the members who were more interested in socializing, and sex, than activism—the same complaint he had had about gay men since 1925. A few items in the chapter's constitution and bylaws also bothered him.

Henry and Huggins were cut from the same cloth. Both were self-assured to the point of being obstinate. Both were straightforward to a fault. Neither was able to back down or back off once his hackles were raised. They were bound to clash, and they did.

Henry sent Huggins a letter of resignation, which has unfortunately been lost, on November 3, 1956, and instead of resigning and letting it go, he felt he had to tell Huggins why he was leaving the group. Huggins took umbrage from some of Henry's comments and wrote back immediately. His letter began, "Your childish letter . . . has been received." He maintained a veneer of professionalism for the next few paragraphs, quoting from then addressing Henry's concerns item by item.

After the debacle with the Society for Human Rights, Henry was very concerned about the group's formal structure. He set up the Society Scouting Sex Superstition as a loosely configured confederation so that members couldn't be easily hunted down by police. The Washington chapter was as formal as it could be. Huggins explained that the chapter's structure suggested permanence and trustworthiness to potential members and attracted them to it, while a "loose, sloppy, informal organization" breeds "suspicion and distrust among both members and those who are solicited to join." He then addressed Henry's points about the constitution and bylaws.

Henry didn't care for the phrase "sex variants" that appeared in article 1, section 1(b) of the constitution because it was too "broad" a term, and he thought the group's motto "We must unite or suffer," found in article 12, section 3 of the bylaws, was "silly." Henry suggested a revision: "Look out for the dogcatcher." Huggins calmly agreed that "sex variants" wasn't specific enough, but he became a little agitated when he responded to Henry's "dogcatcher" quip. Henry meant homosexuals needed to be careful because of the decoys and other tactics the authorities used to hunt them down and arrest them, but Huggins thought Henry was calling them dogs. "Perhaps you consider yourself a dog, but most people don't," he snapped at Henry.

Henry wasn't satisfied with the two pieces of criticism that he gave Huggins, so he took the opportunity to lecture the younger, less-experienced man. He called Connecticut and Massachusetts "provinces of the pope" because contraception was illegal in both states. Huggins countered, "I think you will find that those laws were enacted some time ago by Protestant Puritans, not Catholics." Henry criticized the few books about homosexuality that had recently appeared on newsstands. "All the books that are written about homosexuality are so much trash," Henry claimed. Huggins shot back, "While it's true that some of the books on the subject leave much to be desired, a few are worth keeping. (Have you thrown all of yours away?) A book about you or your organization of 32 years ago might also be considered 'trash' by some people."

They went head-to-head over definitions too. On the offensive, Huggins schooled Henry on *pederasty*: "you ... refer to 'acts per anum (pederasty).' Here again you reveal your ignorance. Pederasty is anal intercourse by an older man with a boy; but anal intercourse between two old men is also an act per anum, or sodomy—but not pederasty." Neither of them understood that the definition had changed over the years.

When Henry called the chapter a "waste of time and money," Huggins went for Henry's jugular. "I know your own project of 1924 went by the board," he snapped, "and finally had to be dissolved, but maybe that was because of you. You'll have to try harder next time and not make an ass out of yourself." To put Henry in his place, Huggins ended his letter with what was perhaps the worst insult anyone could lob at Henry. He quoted the Christian Bible:

> You are beyond doubt a very temperamental and unstable individual, because until now you were the most zealous member of the chapter. Of course, some people won't cooperate at all unless they can have everything their way, and you remind me of what Paul says in I Cor. 13.11, that when one grows up one should put away childish things, and not speak, understand and think as a child.

In his capacity as president of the Washington, DC, chapter, Huggins cc'ed his response to Henry to the heads of the Los Angeles and New York City Mattachine chapters, as well as the national headquarters in San Francisco. When Harold "Hal" Call, Mattachine's national president, received his copy, he called Huggins on the carpet. "I have read your carbon of a letter to Mr. Henry Gerber," he began, "and frankly, Dwight, we are a little distressed about it." Call was concerned over Huggins's "needless alienation of friends of Mattachine," referring to Henry. He was well aware of Henry's work on behalf of gay men in the past, his work with DC's chapter of the society, and the substantial amount of money he had donated regularly over the years.

In case Huggins had misunderstood Call's concern, Call spelled it out:

> Dwight, I believe you are being hasty in bitching back at something which may have offended your own ego, but your skin is thicker than that. Calling Mr. Henry's letter childish, and referring to his views which may not parallel your own as "ignorance," plus the searing appellation of "trash," and making reference to someone's "making an ass out of himself" is, I feel sure, a mistake on your part, an unnecessary and injurious attitude [*sic*] which can greatly harm the Mattachine cause, and at best uncalled for.

He ordered Huggins to stop writing to Henry if he couldn't use "common courtesy due to everyone who writes to us." He took a step further and suggested that Huggins should be "as understanding and tolerant (yes, and as courteous, also) to others as we are asking society to be toward us."

The squabble between Henry and Huggins simply ended, without apologies and without either contacting the other again, but Henry had had it with the group. He eventually admitted other reasons for his disdain for the group to Manuel. Meetings were "too much talking and no results at all," and its leadership's chief topic was "money, money, money. For what?" In his anger over how Huggins had treated him, he doubted "if either ONE or MATTACHINE" would "accomplish anything in the matter of penetrating the lavender curtain of sex regimentation in this country." After his bluster, he told Manuel what had ignited his anger in the first place. The membership included only one man to whom he was attracted, an ironic admission given his persistent judgements aimed at gay men interested in socializing and sex but not liberation.

When he learned about the Washington chapter of the Mattachine Society, Henry was hopeful that it might jump-start his social life, its members becoming his friends and its meetings his social life, but with the DC chapter out of his life, he was on his own again and had few reasons left to get out of the Soldiers' Home. Even his "libido" was "about gone," leaving him without an excuse to visit the parks and movie theaters. He occasionally went to a show or a restaurant over the weekends, but he rapidly devolved into something of a recluse with only the classical music programs on his radio to keep him company.

By the end of August, Henry turned his squabble with Huggins into a denunciation of both the Mattachine Society and ONE Inc. He agreed with several Mattachine members who believed Call and Donald Stewart Lucas, the *Mattachine Review*'s editor and business manager, respectively, were underhandedly using the business they co-owned, Pan-Graphic Press, to print the *Review*. ONE had its faults too. Its newsletter, *ONE Confidential*, disappointed Henry because its reports were "about as confidential as Eisenhower's golf score. And they want me to fork up $25 [about $250 in today's currency] for that nonsense. Nix!"

As the campaign against homosexuals raged and was continually fueled by the government, local police, and news media in DC, Henry became even more concerned "that neither ONE nor MATTACHINE" would "accomplish anything at all" that would help homosexuals. He complained, "They cannot even publish a saucy, meaty story to gladden our hearts like the Swiss publication," the internationally circulated *Der Kreis*, nor did they print "tempting pictures." He was so indignant at the organizations that he "told them both not to send" him "any more publications." "It's a lousy world," Henry concluded, "and I am glad that I am an old man ready to kick the bucket."

At barely sixty-five years old, Henry was hardly at death's door, and despite his grumblings, he didn't cut his ties with ONE Inc. That may have been at least partially owing to Manuel's influence. He had joined ONE and the Mattachine Society at Henry's urging, despite Henry's aggravation at both. "It seems to me that if you want to do something" to "help the cause," Henry had told him, "first of all actively support the organizations that are already on the scene. It surprises me that you neither subscribe to MATTACHINE or ONE." Manuel was just as zealous as Henry had been during his work with the DC chapter of Mattachine and put his efforts behind ONE. At first, he volunteered for any grunt work that needed doing, and it didn't take long for others in its leadership to consider him a "tower of strength." He eventually served as its secretary, as a member of ONE's board of directors, and as its vice president.

It's very likely that it was Manuel's idea for Don Slater, then editor of *ONE Magazine*, to invite Henry to expand the letter to the editor that he had published in it nine years earlier into a full-fledged essay. Henry's "The Society for Human Rights—1925" appeared in the September 1962 issue.* He meant for his reminiscence to be a celebration of the "joyful news that the State of Illinois had recently . . . given up its persecution of homosexuals," referring to the state legislature rescinding its sodomy laws on January 1, 1962, the first state in the nation to do so. His recollections weren't always correct. He recalled that the report of his arrest, which he thought was entitled "Strange Sex Cult Exposed," appeared on the front page of the *Herald-Examiner* when, in fact, the article appeared in the *Chicago Evening American* as GIRL REVEALS STRANGE CULT RUN BY DAD. He also misremembered the dates of several events on the time line. Otherwise, at seventy years old, Henry's recollections held up well.

Henry's memoir brought a letter to the editor. In it Mr. T. from Helena, Montana, complimented Henry's work but objected to Henry referring to the ancient Jewish laws against homosexuality and went so far as to call the reference a "faintly anti-Semitic twist," asserting that Jews weren't against "homosexual behavior" and submitting the story of David and Jonathan and a quote from the Talmud as proof. Instead, Mr. T. put the blame for homophobia on the "followers of Christ."

"The Society for Human Rights—1925" wasn't Henry's only work to appear in ONE's publications. Later that year, Manuel also "cajoled the cantankerous Henry to translate some of Hirschfeld's writing" for ONE's journal, which had been retitled *ONE Institute Quarterly*. The three translations—"Adaptation Treatment of Homosexuality (Adjustment Therapy)" followed by "Classification of Homosexuals as to Age Preferences and Sex Acts" and then "The Role of Homosexual Men and Women in Society"—were from Hirschfeld's *Die Homosexualität des Mannes und des Weibes* (*The Homosexuality of Men and Women*) and appeared in three consecutive issues of the *Quarterly*. Its editor, Dorr Legg, bragged that Henry's translations were the "first time" Hirschfeld's work had appeared in English. Interestingly, *ONE Institute Quarterly* published

---

* Fred Frisbie, who used the pseudonym George Mortenson, served as art director for this issue.

an excerpt from Manuel's *Boys, Men and Love*, "Ancients and the Greek Cult," in the same issue as Henry's first translation.

To celebrate its twelfth anniversary, ONE developed a unique and clever fund-raising scheme that masqueraded as a poll of its members' opinions. It sent a form entitled "Vote 'Yes' on Proposition ONE" to Henry and its other members. The form listed a dozen statements, and its directions took the edge off asking for donations by making fun of the process:

> To vote for a proposition, simply reach into your pocket and remove the required amount. To make your ballot count, total the amounts you have checked and send it to ONE. It is not illegal to send more than you have checked; in fact, we will count your ballot twice if you send double the amount indicated. If you send less than the amount shown, we wont [*sic*] complain either.

The first proposition was introductory. Those that followed addressed the many issues that Henry and other queer people faced day to day:

> 2. A homosexual is no more apt to be a thief, a traitor, a rapist, or a murderer than a heterosexual.
> 3. The homosexual loves his country and can and will defend it as much as a heterosexual.
> 4. I am tired of seeing the phrase, "Drug addicts, homosexuals, and other criminals."
> 5. The Kinsey Reports should be required reading in schools.
> 6. I am so tired of hearing heterosexuals giggle and snicker when talking about "queers."
> 7. Most heterosexuals have an unbelievably naïve conception of what homosexuals are like.
> 8. I think that society is the loser with its prejudice and laws against homosexuals.
> 9. I believe that the feeling of Christ himself toward homosexuals was certainly different from the stand of churches today.
> 10. I believe that homosexual acts are just as "natural" to a homosexual as heterosexual acts are to a heterosexual and that they make him a better and more useful human being.

11. The direction of a person's sexual feelings has no more relationship to living an honorable and useful life than does his skin color or religion.

12. I believe that other minorities have won honorable treatment not by mere passivity but by banding together and fighting to change conditions.

13. I feel that the sensible thing for a homosexual to do is to actively fight and contribute toward changing his position instead of merely complaining about it.

Of course, ONE's staff assumed its members would agree with all the statements, as Henry did, and donate to the cause. He sent ONE a check for six dollars (fifty-six dollars in today's currency).

That following year, ONE faced a revolt in its ranks. A "breakaway group of ONE Inc. staff led by Don Slater secretly removed business records and furniture from ONE Inc., leading to a protracted legal dispute." The records Slater took included the addresses of ONE's members, and he mailed them requests for donations to his new group, the Homosexual Information Center. Although Slater mailed him several requests for donations, Henry remained loyal to ONE Inc. and wouldn't send Slater a cent. For a short time, he was understandably concerned about his name and address falling into the wrong hands. On May 11, 1965, he wrote Legg, "I hope that the privacy of addresses will not be violated" and "We know what eagerness the cops would have to lay hands on it and 'expose' the whole thing by using lies. I went through that myself one time." He promised to "make a contribution soon," but he was "paying off a debt" and couldn't just then.

Later that month, he complimented the staff at ONE on the new issue of the magazine that he had just received and commiserated with them about Slater's actions. "There is always one Judas in each organization," he told them, probably thinking of Al Meininger, and he began scanning publications for news items about homosexuality that he promised to clip and send to them. He enclosed a check for fifty dollars. He donated another fifty dollars three months later, and twenty-five dollars two months after that (a total of more than $1,000 in today's currency), a huge amount for someone living on a pension. He continued to follow the situation between ONE and Slater. The "whole thing is a lousy mess," he wrote Legg and enclosed a few "items on homosexuality" that he had run across in his readings, this time "all taken from the Playboy Magazine." Whether Henry subscribed to *Playboy* or bought issues at a local newsstand is unknown, but at the time, it was one of the few—perhaps the only—heterosexually oriented magazines that espoused sexual freedom and included homosexuals in its fight for it. Evidently, Henry became a member of a tiny clique of men who opened *Playboy* to read its articles, not to ogle its centerfolds.

Henry did subscribe to *Drum*, a gay-focused magazine, for $4.50 annually (about $40 in today's currency), which arrived at the Soldiers' Home in a brown paper envelope. Like *Playboy*, *Drum* addressed its readers' libidos, but with black-and-whites of young men, most in bikini-style trunks or painted-on posing straps. It also published fiction and articles. For example, front and center in the October 1965 issue was editor Clark P. Polak's article "The Story Behind Physique Photography," illustrated with a gallery of covers from the many physique magazines of the early sixties, among them *Big*, *Manual*, *Muscle Boy*, and *Jr*. Notices of news about queer people from around the world, ads for antiaging instruction manuals, two different advice columns, book reviews, a few cartoons, a list of homophile organizations in the United States and internationally, and a satirical piece, "Let's Get the Homos Out of the Comics!" by Oliver (Daddy) Warbucks rounded out the issue.

In January 1966 Henry was struck with a debilitating illness and was admitted to the hospital of the Soldiers' Home. He had been in the hospital for "over a month" when he sent a note to ONE, asking to stop his subscription to the magazine because his life was "all upside down" and he had "no idea" when his physicians might release him from the hospital. Henry's letter crossed paths in the mail with one that Legg sent him. In it, Legg reminded Henry of the "fine account of the Chicago 1925 organization" that Henry had written for *ONE* magazine four years earlier and asked him if he would be interested in writing another piece to be delivered during ONE's midwinter conference January 28–30. A man who worked in ONE's office had told Legg that "about 30 years ago he attended some meetings in New York City" that included Henry. Legg wanted to include Henry's recollections about those meetings at the conference. Henry had a week to jot something down and mail it to Legg.

The man who had mentioned the meetings to Legg must have been Fred Frisbie. Frisbie was twenty-three when he spent the night with one of Henry's soldier friends in 1929. After moving to Los Angeles in 1932, he became an "early advocate for the Gay and Lesbian Rights movement and a leader of the Mattachine Society and co-developer of ONE Incorporated," using the pseudonym George Mortenson with all his ONE-related activities, which included contributing art to ONE's magazines and other publications. He also discovered the love of his life in L.A., Louisa (née Luis) Sola, his "androgynous Puerto Rican angel."

Like Manuel, Frisbie began his work for ONE by doing whatever was necessary and then moved up the organizational ladder until he became its president. Although his friendship with Henry had fallen off nearly forty years earlier, Frisbie hadn't forgotten the elder activist, the stories he told about the Society for Human Rights and its German counterparts, and his battle with legal authorities. Unfortunately, by then, Henry was too ill to respond to Legg's invitation.

The next year, ONE's board of directors briefly shone a spotlight on Henry again in *ONE Confidential*. "Those of us coming on the scene should not forget that all honor is due for the courage and initiative of Henry Gerber as undisputed 'Father of the Homophile Movement' in this country," and in another issue, Anthony Grey referred to Henry as the "Father of the American Homophile Movement" and maintained that Henry had "founded the Homophile Movement in Chicago." Unfortunately, Henry had already canceled his subscription to ONE's publications by then and didn't know that ONE's staff thought of him in such an elevated way. Not quite deemed a "deliverer of the downtrodden, even as Lincoln" had been, Henry would have been pleased that he had been remembered for his plight.

Henry was still on the minds of some of those who worked with ONE Inc. two decades later, especially Fred Frisbie, who often discussed his brief but important relationship with Henry in informal situations as well as during national conferences. During the 1978 Midwinter Institute of ONE held on January 27–29, for example, Frisbie appeared on a panel entitled "Way Back in the 1920s & 1930s." During his time at the podium, he discussed the "legendary Henry Gerber." Jim Kepner appeared at the same conference and delivered a paper on "Henry Gerber, Forerunner of America's Homophile Movement from 1925–1972." By then, many leaders of the gay rights movement considered Henry the "father of homosexual liberation in America."

Fred Frisbie (right) lived with Louisa (née Luis) Sola for many years at 634 West Twenty-Third Street in L.A. *Courtesy of ONE Archives at the USC Libraries*

Nearly a decade later, Henry's old friend Fred Frisbie was the featured speaker at the ONE Institute Extension lecture series. Publicity for his talk promised, "Of prime import will be his recollections of the legendary Henry Gerber founder of the short-lived 1924 Chicago organization earliest [*sic*] documented Homophile group in the U.S." Frisbie's "recollections" were taped. Then as time passed, despite the efforts of those closely involved with the gay liberation movement, Henry was largely forgotten or, occasionally, relegated to a footnote or a paragraph or two in essays and books about it. One of the best and most accurate of the tributes to Henry was cowritten by Kepner and Stephen O. Murray:

> Although his fledgling organization was crushed by a cabal of social control agents, Gerber sowed the seed of gay pride and the idea of fighting for gay rights in scores of correspondents, directly and

indirectly influencing Harry Hay, Jim Kepner, Tony Segura, Donna Smith, Fred Frisbie, Manuel Boyfrank, and others who worked to establish the homophile movement of the 1950s. Gerber is also a clear link between the German movement to remove Paragraph 175 of the German penal code and the 1950s' law reform movement that still remained extremely high-risk activism for people who were not just stigmatized but whose relations—even nonsexual associations—were criminalized.

Unfortunately, Henry never knew the high regard in which many of the activists held him.

Despite his work with the Society for Human Rights and the Society Scouting Sex Superstition, regardless of his letter-writing campaign through the committee of correspondence, Henry was never able to "ameliorate" the plight of homosexuals as he had hoped, but he was wise enough to realize that, no matter what, it wasn't his fault. As he told Manuel in 1946, "It is . . . your and my misfortune to be born 1000 years too soon, or 1000 years too late."

In his last letter to Manuel, he wrote, "It is not a matter of life and death whether homosexuals will ever be admitted as born equal by the hypocrites who enjoy treating us as inferiors. (Thank god for the inferior people; without them we could not feel superior!) We will be dead and buried when this happens!" Manuel was not simply Henry's best friend but also the person with whom he was most intimate for the longest period in his life, although they had been face-to-face with one another only a handful of times. To show Manuel how much he meant to him, Henry ended his last letter to Manuel, "With best wishes and love, as ever your friend, Henry," but that wasn't enough. He added a postscript: "Let me hear from you again soon!"

Henry spent his last months in and out of the hospital with a variety of illnesses. On New Year's Eve 1972, the eighty-year-old Henry J. Gerber died of pneumonia at the hospital of the US Soldiers' Home and was buried in the home's cemetery. Except for the staff member of ONE whose letter to him was returned by the home with the envelope stamped DECEASED, the "Father of the American Homophile Movement" died unnoticed and unmourned by those whom he had spent his entire life trying to free.

NOTES

Epigraph

"To hell with the do-gooders": Gerber to boyFrank, April 14, 1944, 8.

Introductory Note: "Henry's Epistles to the Perverts"

"Henry's epistles to the perverts": boyFrank to McCourt, October 7, 1944, 1.
"repetition, a lot of unnerving": Kepner to Katz, March 19, 1974, 1.
"If it is such a fine invention": Gerber to boyFrank, March 12, 1944, 1.
"There is nothing more beautiful": Ibid., 7.
"ameliorate": Gerber, "Society for Human Rights," 5.
"You have, you must realize": boyFrank to Gerber, December 26, 1944, 1.
"write letters, essays, stories": Ibid., 2.
"If you make letters to me": Ibid.
"boyFrank's . . . copies of the four Gerber books": Kepner to Katz, May 9, 1974, 3.
"We," referring to the staff members: Kepner to Katz, March 4, 1974, 1.

Part I: Chicago

1. "I Had No Idea That I Was a Homosexual"

Spinatener: Gerber to boyFrank, July 5, 1945, 4.
"spinach man": Ibid.
"At the age of 7": Gerber to boyFrank, April 14, 1944, 11.
"it would have been impossible . . . for the old nosey priest": Gerber to boyFrank, October 23, 1945, 4.
"harmony and singing": Gerber to boyFrank, February 18, 1946, 3.
"pestered" by his friends: Ibid.

"Bavarian 'humorist' Ludwig Thoma": Dose, *Magnus Hirschfeld*, 35.

"society wants boys to get interested in girls": Gerber to boyFrank, April 14, 1944, 12.

"women are no good": Ibid.

"1,900 people": "Ellis Island," History.com.

"name, age, destination": Reed, "Going Through Ellis Island."

smitten with "wanderlust": Anderson, *The Hobo*, 82.

"slept in the bunkhouse": Gerber to boyFrank, October 23, 1945, 7.

"boys did not hesitate": Ibid.

"intoxicated persons; deserters": US War Department, *Regulations for the Army*, 175.

"slave pen": Gerber to boyFrank, April 14, 1944, 3.

"colonies" of "men who are thoroughly gregarious": Chicago Vice Commission, *Social Evil in Chicago*, 297.

"Most of us," the investigator later recalled: Sprague, "On the 'Gay,'" 10.

"twenty thousand active homosexuals": Ibid., 11.

"do anything": Sears, *Behind the Mask*, 44.

"active role": Ibid.

"pretty cold": Gerber to boyFrank, January 4, 1945, 3.

"fellow asked me for a match": Ibid.

"swell" in bed: Gerber to boyFrank, July 5, 1945, 2.

"brought along a pal": Ibid.

"disorderly conduct": Gerber to boyFrank, April 14, 1944, 9.

"romantic type": Zorbaugh, *Gold Coast*, 100.

"vermilion kitchenette apartment": Ibid.

"cooking and the usual duties of a wife": Gerber to boyFrank, October 23, 1945, 6.

grips of a "paranoia": Coretto, "'Fountain Pen,'" 10.

"police round-ups": Stibbe, "Enemy Aliens."

"enemy alien": Kepner and Murray, "Henry Gerber," 24.

"three free meals": Sears, *Behind the Mask*, 44.

"psychological examination": Kellogg, *Conscientious Objector*, 30.

"I had no idea": Gerber to boyFrank, July 5, 1945, 4.

"although sexual acts between two people": Somerville, "Scientific Racism," 243.

2. "I Had Always Bitterly Felt the Injustice"

HEAVEN, HELL, OR HOBOKEN: Lurie, "'Heaven, Hell, or Hoboken,'" 13.

"not refight the war": Cornebise, *"Amaroc News,"* 3.

"hoped to maintain an elevated moral tone": Ibid.

"I want to go home": Ibid., 7.

"We're here because we can't": Ibid., 25.

"addressed the issue of homosexual": R. Evans, *U.S. Military Policies*, 7.

"preach the value of non-association": Chicago Vice Commission, *Social Evil in Chicago*, 297.

"on homosexuality within the *German*": Habib, "Chastity, Masculinity, and Military Efficiency," 747.

"increased statistics of homosexuals": Ibid., 747–748.

"one of Berlin's police": Gordon, *Voluptuous Panic*, 90.

"a lot of homosexuality in Berlin": Sprague, "On the 'Gay,'" 10.

"gross indecency": Hitchcock, *Proceedings*.

"Please could you educate": Cox, "Danish Girl."

"opulent villa": Beachy, *Gay Berlin*, 160.

"promoted sex education": Tatchell, "This Week in History."

"fetishes, fantasy pictures": H. Bauer, *Hirschfeld Archives*, 91.

"four quadrants": Taylor, "Magnus Hirschfeld's Institute," 29.

"raids on homosexual gathering": Sears, *Behind the Mask*, 48.

"enforcement" of Paragraph 175: Ibid., 52n35.

"most famous was the so-called gay path": Whisnant, *Queer Identities*, 88.

"classical statue of a marathoner": Waugh, "Strength and Stealth," 20n16.

"were just bare bones pick-up bars": Gordon, *Voluptuous Panic*, 99–100.

"consisted largely of young laborers": Ibid., 52.

"fifty pfennig to ten marks": Beachy, *Gay Berlin*, 202.

"'athletic boxer'": Ibid., 203.

"25,000" male prostitutes: Gordon, *Voluptuous Panic*, 90.

"Doll-Boys": Ibid., 98.

"Line-Boys": Ibid.

"peaked schoolboy hats": Ibid., 277.

"Bubes": Ibid., 80.

"gay balls": Whisnant, *Queer Identities*, 97.

"French observer of the city": Ibid.

"As many": Waugh, *Hard*, 403.

"satirical magazine, an S/M": Ibid.

"few terms from the homosexual magazines": Gerber to boyFrank, July 5, 1945, 7.

"title loosely translates to 'The Self-owner'": Vendeville, "U of T's Fisher Library."

"forum on homosexuality": Tamagne, *History of Homosexuality*, 96.

"personal ads": Waugh, *Hard*, 403.

"beauty of gay personal ads": Carrington, "Love in the Big City," 245.

"Aristocrat, young, belonging": Ibid., 247.

"peaked in the 1920s": Ibid., 248n129.

"homoerotic illustrations and aesthetics": Beachy, *Gay Berlin*, 102.

"social and political organization for homosexual": Rogan, "'Good Nude Photographs,'" 145.

"tens of thousands": Beachy, *Gay Berlin*, 221.

"more of a literary circle": Whisnant, *Queer Identities*, 38.

"peddling pornography": Ibid., 188.

"forces of political conservatism": Ibid., 188.

Presbyterian minister Carl Schlegel: Jonathan Ned Katz, "Carl Schlegel: An Early U.S. Gay Activist, 1906–1907," OutHistory, June 1, 2019, https://outhistory.org/exhibits/show/schlegel/contents.

"for the defense of 'our kind'": Gerber to boyFrank, March 28, 1944, 1.

"I had always bitterly": Gerber, "Society for Human Rights," 5.

"chaos" and "misunderstanding": Ibid.

3. "To Promote and to Protect"

"American soldier is returning home": Cornebise, *"Amaroc News,"* 76.

"ideas" that also needed to be "carried out": Ibid.

"one enlisted man, Private Henry Gerber": Ibid., 224.

"thirty-six [dollars] a month": Claff, "'Thirty' Sounded," 11.

"Hank Gerber came in on the George Washington": Ibid.

"purchased his way out": Hagin to Sprague, December 16, 1982.

"tenderloin district": G. Beemyn, *Queer Capital*, 25.

Pennsylvania Avenue and Ninth and F: B. Beemyn, "Geography of Same Sex Desire," 144.

"young, middle-class white men": G. Beemyn, *Queer Capital*, 25.

"Department of the Interior Building": Ibid., 19.

"made flimsy excuses": Ibid.

"I don't know what you're looking for": Ibid.

"temporary sub. Clerk": US Post Office, "Record of Employe," 1.

"tenacious case of tonsillitis": Gerber to superintendent, April 1, 1924.

"sick leave for five days": Galbraith to Gerber, April 2, 1924.

"Henry Gerber . . . has already had nine": Roloff to Chicago Post Office, April 26, 1924.

"wisely came" to be treated: Ibid.

ranked him at "98 per cent": US Post Office, Statement of Employe's Record." October 1, 1924.

"always fuzzy": Gapp, "Death of Bohemia."

"reading tournaments": Smith, *Chicago's Left Bank*, 9.

"geographical center": Brown and Brown, *Biography of Mrs. Marty Mann*, 19.

"manufacture, transportation and sale of intoxicating": "Prohibition," History.com.

"sexual intercourse": *Oxford English Dictionary*, s.v. "Jazz."

chief slogan was "free love": Zorbaugh, *Gold Coast*, 98.

"Some of my friends said": "Visitors at the Subway Bar."

"Two rooms, boys, or one": Blinstrub, "Follow-Up Work."

"Although Gerber was aware of Chicago's gay subculture": Sprague, "60th," 2.

"fringy areas outside Towertown": Gapp, "Death of Bohemia."

"political forum, theater": Myers, "Chicago's Dill Pickle Club."

"roving lecture forum": Heap, *Slumming*, 236.

"collection of flophouses": Butler, *Hidden History*, 58.

"anything so rash and futile": Gerber, "Society for Human Rights," 6.

"known to history as deliverer of the downtrodden": Ibid.

"preacher who earned his room and board": Ibid., 7.

"job . . . was in jeopardy": Ibid.

"sort of hang-out": Gerber to boyFrank. October 23, 1945, 7.

"romantic type": Zorbaugh, *Gold Coast*, 100.

"forum for discussion": Gerber, "Society for Human Rights," 6.

"self-discipline" would "win": Ibid.

"against the seduction": Ibid.

"organization a purely homophile": Ibid., 8.

"to promote and to protect": Gerber, Application.

"article on 'Self-control'": Fassnacht, "On the Ground," 434.

"I may have funny ideas": Gerber, "Are Indecent."

"If I want to hear 'spiritual'": Ibid.

"Doubtlessly numerous people of the neurotic": Ibid.

"average homosexual": Gerber, "Society for Human Rights," 6.

"as long as some homosexual sex acts": Ibid., 7.

"big, fatal, fearful": Ibid., 7.

"Against human stupidity": Ibid., 7.

4. "Infecting God's Own Country"

"Where is the boy?": Gerber, "Society for Human Rights," 10.

"why her father carried on": "Girl Reveals," *Chicago Evening American*.

"afternoon and night": Ibid.

"publisher of the cult paper": Ibid.

"indigent laundry queen": Gerber, "Society for Human Rights," 7.

Meininger was one of the "bisexuals": Ibid., 8.

"hatchet-faced female": Ibid., 9.

"I love Karl": Ibid., 9.

Meininger's "strange cult": Ibid., 9.

"family disorganization": Pleck, *Domestic Tyranny*, 148.

"overtly feminized role": King, "'Latin Lover.'"

"face-powder dispenser": "Pink Powder," *Chicago Tribune*.

"Homo Americanus!": Ibid.

"And was the pink powder": Ibid.

"Another member of this department": Ibid.

"degeneration" of society "into effeminacy": Ibid.

"more a man": Ferguson, *Idol Worship*, 25.

"To the Man (?)": Leider, *Dark Lover*, 374.

"erotica; contraceptive medications": Earls and Masarik, "Anthony Comstock."

"prize fighting": Ibid.

"lessening sodomy law": Ibid.

"most frequently used against queer people": H. Ryan, *When Brooklyn*, 73.

Wilde, whose life of "gross indecency": Hitchcock, *Proceedings*.

"'shyster' lawyer": Gerber, "Society for Human Rights," 9.

"he would see to it": Ibid.

"shut up or be cited": Ibid.

"Suspension without pay": Bartlett, telegram to postmaster.

"everything had been 'arranged'": Gerber, "Society for Human Rights," 10.

second judge was a "queer himself": Gerber [G.S., pseud.], letter to the editor.

"I had nothing on you": Gerber, "Society for Human Rights," 10.

"What was the idea of the Society": Ibid.

take "life easy": Ibid.

"mixed up in . . . stupid bitches' affairs": Gerber to boyFrank, January 4, 1945, 4.

"only interested in getting as many pieces of trade": Gerber to boyFrank, August 5,
     1944, 3.

"Mr. Gerber is not a suitable person": Bartlett to Lueder.

Part II: New York

5. "Which Way Do YOU Take It, and for How Much?"

"picking up fairies": Geber to boyFrank, August 5, 1944, 3.

"In the 1920s, so many met on the open lawn": Chauncey, *Gay New York*, 182.

"meat rack": NYC LGBT, *Historic Context Statement*, 40.

"East Fourteenth Street between Third Avenue": Chauncey, *Gay New York*, 190.

"Times Square," as historian George Chauncey: Ibid., 191.

"well-dressed, 'mannered' and gay-identified": Ibid.

"effeminate (but not transvestite)": Ibid.

"homosexual solicitation": Polchin, *Indecent Advances*, 40.

"Every tearoom and cabaret": Ibid., 39.

"one of the 'women' was a man": Ibid.

"impudent sissies that clutter Times Square": Chauncey, *Gay New York*, 309.

SEXY SAILORS BLOW!: "Sexy," *Brevities*, 1.

FAG BALLS EXPOSED: Browning, "Fag Balls," 1.

PANSIES BLOW U.S.: "Pansies Blow," *Brevities*, 1.

"thirteen-part series, 'A Night in Fairy-land'": Barbas, *Confidential Confidential*, 97.

"sensational articles": Straw, "Remembering."

"Tear off an hour": Ad for *Confessions*, *Brevities*.

"red-handed with a lad": "The Fag," *Brevities*.

"The pickings are perfectly glorious": Ibid.

"always sure" to find "a ringer": Gerber to boyFrank, February 19, 1940, 2.

"usually psychopathic individuals": Gerber to boyFrank, July 5, 1945, 5.

"anyone over 22": Gerber to boyFrank, March 12, 1944, 1.

"about 4" orgasms: Gerber to boyFrank, January 4, 1945, 4.

"string of 'prostitutes'": Gerber to boyFrank, March 12, 1944, 1.

"too self-centered": Gerber to boyFrank, June 20, 1945, 1.

"There are thousands of boys": Ibid.

"I want you for the U.S. Army": Flagg, "I Want You."

"old theory that only a man fed on rum": Gerber, "Evolution."

"Frederick the Great": Humphries, Did You Know That—.

"over 50,000 copies": Tobin, "On Research Trip."

"What heterosexual would not turn highly neurotic": Gerber, "Defense," 221.

"by social conditions": Ibid., 224.

"solitude" as "the great blessing": Gerber, self-description.

"three square meals a day": "Some of the Advantages," *Recruiting News*.

"younger" than Henry: Kepner to Katz, March 11, 1974, 2.

"overconfidence in stock market investments": Amadeo, "Stock Market Crash."

"Wages fell 42%": Ibid.

"comfortable" or even "healthful": "Some of the Advantages," *Recruiting News*.

"stark and functional": US Department of the Interior, *Historic American Buildings*, 2.

"those intellectuals who are mentally marooned": "Baker Memorial," *ONEletter*, 6.

CONTACT WITHOUT FRICTION: "Contact Without Friction," GraduateWay.

"came to the rescue by volunteering": "Baker Memorial," *ONEletter*, 6.

"The Only Correspondence Club": Ibid., 5.

6. "Escape from the Bughouse of This Fairytale Kultur!"

"Escape from the Bughouse": Gerber, "Escape from the Bughouse."

"23%" went "for postage": Gerber, information sheet.

"addressographs, graphotypes and mimeographs": Gerber to boyFrank, March 12, 1944, 2.

"ideal friend": Gerber, "Contacter."

"Surrounded by Millions of Cracked Brains": Gerber, "Surrounded."

"'More fun than the Theatre'": Gerber, "More Fun."

"'Not a Brain Cell in a carload'": Gerber, "Not a Brain."

"CONTACTS, an unusual correspondence club": Gerber, "Contacts, an Unusual."

"Are you without congenial contacts?": Gerber, "Are You Without."

"unusual": Gerber, "Excess Leisure."

"uncommon": Gerber, "Love of Solitude."

"Escape": Gerber, "Escape from the Bughouse."

"very large": Gerber, information sheet.

"liberal": Ibid.

"very nature": Ibid.

"to exchange": Gerber, "Descriptions." 2.

"official representative of Contacts": Ibid.

"Postal inspectors subscribed": D'Emilio, *Sexual*, 47.

"'normals' and 'perverts'": Sears, *Behind the Mask*, 84.

"inner sanctum": Gerber to boyFrank, March 28, 1944, 1.

"Probably a few men made homosexual contacts": boyFrank to Horvath, December 15, 1944, 6.

"1744 and 2573 are allright": Gerber to boyFrank, January 27, 1940, 2.

"To me," he said, "Contacts was a means": Gerber to boyFrank, March 12, 1944, 3.

"art model": Gerber, "Sample Descriptions."

"preferred" contact with "male correspondents": Ibid.

"inversion," the "psychology of the abnormal": Ibid.

"quite a lot of men": boyFrank to Horvath, December 15, 1944, 6.

"anatomical studies": "Bodybuilding," Archives West.

"beautiful set of poses": Chapman, *Sandow the Magnificent*, 33.

"part diatribe against medical doctors": Mullins, "Nudes, Prudes, and Pigmies," 28.

"his advocacy of muscular development": Johnson, "Physique," 871.

"painted, perfumed": Ibid.

"more than a whiff of eroticism": Black, "Charles Atlas."

"house organs": Johnson, "Physique," 870.

Physical Culture obviously": Mullins, "Nudes, Prudes, and Pigmies," 28.

"Dr. Magnus Hirschfeld ha[d] come here": H. Bauer, *Hirschfeld Archives*, 104.

"discuss 'love's natural laws'": Ibid., 104.

"As a freedom-loving person": Dose, *Magnus Hirschfeld*, 37.

"small multigraphed page": Gerber, "Among," 1.

"Sure nuf, Honey": Ibid., 2.

"quite a library": Gerber, self-description.

"handle books considered 'obscene'": Gerber, information sheet.

"pessimistic" and "bitter": Kepner, "Who Founded," 9.

"makeshift" and "impromptu": Hauser, "Dedication."

"In our despondent and chop-fallen": Ibid.

"take the initiative to proclaim": Ibid.

"avowed atheist country": Gerber, "Theism," 3.

"sending of American Christian missionaries": Ibid.

"newspapers forgot to say": Ibid.

"religionists" in "What Is Atheism?": Gerber, "What Is Atheism?," 5.

"universe is run on a harmonious order": Ibid.

Church's "criminal history": Ibid., 6.

"It ain't' no sin": Ibid.

"'by 1934 more than 46 million'": Toledo, "She Would Not," 5.

"producing an immoral show": Ibid., 2.

"crimes against the law": Association of Motion Picture Producers, "Motion Picture Production Code."

"greatest menace to faith": Shank, "Dougherty's Movie Boycott."

"over 300,00 Catholics": Ibid.

"sex suppression": Gerber, "Moral," 6.

"The war brought our yokels": Ibid.

"poor, misguided Mae West": Ibid., 8.

"Hitler edict": Ibid.

"defended" Röhm "more than once": Babst, "Ernst Röhm."

"newspapers of America": Gerber, "Hitler," 1.

"waning of capitalism": Ibid., 2.

"homosexuals will go on fighting": Ibid.

"Politicians and priests": Gerber, "Recent," 4.

"to convey the impression that ALL": Ibid., 5.

"hero on the battlefield": Ibid.

"could be classed as anti-homosexual propaganda": Ibid. 5.

"it is not the various modes of sex pleasure": Gerber, "A New," 4.

"Rene Guyon goes deeply into the sexual taboo": Ibid.

"grand," but he called the lyrics "bunk": Gerber, "Tannhaeuser," 8.

"that the medical authorities in America": Gerber, "More Nonsense," 1.

"It is only the attitude of Anglo-Saxon society": Ibid., 3.

"Homosexuality has until recently been strictly taboo": Gerber, "Recent," 1.

7. "For Christ's Sake, Leave Me Out of It"

"queer people went from 'novelty'": H. Ryan, *When Brooklyn*, 179.

"earliest known American crusade": NYC LGBT, *Historic Context Statement*, 35.

"flamboyantly effeminate 'fairies'": Ibid.

"degenerate resort": Chauncey, *Gay New York*, 38.

"surveillance of homosexuals": Ibid., 185.

"arrested 88 (30 percent)": Ibid., 419n18.

"'homosexual solicitation'": NYC LGBT, *Historic Context Statement*, 35.

"rendezvous for perverts": Ibid., 36.

"Times Square clubs featuring pansy": Chauncey, *Gay New York*, 332.

"thousands" to Harlem, Madison Square Garden: Ibid., 291.

"bar or restaurant": Ibid., 356.

"all the fairy round-ups": Martin, "Third Sex Plague," 1.

"third sex is flooding America": Browning, "Fag Balls," 1.

"Germans are turning queerer": Schultz, "Fags Ram Heinies!," 1.

"New York's hordes": "B'Way," *Broadway Brevities*, 1.

"Beebles uff Chermany": Untitled cartoon strip, *Broadway Tattler*, 2.

"zex perverts": Ibid.

"Thanks for yoor noht": boyFrank to Gerber, September 22, 1935, 1.

"self-abasement": boyFrank [J. P. Starr, pseud.], "His Was a Monkey-Puzzle," 1.

"'At first they'd solace'": Boag, "Sexuality, Gender, and Identity," 332.

"wounded twice": boyFrank [J. P. Starr, pseud.], "His Was a Monkey-Puzzle," 11.

"With all yu say about churches": boyFrank to Gerber, September 22, 1935, 1.

"Wun ov the thingz": Ibid., 2.

Manuel and Maki called their group a "convent": Gerber to boyFrank, n.d. ["Thanks for your"].

"Since I am neither a radical": Ibid.

"I am never again recommending anything": Ibid.

"chief monkey-monk": boyFrank to Gerber, September 27, 1936, 1.

"But for Christ's sake": Gerber to boyFrank, n.d. ["Thanks for your"].

"sex criminal": Polchin, *Indecent Advances*, 13.

"sex fiend": Ibid.

"queer as an effeminate fairy": Chauncey, *Gay New York*, 359.

"Uncle Sam's official snooper": Tucker, "Hist! Who's That?," 15.

"He is short, fat": Ibid., 49

"Eleanor blue" was associated with the First Lady: Ibid.

"compact body": Newton, "Tucker, Ray."

"Hoover stride has grown noticeably": Ibid.

"The sex fiend, the most loathsome": Hoover, "War on the Sex Criminal."

"isn't some fabled monster": Ibid.

"He often begins with annoyances": Ibid.

"orderly homosexual, the exhibitionist": Polchin, *Indecent Advances*, 91.

"present apathy of the public": Ibid., 13.

"war" against them "made homosexuality a national policing concern": Ibid., 13.

"post-pansy panic": Morris, "Pink Herring," 233.

"500 . . . sex offenders": Terry, *American Obsession*, 277.

"In preparation for the 1939 World's Fair": Ibid.

"highly publicized murders": Elias, "Lavender Reading."

"to frequent or loiter": Painter, "New York."

"As long as I am in the ARMY": Gerber to boyFrank, February 19, 1940, 1.

"romance and love": Gerber to McCourt, June 20, 1945, 1.

"intellectual riff-raff": Gerber to boyFrank, March 12, 1944, 3.

"used as a pimp": Gerber to boyFrank, February 19, 1940, 1.

8. "Favored by Nature with Immunity to Female 'Charms'"

"any connexion with Contacts": boyFrank to [Grace Bowes].

"I'll try not to be a pest": boyFrank to Gerber, January 15, 1940.

"Contacts," Henry assured him: Gerber to boyFrank. January 22, 1940.

"mood . . . to put it back into active service": Ibid.

"Am home every evening": Ibid.

"NYC Male, secretary": McCourt, self-description.

"male only": Ibid.

"NYC Male, 44, proofreader": Gerber, self-description.

"In studying a man's listing": boyFrank to 10, January 25, 1940.

"fond of reading nonfiction": Gerber, self-description.

"ought to read some fiction": boyFrank to 10, January 25, 1940.

"Can I come up and see you": Ibid.

"interested in photography": McCourt, self-description.

"thousand . . . negatives and innumerable prints": Sears, *Behind the Mask*, 93.

"hard-to-get": boyFrank, to 1744, January 25, 1940, 2.

"I'm 45, and look it": McCourt to boyFrank, January 30, 1940.

"limited in scope": Ibid.

"I am intensely interested": Ibid.

"As I meet a man": boyFrank to 1744, January 25, 1940. 3.

"As to the negro": McCourt to boyFrank, February 1, 1940, 1.

"Everybody regrets the passing of Contacts": boyFrank to Gerber, n.d. ["Realization that"], 1.

"Let me tell you from experience": Gerber to boyFrank, January 27, 1940, 1.

"I would like to see": Ibid., 2.

"You would not last long": Ibid., 1.

"private affairs": Gerber, self-description.

"Personally," he admitted, "I am only interested in young": Ibid., 1.

"hundred soldiers": Gerber to boyFrank, February 19, 1940, 4.

"Of course if I were a fairy": Ibid.

"I like young meat": Ibid.

"I did *not* give my new address": Ibid., 5.

"for replenishing the larder": Ibid., 5.

"Sorry you are not 20": Ibid., 4.

"Henry Gerber didn't have anything": McCourt to boyFrank, January 30, 1940.

"I don't know of anyone who would seriously": Ibid.

"There is good food": McCourt to Al, March 1.

"Abbey of Thelema": McCourt to boyFrank, February 11, 1940, 2.

"complicated set of magical": Beyer, "Understanding the Religion."

"You have so MANY": McCourt to boyFrank, February 7, 1940, 1.

"concentrate on one a time": Ibid.

"preferably after eight o'clock": Ibid.

"Santa Claus service": Gerber to boyFrank, February 19, 1940, 2.

Henry called it "fantastic": Ibid., 1.

"pass around" a "list": Ibid., 2.

"weekly schedule: Henry's Paul": Ibid.

"told" him of one "run by a hospital orderly": Ibid.

"so many interesting young men": boyFrank to McCourt, July 7, 1941, 1.

"half-a-dozen fine men": boyFrank to George [Bosch], December 26, 1943, 7.

"As you know, I give and take": boyFrank to McCourt, March 16, 1941, n.p.

"We are working in a field": Kosar and Todd, "*Physical Fitness* Magazine," 9.

"advised Birger to consider establishing": Ibid.

"stony broke": boyFrank to Lee Birger, September 1, 1940, 1.

"full of old Contacts members": Gerber to boyFrank, February 19, 1940, 1.

"'surprise' (and stag)": McCourt to boyFrank, September 21, 1940.

"Heart of Screenland": Masters, "Culver City."

"grand guy": boyFrank to McCourt, September 24, 1940.

"do something in the way": boyFrank to McCourt, December 16, 1940, 2.

"to have homosexual intercourse": Gerber to boyFrank, March 12, 1944, 6.

"That of course is so much horseshit": Ibid.

"I hate such hypocrisy": Ibid.

"rare group of about fifteen interwar films": Waugh, *Hard*, 310.

"male same-sex activity ranged": Ibid., 309–310.

"all presented male homosexual behavior": Ibid., 310.

"In such films," Waugh discovered: Waugh, "Homosociality," 282.

"hard to catch free": boyFrank to McCourt, March 16, 1941, 1.

"Henry's epistles": boyFrank to McCourt, October 7, 1944, 1.

9. "I Nearly Fell Out of My Chair!"

"I nearly": Gerber to boyFrank, April 14, 1944, 9.

"passed the nation's first peacetime": Bérubé, *Coming*, 2.

"armed forces decided to exclude": Ibid.

"more than 16 million": Ibid.

"draft": boyFrank to McCourt, February 2, 1943, 6.

"disability with a 3/4 pay pension": Gerber to boyFrank, March 27, 1941, 2.

"enlisted": *US Statutes at Large*, chapter 263, 394–395.

"only civilized city": Gerber to boyFrank, March 27, 1941, 2.

BECOME A PARATROOPER: Library and Archives, Hoover Institution.

NURSES ARE NEEDED: US Capitol Visitor Center, *Nurses Are Needed!*

"mill-stone": Gerber to boyFrank, March 27, 1941, 1.

"old soldier friend": Ibid.

"long been popular with queer people": Walsh, "Florida's Anything-Goes."

"had little time to do any cruising": Gerber to boyFrank, March 27, 1941, 1.

"b.i.o.n."—believe it or not: McCourt to boyFrank, March 16, 1941, 2.

"Dick S." dropped by Frank and Chuck's: McCourt to boyFrank, October 8, 1940.

"8½" but the "fellow from Connellsville: Ibid.

"remove their nether garments": McCourt to boyFrank, July 17, 1942, 2.

"8 or 9 old bitches": Gerber to boyFrank, April 14, 1944, 10.

"dozen elderly men": Gerber to boyFrank, January 4, 1945, 2.

"In San Diego, years ago": boyFrank to McCourt, February 2, 1943, 5–6.

"Forest Ranger" who wrote fictional: Ibid.

"made quite an impression": McCourt to boyFrank, July 19, 1940, 1.

"good," Manuel recalled, "but inhibited": boyFrank to McCourt, March 16, 1941, 1.

"We've been been having some exciting parties": McCourt to boyFrank, August 15, 1943, 1

"numbered 4,000": Buhs, "Robert L. Farnsworth."

"Rocket to the Moon?": Ad for US Rocket Society, *Popular Science*.

"indulging" himself with "any extravagant": McCourt to boyFrank, January 24, 1942, 1.

"2 legal-size hectographed": Gergen, *MFS Bulletin*, 1.

"very closety, with a sprinkling": Kepner to Katz, January 31, 1974, 5.

"Letters censored": McCourt, "Rocketeers: Members."

"Christmas story" at the end: McCourt, "Supplement."

"It seems to me it would be": Gerber to boyFrank, March 19, 1944.

"I am only interested in getting": Gerber to boyFrank, December 3, 1944, 1.

"There is nothing more beautiful": Gerber to boyFrank, March 12, 1944, 7.

"romance and love": Gerber to McCourt, June 20, 1945, 1.

"What could be a nicer hobby": Woycke, *Espirit de Corps*.

"substantial portion": O'Brien and Fair, "'As the Twig Is Bent,'" 30.

"bronze medal for touching the palms": "S & H Leaguers' Page," *Strength and Health*.

"Department of Justice through physical": Ibid.

"employment in a gymnasium": Ibid.

"interested in photographic studies": Ibid.

"interested in writing music": Ibid.

"interested in French": Ibid.

"only received twelve replies": O'Brien and Fair, "'As the Twig Is Bent,'" 30.

"It takes all sorts of people": Ibid.

"U.S. district attorney shouting": Ibid.

"four or five times": Gerber to boyFrank, October 23, 1945, 6.

"punk" whom he had propositioned: Gerber to boyFrank, April 14, 1944, 3.

"tried to get me out of the army": Gerber to boyFrank, August 31, 1957, 2.

"No partner in sex": Ibid.

"It takes a cocksucker": Ibid.

"mutual masturbation with men": Gerber to boyFrank, February 19, 1940, 3.

"*not a homosexual*": Gerber to boyFrank, April 14, 1944, 9.

"I nearly fell out of my chair!": Ibid.

"disability existed prior": Gerber to boyFrank, August 5, 1944, 1.

"dopey old fellow": Gerber to boyFrank, May 25, 1944, 2.

"I never saw anyone there": Gerber to boyFrank, February 18, 1946, 2.

"When one of my friends came up": Ibid.

quean initially denoted: *The Concise New Partridge Dictionary of Slang and Unconventional English*, 2nd ed. (New York: Routledge, 2015), 628.

"served as Henry Gerber": "Dittmar," registration card, Ancestry.com.

"my dear old friend": Gerber to boyFrank, February 20, 1944.

Part III: Washington, DC

10. "What Homosexual in His Right Mind Wants to Marry or to Be 'Cured'?"

"haven of refuge": Gerber to boyFrank, March 12, 1944, 3.

"old boozehounds": Gerber to boyFrank, February 18, 1946, 1.

"They don't let you forget": Gerber to boyFrank, March 12, 1944, 3.

"They turn on the lights": Gerber to boyFrank, March 28, 1944, 2.

"Recreational Bulletin": Kepner, "Henry Gerber: Grandfather," 1.

"Barton R. Horvath wishes to announce": Horvath, ad for photographs.

"very puritanical influences": boyFrank to McCourt, January 12, 1944, 3.

"I am dissatisfied with the amount": boyFrank to Horvath, March 26, 1944, 1.

"express or by courier": Ibid.

"most artistic and photographically perfect": Horvath, ad for *Art*.

"know a single": Gerber to boyFrank, April 20, 1944, 1–2.

"daily intercourse": Ibid., 1.

"may be all right": Ibid., 1.

"Damn it all": McCourt to Gerber, April 22, 1944, 2.

"Judging by the way he lived": Ibid.

"Hearing about your $10,000": boyFrank to Horvath, December 15, 1944, 2.

"I . . . think you waste": McCourt to boyFrank, January 5, 1945, 1.

"going into business with Melan": Ibid.

"if he intended to participate": Ibid.

"careful of his 'manly reputation'": Ibid.

"Post Office Insp. L.A. Miller": "Accused," *Jersey Journal*.

"obscene, lewd and lascivious": Ibid.

"Barton Horvath . . . is putting out his own": "Iron," *Strength and Health*.

"numbed by this endless, senseless war": McCourt to Gerber, April 22, 1944, 1.

"healthy young Rocketeers": McCourt to boyFrank, January 29, 1945, 1.

"Most homosexuals," he observed: Gerber to *Time*, April 5, 1944, 5.

"extortionists and blackmailers": Ibid.

"As long as there are laws": Gerber to boyFrank, February 19, 1940, 3.

"What homosexual in his right mind": Gerber to boyFrank, August 9, 1947, 1.

"imperialistic politicians": Gerber to *Time*, April 5, 1944, 4.

"Hitlers, the Mussolinis": Gerber to boyFrank, March 12, 1944, 4.

"religious fanatics": Gerber to *Time*, April 5, 1944, 4.

"put her foot": Gerber to boyFrank, September 6, 1946.

"Now with the rubber shortage": Gerber to boyFrank, March 12, 1944, 4.

"Many errors occur in the translation": Gerber, "Excerpts," 29.

"repentant thief": Ibid.

"Verily I say unto you": Ibid.

"Quite a lot of 'bitches'": Gerber to boyFrank, August 9, 1944, 1.

"Unless he meant it as a joke": Gerber to boyFrank, May 25, 1944, 2.

"I do not quite agree": Gerber to McCourt, April 25, 1944, 1.

"we all have become hypocrits": Ibid.

"started in on religion": Gerber to boyFrank, May 25, 1944, 3–4.

"I am a pessimist": Ibid., 2.

"I was once married": Gerber to boyFrank, October 23, 1945, 6.

"I once was in love": Ibid.

"first degree Baptist": Ibid., 5.

11. "Notorious as a Homosexual Paradise"

"keeping a boy": Gerber to boyFrank, February 19, 1940, 4.

"struggle to do something": Gerber to boyFrank, October 23, 1945, 1.

"samizdat fashion": Kepner, "My First 66."

"extensive account of Male love": Kepner to Katz, January 21, 1974, 4.

"practical tips on how to stretch": Kepner, "Monwell boyFrank" 3.

"repetitious . . . personal accounts": Gerber to boyFrank, April 12, 1944.

"not read about": Ibid.

"I am surrounded by a bunch of dirty": Gerber to boyFrank, April 14, 1944, 1.

Frank retuned the "translations": McCourt to Gerber, April 22, 1944, 2.

"nucleus of a valuable work": boyFrank to Gerber, August 2, 1946, 1.

"I never intended it for publication": Gerber to boyFrank, February 18, 1946, 2.

"You must have Jewish blood": Ibid.

"Jew and all profit-minded": Gerber to boyFrank, March 26, 1946, 2.

"bunch of Jews": Gerber to boyFrank. December 7, 1946.

"philosophy of life": Gerber to boyFrank, March 12, 1944, 8.

"'pervert's-defense' book": boyFrank to McCourt, January 14, 1947, 6.

"candid advice a boy needs": Ibid., 5.

"ancient Greeks" who "spent all the time": Ibid.

"Thinkers have often wondered why": Sears, *Behind the Mask*, 91.

"probably in Guadalcanal": Gerber to boyFrank, February 20, 1944.

"knew anyone in or near Washington": Ibid.

"Since writing that article": Gerber to boyFrank, October 23, 1945, 4.

"only physical things": Ibid., 5.

"sex *instinct* is inherited": Ibid.

"normal bisexuality underlies all sex": Gerber to boyFrank, April 14, 1944, 12.

"After all, the whole business of sex": Gerber to boyFrank, July 5, 1945, 5.

"pity for the poor suckers": Gerber to boyFrank, April 14, 1944, 8.

"Some people are still able to see the racket": Gerber to boyFrank, July 5, 1945, 5.

"Whether homosexuals are born that way": Gerber to boyFrank, October 23, 1945, 5.

"academic matter and it does not matter": Ibid.

"not extinguished": Gerber to boyFrank, February 20, 1944.

couldn't be a "father!": Ibid.

"contact with some young and handsome": Gerber to boyFrank, March 12, 1944, 2.

"I think 'Contacts' did more good": boyFrank to Gerber, March 6, 1944, 2.

"Why don't you take Contacts?": Gerber to boyFrank, March 12, 1944, 2.

"The homosexual knows that although his condition": Ibid., 8.

"That it is nobody's business": Gerber, "Society Scouting."

"founders," "contributing members": Ibid.

"committee of correspondence": Gerber to boyFrank, March 28, 1944, 3.

"All great causes start": Gerber to boyFrank, October 23, 1945, 3.

"FEAR," he explained to Manuel: Gerber to boyFrank, January 4, 1945, 2.

"Superb Steam and Hot Rooms": Ad for Riggs, *Evening Star*.

"spend the night": Ibid.

raid on a "Turkish bath": Gerber to McCourt, June 20, 1945, 1.

"special investigators and military": "50 Taken," *Evening Star*.

"many service men frequented": Gerber to McCourt, June 20, 1945, 1.

"old-fashioned idea": Gerber to boyFrank, October 23, 1945, 3.

"Homophiles want no pity": Ibid.

"efforts of other great liberators": Gerber to boyFrank, March 28, 1944, 1.

"known to history as deliverer": Gerber, "Society for Human Rights," 6.

"Our movement," he gushed: boyFrank to Gerber, March 25, 1944, 1.

"That would be only a drop": Ibid.

"That is the main thing": Gerber to boyFrank, March 28, 1944, 1.

"enthusiastic about the plan": McCourt to boyFrank, October 7, 1944, 1.

"to help those who don't": Ibid.

"eight sibilants": boyFrank to Gerber, March 25, 1944, 2–3.

"it does not . . . matter much": Gerber to boyFrank, March 28, 1944, 2.

"Band of brothers is inappropriate": Ibid., 3.

"I can call you Doris": Ibid., 2.

"Instead of" calling the new group: Ibid.

"God—homosexuality": Gerber to McCourt, April 25, 1944, 3.

"left out Jesus": Gerber to boyFrank, July 5, 1945, 3.

"I have studied your code": boyFrank to Gerber, June 30, 1945, 6.

"Very interesting to know about": Gerber to boyFrank, April 20, 1944, 1.

"Henry would be mortified": boyFrank to McCourt, October 14, 1944, 3.

"delighted" Henry, who assumed: Gerber to boyFrank, October 23, 1945, 5.

"When I was at the concert": Ibid.

"had several homes, a wife, a daughter": Thomas and Batten, "Wife Killer," 20.

"Since suppression of all 'non-procreative'": Gerber to *Time*, April 5, 1944. 1.

"*not a homosexual*": Ibid.

"sodomy or incest": Ibid., 2.

"not 'inborn' but . . . acquired": Ibid.

"when the rights": Ibid., 4.

"Having arrived at the age of discretion": Gerber to boyFrank, March 12, 1944, 8.

"We are in possession": Gerber to boyFrank, October 23, 1945, 2.

"one of gross stupidity": Gerber to *American Mercury*, April 9, 1944, 1.

"remove restrictions on *natural* forms": Ibid., 3.

"You are, of course, free to publish": Ibid.

12. "This Fascist World"

"nice time was had by all": Gerber to boyFrank, September 25, 1944, 1.

"in France or Switzerland where": Ibid., 3.

"Everytime I talk to one of the soldiers": Gerber to boyFrank, January 4, 1945, 3.

"reading, writing and going to the movies": Gerber to boyFrank, September 25, 1944, 5–6.

"One day," he told Manuel: Gerber to boyFrank, January 4, 1945, 3.

"112-day furlough": Gerber to boyFrank, February 8, 1945.

"Retirement means just that": Gerber to boyFrank, July 5, 1945, 2.

"less expensive and shabbier": Williams, *Notebooks*, 418.

"packed with gay servicemen": Bérubé, "History," 196.

"notorious as a homosexual paradise": Gerber to boyFrank, March 6, 1945, 2.

"steam room, massage rooms": Bérubé, "History," 196.

"brazen bitches": Gerber to boyFrank, June 20, 1945, 2.

"2 days a week in the library": Gerber to boyFrank, April 16, 1945, 4.

"there is nothing like a big city": Ibid., 3.

"positively the most bacchanalian": Gerber to McCourt, June 20, 1945, 1.

"romance and love": Ibid.

"self-centered": Ibid.

"I have always haughtily disdained": Gerber to boyFrank, June 22, 1945, 3.

"around public toilets": Gerber to McCourt, June 20, 1945, 1.

"ad in the Writers' Digest": Gerber to boyFrank, October 23, 1945, 8.

"chap in Chicago who wanted exciting letters": Ibid.

"got about three nice correspondents": Ibid.

"Louisiana bitch": Ibid., 1.

"You cannot talk to these young": Ibid.

"total of 244,300 individuals": New, "Ending Citizenship," 554.

"angels" in Pershing Square: Gerber to boyFrank, March 6, 1945, 1.

"fed up with Washington": Gerber to boyFrank, October 23, 1945, 8.

"romantic fool": Gerber to boyFrank, March 6, 1945, 1.

"fanatical Jesus-lover": Gerber to McCourt, June 20, 1945, 1.

"Whenever I see a handsome thing": Gerber to boyFrank, February 18, 1946, 2.

"To a practical man": boyFrank to Gerber, April 30, 1945, 1.

hadn't let "Henry discourage": McCourt to boyFrank, January 5, 1945, 1.

"Within his limitations": Ibid.

"25%" interested in being involved: Gerber to boyFrank, October 23, 1945, 2.

"I have not only no ambition": McCourt to boyFrank, n.d. ["So far unable"], 2.

"some pictures": McCourt to boyFrank, n.d. ["Midway in a reply"], 1.

"P.O. Gestapo": Gerber to boyFrank, February 18, 1946, 2.

"canoeing marathons": Boyle, "Mysterious Major Raven-Hart."

"friend of a friend": Raven-Hart, Down the Mississippi, 1.

"boy" named Phil: Gerber to boyFrank, July 5, 1945, 2.

"boys 10–12": Ibid.

"nursed along for some time": McCourt to boyFrank, October 7, 1944, 2.

"philosophy" would emphasize "this life": Ibid., 1.

"THE RELIGION OF BEAUTY": Ibid., 2.

"on exactly the right track": boyFrank to McCourt, October 14, 1944, 7.

"Your Religion of Beauty advertisement": Ibid., 9.

"it would but upset": McCourt to boyFrank, October 7, 1944, 2.

"hardly Henry's dish": boyFrank to McCourt, October 14, 1944, 9.

"Actually, the things we are doing": Ibid.

"There is plenty of enthusiasm": McCourt to boyFrank, n.d. ["Midway in a reply"], 1.

"Two healthy young Rocketeers": McCourt to boyFrank, January 29, 1945, 1.

"encyclopedia, or perhaps better a symposium": Ibid.

"interested in extreme youth": McCourt to boyFrank, July 19, 1940, 1.

"contribute valuable critique": McCourt to boyFrank, January 5, 1945, 1.

"It is an interesting attempt": Schafer to McCourt, February 26, 1945.

"fed up on a lot of this 'apologia for sin'": Schafer to McCourt, n.d. ["This letter is for yourself"].

"opus to Stenberg or Frank": Gerber to boyFrank, February 18, 1946, 4.

"said that the two, Frank and Chuck": Ibid., 2.

"Frank is going to the dogs": Gerber to boyFrank, October 23, 1945, 1.

"this fascist world": Ibid., 2.

"Had the heat turned on": McCourt to boyFrank, n.d. ["Had the heat"].

"retired Coastguardsman": Ibid.

"were plain poses": Gerber to boyFrank, February 18, 1946, 2.

"The way Frank and Chuck have been living": Gerber to boyFrank, June 22, 1945, 3.

"When I lived with him": Gerber to boyFrank, October 23, 1945, 1.

"That taxpayers' money": Gerber to boyFrank, February 18, 1946, 2.

13. "So Much Poppycock"

"In such a cosmic holocaust": Gerber to boyFrank, October 23, 1945, 2.

"Perhaps in a year": Gerber to McCourt, June 20, 1945, 2.

"bloodiest battle": Paterson, "Revealed."

"thousands were willing to make": Gerber to boyFrank, July 5, 1945, 3.

"One got away with murder": Gerber to boyFrank, June 22, 1946, 3.

"swankily furnished apartment": "Late Bulletin," *Evening Star.*

"indecent proposal": "Youth Held for Jury," *Evening Star.*

"prayed over the body": Ibid.

"man who made the phone call": "Lennon," *Evening Star.*

"improper advances to him": Ibid.

"one who bled freely": "Jury Considers," *Evening Star.*

"blood-soaked bed": "Slaying Victim's," *Evening Star.*

"about 5 feet 8 inches": Ibid.

"elaborately furnished": Ibid.

"some pictures of servicemen": Ibid.

"sex offenses": Ibid.

"Glendening took a liking to the youth": Ibid.

"sex affair": Gonzalez, "Police Seek Ex-G.I."

because he made "improper advances": "Eisenbarth Ordered," *Evening Star*.

"5 feet 6": "Fort Belvoir," *Evening Star*.

"hanger-on in taverns": Ibid.

had made "improper advances": "Glendening Suspect," *Evening Star*.

"expelled on sex charges": Ibid.

"illegally wearing a naval uniform": Ibid.

"5-to-15 year prison term": "Eisenbarth Starts," *Evening Star*.

"A young man named Samuel": Crain, "Theory That Justified."

"restless ever since the death of his father": "D.C. Youth," *Evening Star*.

"older youths and men": "City's Pervert Fringe," *Washington Post*.

"blamed her son's death": "Stiff Penalties," *Evening Star*.

"victimized by perverts": Neff, "2 Doctors Urge."

"homosexual arrests": Cervini, *Deviant's War*, 4.

"adult perverts convicted of molesting minors": Neff, "2 Doctors Urge."

"They seemed charming": Gerber to boyFrank, July 5, 1945, 2.

"most of these boys": Gerber to boyFrank, July 9, 1946.

"I can't think of anything": boyFrank to Gerber, August 2, 1946, 5.

"sex pervert, in his more innocuous": Faderman, *Gay Revolution*, 643n5.

"cited the case of a 15-year-old": "Murphy Tells," *Evening Star*.

"We've had a lot of robberies": "Park Police to Act," *Washington Post*.

"with disorderly conduct, loitering": Johnson, *Lavender*, 59.

"warned" 467 others: US House Committee on the District of Columbia, "Table 9."

"pervert file": Johnson, *Lavender*, 59.

"ninth-grader from Jefferson Junior": Ibid., 59–60.

"Having once fondled": Ibid., 60.

"obvious surveillance technique": Ibid., 47.

a nickname, the "Sneak": Ibid., 47.

"popular bars, restaurants, and theaters": Lvovsky, "Queer Expertise," 180–181.

"on the basis of two factors: age and physical attractiveness": Ibid., 181–182.

"one-man vice squad": "Official Waits," *Evening Star*.

"150 vice convictions": Lvovsky, "Queer Expertise," 198.

"simply pled guilty": Ibid., 189.

14. "Everyone Is After Their Scalp"

"had many nice parties": Gerber to boyFrank, August 9, 1947, 2.

"boy-boy sexercise": boyFrank to McCourt, May 28, 1947, 5.

"By that means," Manuel fantasized: Ibid., 6.

"few hundred men": Ibid.

"come right out and say": Ibid., 7.

"'Mr. DuTell,' we might lead off": Ibid.

"[The] man may give his son": Ibid., 23.

"Your [sic] are entirely off your nut": Gerber to boyFrank, August 9, 1947, 2.

"barbaric laws": B. Evans, "That Homosexuals," 598.

"I do not think that women": Gerber, "Homosexuals," 124.

"Dr. Gerber certainly knows": Brinkman, "Homosexuality Again," 507.

"it was too much definition": Gerber to boyFrank, August 9, 1947, 1.

"three theoretical psychoanalyses": Ibid.

"statistics of how many homosexuals": Ibid.

"run-around": Ibid.

"Your editorial," he wrote: Gerber to *Times-Herald*, September 4, 1947, 3.

"was strictly": Gerber to boyFrank, September 15, 1947, 2.

"What's up, bud?": Ibid.

"He was broke": Ibid.

"16-year-old boy": Ibid.

"100% heterosexual": Ibid.

"Your editorial of September 3": Gerber to the *Times-Herald*. September 4, 1947, 1.

"rape of a 14-year old girl": Ibid.

"I suppose you do not read your own crap": Ibid.

"thousands of priests, nuns, and monks": Ibid., 1.

"*moral depravity*": Gerber to boyFrank, September 15, 1947, 1.

"wave of homosexual offenses": Ibid.

"large army of Wacs": Ibid.

"married men are their best": Gerber to *National Defense*, September 15, 1947, 1.

"normal homosexual does not hate": Gerber to boyFrank, April 14, 1944, 7.

"romance and love": Gerber to boyFrank, June 20, 1945, 1.

"Women are good psychologists": Gerber to boyFrank, January 4, 1945, 2.

"by hook and crook": Gerber to boyFrank, March 12, 1944, 4.

"Why should anyone take upon himself": Gerber to boyFrank, July 5, 1945, 5.

"Why rear children": Ibid.

"Editors want things concise": boyFrank to Gerber, September 29, 1947, 3.

"brief, brief, brief": Ibid., 7.

"Everyone is after their scalp": Gerber to boyFrank, August 9, 1947, 1.

"insure full prosecution": "Bar Committee," *Evening Star*.

"fine of up to $100": Painter, "District of Columbia."

"penalty of 10 years": "Changes in Sex Laws," *Evening Star*.

"mandated that anyone accused": Graham and Hooks, *Historic Context Statement*, 2, 14.

"provided for the indefinite": Burroway, "Today."

"psychopathic child molester": Chauncey, *Gay New York*, 359.

"improper advances": "First Sex Law Case," *Evening Star.*

"on the Mall": Johnson, *Lavender*, 59.

"would have been charged with": Ibid.

"suspended sentence and place on probation": "Man Gets," *Evening Star.*

"One of the benches": Lait and Mortimer, *Washington Confidential*, 25.

15. "As If We Did Not Know!"

"to ameliorate the plight": Gerber, "Society for Human Rights," 5.

"avoid Pershing Square": Kepner, "My First 66," 1.

"enticed an 'older' gentleman": Burroway "Daily."

"Poor guy": Ibid.

"friend of Henry Gerber in Chicago": Kepner, "My First 66," 1.

"So I first heard about that group": Burroway, "Daily."

"society was primarily a social thing": Ibid.

"idea of gay people getting together": Ibid.

"five-page organizational outline": Feinberg, "'Bachelors for Wallace.'"

"10 percent of white males": Johnson, *Lavender*, 62.

"thirty-seven percent had had at least": Ibid.

"it is difficult to maintain the view that psychosexual": Ibid., 54.

"watershed moment": Ibid.

"There wasn't a radio stand-up": Ibid.

"as though it were a Bible": Ibid.

"Kinsey reported that 95 percent": Heatley, "'Commies and Queers,'" 32.

"article debunks socalled": Gerber to boyFrank, December 25, 1947, 1.

"37 percent" also became a trigger: Freedman, "'Uncontrolled Desires,'" 105.

"Kinsey's evidence of a 'gap'": Ibid.

"pervert file": Johnson, *Lavender*, 59.

"FBI records": Waldrop, "Murder as a Sex Practice," 144.

"Arrests of homosexuals": Ibid.

"sensationalized exposé on so-called": Belonsky, "How Fake News from 1949."

"sex pervert, whether a homosexual": "Queer People," *Newsweek.*

"stern attitude is required if the degenerate": Ibid.

"white supremacist": Johnson, *Lavender*, 101.

"in parentheses": Investigations Subcommittee, *Report*, 2082.

"those who engage in acts": US Senate Committee on Expenditures, *Employment of Homosexuals*, 19.

"purge," as historian David Johnson calls it: Johnson, *Lavender*, 167.

"hot to emulate Gerber": Kepner, "My First 66," 1.

"They blame us for everything": Freedman, "'Uncontrolled Desires,'" 94.

"paranoia" that many queer men: Kepner to Katz, March 19, 1974, 3.

"homosexuality an illness": Baxter, "'Homo-Hunting,'" 121.

"too scared to give their names": Gerber to boyFrank, January 27, 1940, 1.

"news, book reviews, opinion pieces": "*ONE* Magazine," ONE Archives.

"Dear Friends": Gerber to *One*, July 1953, 22.

"criminal, infamous": "Executive Order 10450," Mattachine Society.

"intoxicants to excess": Ibid.

"There was not a single example": Lim and Kracov, "Lavender Scare."

"very hard to overcome": Gerber to ONE Inc., August 12, 1954.

"included scholarly and philosophical": "*Mattachine Review*," ONE Archives.

"Your magazine is as fine": Gerber to *Mattachine Review*, April 1956, 39.

"The Review and the Society": Editor, *Mattachine Review* to H.G., April 1956, 39.

"observed in Lafayette Park": Johnson, *Lavender*, 61.

"act of perversion": Ibid.

"arrested for kissing": Ibid.

16. "Born 1000 Years Too Soon, or 1000 Years Too Late"

"best thing": Gerber to boyFrank, February 18, 1946, 1.

"sparkplug of the whole organization": Strub, "In Hispanic Heritage Month."

"furious pace": Sears, *Behind the Mask*, 343.

"Forward and Foreward": "Forward and Foreward," *Washington Newsletter*.

"to guard": *Collins Dictionary*, "Foreward."

"all homosexuals of good will": "What Is the Mattachine Society," *Washington Newsletter*.

"education of the heterosexual public": "Aims and Principles," *Washington Newsletter*.

"organized to blackmail": "First Organization," *Washington Newsletter*.

"promised to fight antihomosexual": Cervini, *Deviant's War*, 73.

"It seems the first American organization": "First Organization," *Washington Newsletter*.

"arms . . . crippled": Gerber to boyFrank, August 31, 1957, 1.

"most zealous": Sears, *Behind the Mask*, 344.

"Your childish letter": Huggins to Henry Gerber, November 8, 1956, 1.

"loose, sloppy, informal organization": Ibid.

"sex variants": Ibid.

"We must unite": Huggins to Morford, November 6, 1956, enclosure, 5.

section 3 of the bylaws, was "silly": Huggins to Gerber, November 8, 1956, 2.

"Look out for the dogcatcher": Ibid.

"sex variants" wasn't specific enough: Ibid.

"Perhaps you consider yourself a dog": Ibid.

"provinces of the pope": Ibid.

"I think you will find": Ibid., 1.

"All the books that are written": Ibid., 2.

"While it's true that some": Ibid.

"you . . . refer to 'acts per anum'": Ibid., 2.

"waste of time": Ibid., 2.

"I know your own project": Ibid., 1.

"You are beyond doubt": Ibid., 2.

"I have read your carbon": Call to Huggins, November 9, 1956, 1.

"needless alienation": Ibid.

"Dwight, I believe you are being hasty": Ibid.

"common courtesy": Ibid., 2.

"as understanding and tolerant": Ibid.

"too much talking and no results": Gerber to boyFrank, June 18, 1957, 3.

"if either ONE or MATTACHINE": Ibid., 2.

"libido" was "about gone": Ibid., 3.

"about as confidential as Eisenhower's": Gerber to boyFrank, August 31, 1957, 1.

"that neither ONE nor MATTACHINE": Ibid.

"They cannot even publish": Ibid.

"told them both not to send": Ibid.

"It's a lousy world": Ibid., 2.

"It seems to me that if you want": Gerber to boyFrank, June 18, 1957, 2.

"tower of strength": Legg to Gerber, May 19, 1965.

"joyful news": Gerber, "Society for Human Rights," 5.

"faintly anti-Semitic": T. to ONE.

"followers of Christ": Ibid.

"cajoled the cantankerous Henry": Sears, Behind the Mask, 460.

"first time" Hirschfeld's work: Legg, editorial, 40.

"To vote for a proposition": "Vote 'Yes' on Proposition ONE."

"A homosexual is no more apt": "Vote 'Yes' on Proposition ONE."

"breakaway group": Morgan, "Timeline."

"I hope that the privacy": Gerber to Legg, May 11, 1965.

"make a contribution": Ibid.

"There is always one Judas": Gerber to ONE Inc., May, 27 1965.

"whole thing is a lousy mess": Gerber to Legg, August 19, 1965.

"over a month": Gerber to ONE Inc., January 17, 1966.

"fine account of the Chicago": Legg to Gerber, January 20, 1966.

"about 30 years ago": Ibid.

"early advocate": Childs, "Fredric Frisbie," 2.

"androgynous Puerto Rican": Frisbie, "One Among Us," 9.

"Those of us coming on": "To the Friends," ONE Confidential.

"Father of the Homophile Movement": Grey, "To the City," 3.

"deliverer of the downtrodden": Gerber, "Society for Human Rights," 6.

"legendary Henry Gerber": Kepner, "Henry Gerber, Forerunner," 2.

"father of homosexual liberation": Ibid.

"Of prime import": "A Bold Pioneer," One Calendar.

Frisbie's "recollections": Ibid.

"Although his fledgling organization": Carpenter, "Born in Dissent," 383.

"ameliorate" the plight: Gerber, "Society for Human Rights," 5.

"It is . . . your and my misfortune": Gerber to boyFrank, February 18, 1946, 1.

"It is not a matter of life and death": Gerber to boyFrank, August 31, 1957, 1.

"With best wishes": Ibid.

envelope stamped DECEASED: Kepner to Katz, January 31, 1974, 4.

"Father of the American Homophile": "To the Friends," ONE Confidential.

BIBLIOGRAPHY

Archives

AB   Allan Bérubé Papers. Gay, Lesbian, Bisexual, and Transgender Historical Society, San Francisco, CA.

bF   Manuel boyFrank Papers. ONE: National Gay and Lesbian Archives, Los Angeles, CA.

EWB   Ernest Watson Burgess Papers. Special Collections, Regenstein Library, University of Chicago, Chicago, IL.

FEK   Franklin E. Kameny Letters. ONE Inc. Records, ONE: National Gay and Lesbian Archives, Los Angeles, CA.

GS   Gregory Sprague Papers. Research Center, Chicago History Museum, Chicago, IL.

HIC   Homosexual Information Center. Special Collections and Archives, Oviatt Library, California State University, Northridge, CA.

JK   Jim Kepner Papers. ONE: National Gay and Lesbian Archives, Los Angeles, CA.

JNK   Jonathan Ned Katz Papers, 1947–2004. Manuscripts and Archives Division, New York Public Library, New York, NY.

JPA   Juvenile Protective Association Papers. Special Collections and University Archives, University of Illinois at Chicago.

LM   Lyon Martin Papers. Gay, Lesbian, Bisexual, and Transgender Historical Society, San Francisco, CA.

NPRC   National Personnel Records Center. National Archives and Records Administration, St. Louis, MO.

OIMC   One, Incorporated Magazine Collection. One: National Gay and Lesbian Archives, Los Angeles, CA.

OIR   One, Incorporated Records. One: National Gay and Lesbian Archives, Los Angeles, CA.

SHR   Society for Human Rights. Illinois State Archives, Springfield, IL.

Note: A few of the letters written by Gerber and others were undated. I've added the first few words of the letter in brackets after "n.d." (no date) in their citations to distinguish them from the others without dates.

Adams, James G. *Review of the American Forces in Germany*. Koblenz, Germany: James G. Adams, 1921.

Adkins, Judith. "'These People Are Frightened to Death:' Congressional Investigations and the Lavender Scare." *Prologue* 48, no. 2 (2016).

Albertson, Clinton E. "In Defense of Marriage." Letter to the editor. *American Mercury*, October 1947, 505–506.

Amadeo, Kimberly. "Stock Market Crash of 1929: Facts, Causes, and Impact." The Balance, March 17, 2020. https://www.thebalance.com/stock-market-crash-of -1929-causes-effects-and-facts-3305891.

Ancestry.com. "Army List of Organizations and Casuals Returning to the United States." Records of the Office of the Quartermaster General, 1774–1985. Record group no. 92. Roll or box no. 56. National Archives, College Park, MD.

———. "Daily Report: 22 December 1911." Belgique, Anvers, index de police de l'immigration, 1840–1930. Antwerp, Belgium. Ancestry.com Operations, 2014.

———. "Dittmar, Josef." List or Manifest of Alien Passengers for the United States Immigration Officer at Port of Arrival. Arriving Passenger and Crew Lists (including Castle Garden and Ellis Island), 1820–1957. New York. Ancestry.com Operations, 2010.

———. "Dittmar, Joseph H." Registration card, October 2, 1942. World War II Draft Cards Young Men, 1940–1947. Ancestry.com Operations, 2011.

———. "Gerber, Henry." List of Outward-Bound Passengers (United States Citizens and Nationals). Arriving Passenger and Crew Lists (including Castle Garden and Ellis Island), 1820–1957. New York, April 5, 1951. Ancestry.com Operations, 2010.

———. "Gerber, Henry." "List of United States Citizens (for the Immigration Authorities). Army Transport Service Arriving and Departing Passenger Lists, 1910–1939. Ancestry.com Operations, 2016.

Anderson, Nels. *The Hobo: The Sociology of the Homeless Man*. New York: Routledge, 2006.

Archives West. "Bodybuilding Photograph Collection, Circa 1930s." January 1, 2020. http://archiveswest.orbiscascade.org/ark:/80444/xv46411.

Ashkenasi, Danny. "Das lila Lied—The Lavender Song—'We Just Happen to Be Different from the Others!'" Notes from a Composer, November 7, 2016. https: //dannyashkenasi.com/2016/11/07/das-lila-lied-the-lavender-song-we-just-happen -to-be-different-from-the-others.

Association of Motion Picture Producers. "The Motion Picture Production Code (as Published 31 March 1930)." https://www.asu.edu/courses/fms200s/total-readings/MotionPictureProductionCode.pdf.

Austin, Roger. *Playing the Game: The Homosexual Novel in America.* Indianapolis: Bobbs-Merrill, 1974.

Babst, Gordon. "Ernst Röhm (1887–1934)." GLBTQ Archive, 2015. http://www.glbtqarchive.com/ssh/rohm_e_S.pdf.

Barbas, Samantha. *Confidential Confidential: The Inside Story of Hollywood's Notorious Scandal Magazine.* Chicago: Chicago Review Press, 2018.

Barbera, Gianni. "Denied to Serve: Gay Men and Women in the American Military and National Security in World War II and the Early Cold War." M.A. thesis, Wilkinson College of Arts, Humanities, and Social Sciences, Chapman University, 2019.

Barkin, Kenneth and James J. Sheehan. "Germany: Germany from 1871 to 1918." *Encyclopedia Britannica.* Accessed November 20, 2019. https://www.britannica.com/place/Germany/Germany-from-1871-to-1918.

Barnes, Alexander F. "'Representative of a Victorious People': The Doughboy Watch on the Rhine." *Army History,* Fall 2010, 6–19.

Bartlett, John H. Letter to Arthur C. Lueder, August 10, 1925. GS. Box 25, folder 4.

———. Telegram to postmaster [Arthur C. Lueder], July 17, 1925. GS. Box 25, folder 4.

Bauer, Heike. *The Hirschfeld Archives: Violence, Death, and Modern Queer Culture.* Philadelphia: Temple University Press, 2017.

Bauer, J. Edgar. "Magnus Hirschfeld (1868–1935)." GLBTQ Archive, 2015. Accessed November 14, 2019. http://www.glbtqarchive.com/ssh/hirschfeld_m_S.pdf.

Baugher, Shirley. *Hidden History of Old Town.* Charleston, SC: History Press, 2011.

Baxter, Randolph W. "'Homo-Hunting' in the Early Cold War: Senator Kenneth Wherry and the Homophobic Side of McCarthyism." *Nebraska History* 84 (2003): 118–132.

Beachy, Robert M. *Gay Berlin: Birthplace of a Modern Identity.* New York: Knopf, 2014.

Beemyn, Brett. "The Geography of Same Sex Desire: Cruising Men in Washington, DC in the Late Nineteenth and Early Twentieth Centuries." *Left History* 9 (Spring/Summer 2004): 142–159.

Beemyn, Genny. *A Queer Capital: A History of Gay Life in Washington, D.C.* New York: Routledge, 2014.

Beisert, Oscar, and J. M. Duffin. *Nomination to the Philadelphia Register of Historic Places: The Camac Baths.* Philadelphia: Keeping Society of Philadelphia, 2018.

Belonsky, Andrew. "How Fake News from 1949 Painted Gay Men as Predators for Decades." LGBTQ Nation, October 24, 2017. https://www.lgbtqnation.com/2017/10/fake-news-1949-painted-gay-men-predators-decades.

Bérubé, Allan. *Coming Out Under Fire: The History of Gay Men and Women in World War II*. New York: Free Press, 1990.

———. "The History of Gay Bathhouses." In *Policing Public Sex: Queer Politics and the Future of AIDS Activism*, edited by Dangerous Bedfellows, 187–238. Boston: South End, 1996.

Beyer, Catherine. "Understanding the Religion of Thelema." Learn Religions. Last updated January 27, 2019. https://www.learnreligions.com/thelema-95700.

Biographical Directory of the United States Congress. "Hoeppel, John Henry." Accessed February 10, 2021. https://bioguide.congress.gov/search/bio/H000677.

Black, Jonathan. "Charles Atlas: Muscle Man." *Smithsonian*, August 2009. https://www.smithsonianmag.com/history/charles-atlas-muscle-man-34626921.

Blinstrub, Benjamin. "Follow-Up Work on Mr. Kinsie's Investigation." December 27, 1927. JPA. Box 6, folder 96.

Boag, Peter. "Sexuality, Gender, and Identity in Great Plains History and Myth." *Great Plains Quarterly* 18 (Fall 1998): 327–340.

Boundless US History. "The Great Depression." Accessed August 28, 2020. https://courses.lumenlearning.com/boundless-ushistory/chapter/the-great-depression.

Boyd, Nan Alamilla. *Wide-Open Town: A History of Queer San Francisco to 1965*. Berkeley: University of California Press, 2003.

boyFrank, Manuel. [Contact letterhead mock-up]. bF. Box 5, folder 28.

——— . [J. P. Starr, pseud.]. "His Was a Monkey-Puzzle Family Tree." September 18, 1978. bF. Box 6, folder 17.

———. Letter to Barton Horvath, March 26, 1944. Box 1, folder 26.

———. Letter to Barton Horvath, December 15, 1944. bF. Box 1, folder 26.

———. Letter to Frank McCourt, September 24, 1940. bF. Box 1, folder 33.

———. Letter to Frank McCourt, December 16, 1940. bF. Box 1, folder 33.

———. Letter to Frank McCourt, September 24, 1940. bF. Box 1, folder 33.

———. Letter to Frank McCourt, March 16, 1941. bF. Box 1, folder 33.

———. Letter to Frank McCourt, July 7, 1941. bF. Box 1, folder 33.

———. Letter to Frank McCourt, February 2, 1943. bF. Box 1, folder 34.

———. Letter to Frank McCourt, July 19, 1943. bF. Box 1, folder 34.

———. Letter to Frank McCourt, January 12, 1944. bF. Box 1, folder 34.

———. Letter to Frank McCourt, October 7, 1944. bF. Box 1, folder 34.

———. Letter to Frank McCourt, October 14, 1944. bF. Box 1, folder 34.

———. Letter to Frank McCourt, August 29, 1945. bF. Box 1, folder 34.

———. Letter to Frank McCourt, January 14, 1947. bF. Box 1, folder 35.

———. Letter to Frank McCourt, May 28, 1947, 5. bF. Box 1, folder 35.

———. Letter to Frank McCourt, October 6, 1947. bF. Box 1, folder 35.

——. Letter to Frank McCourt, July 9, 1948. bF. Box 1, folder 35.

——. Letter to Frank McCourt, n.d. ["You may, I surmise."]. bF. Box 1, folder 32.

——. Letter to George [H. Bosch], December 26, 1943. bF. Box 5, folder 15.

——. Letter to [Grace Bowes], American Service. November, 18 1939. bF. Box 4, folder 29.

——. Letter to Henry Gerber, September 22, 1935. bF. Box 4, folder 29.

——. Letter to Henry Gerber, September 27, 1936. bF. Box 4, folder 29.

——. Letter to Henry Gerber, January 15, 1940. bF. Box 4, folder 29.

——. Letter to Henry Gerber, March 6, 1944. bF. Box 1, folder 21.

——. Letter to Henry Gerber, March 25, 1944. bF. Box 1, folder 21.

——. Letter to Henry Gerber, April 9, 1944. bF. Box 1, folder 21.

——. Letter to Henry Gerber, December 26, 1944. bF. Box 1, folder 21.

——. Letter to Henry Gerber, April 30, 1945. bF. Box 1, folder 15.

——. Letter to Henry Gerber, June 30, 1945. bF. Box 1, folder 15.

——. Letter to Henry Gerber, August 2, 1946. bF Box 1, folder 16.

——. Letter to Henry Gerber, September 29, 1947. bF. Box 1, folder 17.

——. Letter to Henry Gerber, September 30, 1948. bF. Box 1, folder 18.

——. Letter to Henry Gerber, n.d. ["Realization that he is 'favord."]. bF. Box 1, folder 21.

——. Letter to Jim Kepner, July 13, 1970. bF. Box 1, folder 27.

——. Letter to Lee Birger, September 1, 1940. bF. Box 1, folder 1.

——. Letter to 10 [Henry Gerber], January 25, 1940. 1. bF. Box 1, folder 32.

——. Letter to 1744 [Frank McCourt], January 25, 1940. bF. Box 1, folder 32.

Boyle, Richard. "The Mysterious Major Raven-Hart." *Sunday Times* (Sri Lanka), February 19, 2017. http://www.sundaytimes.lk/170219/plus/the-mysterious-major-raven-hart-229159 .html.

Brevities. June 20, 1933, n.p. https://www.queermusicheritage.com/gayephemera5.html.

——. November 23, 1933, 12.

——. Ad for *Confessions of a "Pansy."* November 30, 1933, 7.

——. "Confessions of a 'Pansy.'" November 30, 1933, 7.

——. "The Fag." October 19, 1933, 7.

——. "Pansies Blow U.S." May 9, 1932, 1.

——. "Sexy Sailors Blow." October 12, 1933, 1, 12.

Brinkman, Paul, Jr. "Homosexuality Again." Letter to the Editor. *American Mercury*, October 1947, 506.

Broadway Brevities. "B'way Queers Brazen!" May 15, 1933, 1.

Broadway Tattler. Untitled cartoon strip. January 1934, 2.

Brown, Sally, and David R. Brown. *A Biography of Mrs. Marty Mann: The First Lady of Alcoholics Anonymous.* Center City, MN: Hazelden, 2013.

Browning, Buddy. "Fag Balls Exposed." *Broadway Brevities*, March 14, 1932, 1, 12.

Buhs, Joshua Blu. "Robert L. Farnsworth as a Fortean." *From an Oblique Angle* (blog), December 3, 2014. https://www.joshuablubuhs.com/blog/robert-l-farnsworth-as-a-fortean.

Bunson, Matthew. "German Catholics Under the Iron Fist." Catholic Answers, December 1, 2008. https://www.catholic.com/magazine/print-edition/german-catholics-under-the-iron-fist.

Burnette, Brandon R. "Comstock Act of 1873 (1873)." First Amendment Encyclopedia. Free Speech Center. https://www.mtsu.edu/first-amendment/article/1038/comstock-act-of-1873.

Burroway, Jim. "The Daily Agenda for Thursday, April 7." Box Turtle Bulletin, April 7, 2016. www.boxturtlebulletin.com/2016/04/07/71931.

———. "'Something Twisted Mentally': McCarthy Links 'Flagrantly Homosexuals' to Communism." *[Emphasis Mine]* (blog), May 11, 2018. http://jimburroway.com/history/something-twisted-mentally-mccarthy-links-flagrantly-homosexuals-to-communism.

———. "Today In History, 1948: Congress Allows Indefinite Confinement of Gay People as 'Sexual Psychopaths' in Washington, D.C." Box Turtle Bulletin, June 9, 2016. http://www.boxturtlebulletin.com/2016/06/09/72981.

Butler, Patrick. *Hidden History of Lincoln Park.* Charleston, SC: History Press, 2015.

Byers, John Andrew. "The Sexual Economy of War: Regulation of Sexuality and the U.S. Army, 1898–1940." PhD diss., Department of History, Duke University, 2012.

Call, Harold L. Letter to Buell Dwight Huggins, November 9, 1956. Homophile organizations, Mattachine Society correspondence, January 10, 1955–January 11, 1957. Gay, Lesbian, Bisexual, and Transgender Historical Society, Archives of Sexuality and Gender.

Carpenter, Dale. "Born in Dissent: Free Speech and Gay Rights." *Southern Methodist University Law Review* 375 (2019): 375–387.

Carpentier, Charles F. Memo to Latham Castle, November 15, 1956. "Dissolved Domestic Corporation Charters, May 1, 1849–March 7, 1980." SHR. Record series 103.112, Corporations, box 1783, no. 125058.

———. Memo to William G. Clark, November 15, 1963. Dissolved Domestic Corporation Charters, May 1, 1849–March 7, 1980." SHR. Record series 103.112, Corporations, box 1783, no. 125058.

Carrington, Tyler. "Love in the Big City: Intimacy, Marriage, and Risk in Turn-of-the-Century Berlin." PhD diss., Department of History, University of Illinois at Urbana-Champaign, 2014.

Castle, Latham. Memo, July [18?,] 1956. "Dissolved Domestic Corporation Charters, May 1, 1849–March 7, 1980." SHR. Record series 103.112, Corporations, box 1783, no. 125058.

Cervini, Eric. *The Deviant's War: The Homosexual vs. the United States of America*. New York: Farrar, Straus and Giroux, 2020.

Chapman, David L. *Sandow the Magnificent: Eugen Sandow and the Beginnings of Bodybuilding*. Urbana: University of Illinois Press, 1994.

Chauncey, George. *Gay New York: Gender Urban Culture, and the Making of the Gay Male World, 1890–1940*. New York: Basic Books, 1994.

Chicago Evening American. "Girl Reveals Strange Cult Run by Dad." July 13, 1925.

Chicago Tribune. "Pink Powder Puffs." July 18, 1926.

Chicago Vice Commission. *The Social Evil in Chicago: A Study of Existing Conditions*. Chicago: Gunthorp Warren, 1911.

Childs, Jim. "Fredric Frisbie: Early Gay Rights Advocate." *West Adams Matters*, March 2004, 2.

Chiles, William H. "A Heterosexual Looks at Homosexuality." *Chanticleer*, May 1934, 1–3.

Claff, Julian B. "'Thirty' Sounded for *Amaroc News*, Most Unique of American Dailies." *Editor and Publisher*, March 17, 1923, 11, 31.

Collins Dictionary. "Foreward." 2021. https://www.collinsdictionary.com/us/dictionary /english/foreward.

Coretto, Elizabeth. "'The Fountain Pen and the Typewriter': The Rise of the Homophile Press in the 1950s and 1960s." Honors thesis, Department of History, Oberlin College, Spring 2017.

Cornebise, Alfred E. *"The Amaroc News": The Daily Newspaper of the American Forces in Germany, 1919–1923*. Carbondale: Southern Illinois University Press, 1981.

Cox, David. "The Danish Girl and the Sexologist: A Story of Sexual Pioneers." *Guardian*, January 13, 2016. https://www.theguardian.com/science/blog/2016/jan/13/magnus -hirschfeld-groundbreaking-sexologist-the-danish-girl-lili-elbe.

Crain, Caleb. "The Theory That Justified Anti-gay Crime." *New Yorker*, June 26, 2019. https://www.newyorker.com/books/under-review/the-theory-that-justified -anti-gay-crime.

Dalzell, Tom, and Victor, Terry, eds. *New Partridge Dictionary of Slang and Unconventional English*. Vol. 2, J–Z. New York: Routledge, 2006.

Davis-Monthan Aviation Field Register: First Municipal Aviation Field in the U.S. "Horace Neveille Heisen." February 16, 2007. https://dmairfield.org/people/heisen_hn /index.html.

de la Croix, St. Sukie. *Chicago Whispers: A History of LGBT Chicago Before Stonewall*. Madison: University of Wisconsin Press, 2012.

DeCosta-Klipa, Nik. "The Checkered History and Doubtful Future of New England's 'Alcatraz of the East,'" *Boston Globe*, July 5, 2017. https://www.boston.com/news /history/2017/07/05/the-checkered-history-and-doubtful-future-of-new-englands -alcatraz-of-the-east.

D'Emilio, John. *Making Trouble: Essays on Gay History, Politics, and the University.* New York: Routledge, 1992.

———. *Sexual Politics, Sexual Communities: The Making of a Homosexual Minority in the United States 1940–1970.* 2nd ed. Chicago: University of Chicago Press, 1983.

Dose, Ralf. *Magnus Hirschfeld: The Origins of the Gay Liberation Movement.* Translated by Edward H. Willis. New York: Monthly Review Press, 2014.

Drum. "Frontal Nudes." October 1965, 38.

Earls, Avrill, and Elizabeth Garner Masarik. "Anthony Comstock: Sex, Censorship, and the Power of Policing the Subjective." *Dig: A History Podcast*, March 24, 2019. Transcript and audio, 1:01:58. https://digpodcast.org/2019/03/24/anthony-comstock.

Elias, Christopher. "A Lavender Reading of J. Edgar Hoover." *Slate.* September 2, 2015. https://slate.com/human-interest/2015/09/how-colliers-suggested-j-edgar-hoover -was-gay-back-in-1933.html.

Emmerson, Louis L. Certificate of Incorporation. December 1924. "Dissolved Domestic Corporation Charters, May 1, 1849–March 7, 1980." SHR. Record series 103.112, Corporations, box 1783, no. 125058.

Encyclopaedia Britannica. "Montgomery Ward and Company." April 26, 2002. https:// www.britannica.com/topic/Montgomery-Ward-and-Co.

Eskridge, William N., Jr. "Privacy Jurisprudence and the Apartheid of the Closet, 1946– 1961." *Florida State University Law Review* 24 (1997): 703–840.

Evans, Bergen. Letter to Henry Gerber. *American Mercury*, June 1947, 124–125.

———. "That Homosexuals Are Always Effeminate." *American Mercury*, May 1947, 598.

Evans, Rhonda. *U.S. Military Policies Concerning Homosexuals: Development, Implementation and Outcomes.* Center for the Study of Sexual Minorities in the Military, University of California at Santa Barbara, 2001.

Evening Star (Washington, DC). Ad for Riggs Turkish Baths. March 29, 1946.

———. "Army Clears Up Mystery of Bench 'Wired for Sound.'" November 11, 1947.

———. "Bar Committee to Aid in Writing Strong Sex Law. August 26, 1947.

———. "Body of Man, Believed Beaten with War Club, Found Here." June 3, 1946.

———. "Changes in Sex Laws with 20-Year Penalty Are Prepared by Fay." December 14, 1947.

———. "D.C. Heads Approve 26 as Police Rookies." March 31, 1948.

———. "D.C. Youth, 16, Found Hanging from Necktie During Party." July 2, 1946.

———. "District Heads to Hear Wallace and Manthos on Appeal by Grill." December 21, 1948.

———. "Eisenbarth Ordered Held Without Bond in Slaying of Glendening." June 15, 1946.

———. "Eisenbarth Starts Serving 3 to 15 Years for Slaying." December 18, 1946.

———. "50 Taken in Raids at Turkish Baths." March 25, 1945.

———. "First Sex Law Case Ends in Commitment." July 21, 1948.

———. "Fort Belvoir Soldier Wanted as Suspect in Glendening Slaying." June 6, 1946.

———. "Four to Face Jury Trial in Congress Hotel Raid." October 30, 1948.

———. "Glendening Suspect, Caught at Niagara, to Be Returned Here." June 14, 1946.

———. "Indictment Charges Murder to Soldier in Traffic Fatality." March 18, 1946.

———. "Jury Considers Fate of Lennon on Trial in Slaying of Nault." June 14, 1946.

———. "Late Bulletin." February 26, 1945.

———. "Lennon Takes Stand Tells of Hitting Victim." June 13, 1946.

———. "Man Gets 3 to 9 Years for Firing 2 Shots in Bus Station Dispute." December 24, 1948.

———. "Man Held on Sex Charge Brought by Boy, 16." October 8, 1947.

———. "Manthos to Walk Beat in 6th Precinct After Shift from Vice Squad." November 14, 1948.

———. "Murphy Tells How Degenerates Ruin Lives of Many Youngsters." August 23, 1947.

———. "Official Waits Sentencing in Second Sex Conviction." October 27, 1949.

———. "Old Soldier, 84, Slain; Pal, 78, Cut, Found with Knife in Hand." October 21, 1941.

———. "Police in 13 States Join Hunt for Youth in War Club Slaying." June 8, 1946.

———. "Police Seek Identity of Youth Hunted in Glendening Murder." June 5, 1946.

———. "Publicity for Sex Prime Praised by Judge, Prosecutors, Police." August 28, 1947.

———. "Sanity Examination Bill Sought for D.C. as Sex Crime Check." August 18, 1942.

———. "Slaying Victim's Auto Found; Saw Man Park It, Woman Says." June 4, 1946.

———. "Stiff Penalties Backed in Sex Perversion Involving Children." July 4, 1946.

———. "Two Are Fined $50 Each on Soliciting Charges." July 19, 1948.

———. "Two Held in $500 Bond on Sex Charges." November 7, 1948.

———. "Veteran's Body Found in Sand at Soldiers' Home." March 7, 1946.

———. "Vice Arrests Bring 4 More Men to Court." July 11, 1948.

———. "Youth Held for Action at Inquest Today in Apartment Death." February 28, 1946.

———. "Youth Held for Jury Action in Slaying." March 1, 1946.

Faderman, Lillian. *The Gay Revolution: The Story of the Struggle.* New York: Simon & Schuster, 2015.

Faderman, Lillian, and Stuart Timmons. *Gay L.A.: A History of Sexual Outlaws, Power Politics, and Lipstick Lesbians.* Berkeley, CA: University of California Press, 2009.

FamilySearch.org. Belgique, Anvers, immigration recorde par la police de la ville, 1840–1930. Stadsarchief Antwerpen (Antwerp City Archives), Belgium. Accessed December 2, 2019.

———. Belgique, Anvers, index de police de l'immigration, 1840. Stadsarchief Antwerpen, Belgie (Municipal Archives, Antwerp). Accessed December 2, 2019.

Fassnacht, Max. "On the Ground of Nature: Sexuality and Respectability in *Die Freundschaft*'s *Wandervogel* Stories." *Journal of Homosexuality* 68, no. 3 (September 2019): 434–460. https://doi.org/10.1080/00918369.2019.1656030.

Feinberg, Leslie. "'Bachelors for Wallace.'" *Workers World*, May 26, 2005. https://www.workers.org/2005/us/lgbtseries-0602.

Ferguson, Michael. *Idol Worship: A Shameless Celebration of Male Beauty in the Movies*. 2nd ed. Sarasota, FL: Star Books, 2005.

Flagg, James Montgomery. "I Want You for the U.S. Army." Poster. New York: Recruiting Publicity Bureau, 1941. University of North Texas Libraries, UNT Digital Library, UNT Libraries Government Documents Department. Accessed April 15, 2020. https://digital.library.unt.edu/ark:/67531/metadc445/.

Freedman, Estelle B. "'Uncontrolled Desires': The Response to the Sexual Psychopath, 1920–1960. *Journal of American History* 74 (June 1987): 83–106.

Friedman, Mack. *Strapped for Cash: A History of American Hustler Culture*. New York: Alyson, 2003.

Frisbie, Fred. "One Among Us." In *Don Slater: A Gay Rights Pioneer Remembered by His Friends*, 9–10. Rev. ed. Los Angeles: Homosexual Information Center, 1997.

Galbraith, Frank H. Letter to Henry Gerber, April 2, 1924. GS. Box 25, folder 4.

Gapp, Paul. "Death of Bohemia." *Chicago Tribune*, February 14, 1988. https://www.chicagotribune.com/news/ct-xpm-1988-02-14-8803300313-story.html.

Gerber, Henry, trans. "Adaptation Treatment of Homosexuality (Adjustment Therapy)." *ONE Institute Quarterly* (Spring/Summer/Fall 1962): 41–54.

———. "Among Our Competitors." *Commentary*, April 1935, 1–2.

———. Application for Incorporation. December 1924. "Dissolved Domestic Corporation Charters, May 1, 1849–March 7, 1980." SHR. Record series 103.112, Corporations, box 1783, no. 125058.

———."Are Indecent Shows Realistic?" *Chicago Daily Tribune*, March 2, 1925.

———. "Are You Without Congenial Contacts? Ad for Contacts. *American Mercury*, August 1939, 518.

———, trans. "Classification of Homosexuals as to Age Preferences and Sex Acts." *ONE Institute Quarterly* (Winter 1962): 20–29.

———. Contacter 1366. 1935. bF. Box 8, folder 9.

———. "Contacts, an Unusual Correspondence Club." Ad for Contacts. *American Mercury*, December 1936, 376.

———. "Descriptions." 1935. bF. Box 3, folder 1.

———. "Englische Heuchelei." *Blätter für Menschenrecht* 6 (October 1928): 4–5.

———. "Escape from Reality." *Chanticleer*, May 1934, 7–8.

———. "Escape from the Bughouse of This Fairytale Kulture!" Ad for Contacts. *American Mercury*, November 1935, 253.

———. "The Evolution of the Army Ration." *United States Army Recruiting News*, July 1, 1927, 4.

———. "Excerpts from After-Thoughts." *Truth Seeker*, February 1944, 29.

———. "Excess Leisure Problems." Ad for Contacts. Saturday Review of Literature, July 7, 1934, 799.

———. Expiration notice to 1366 [Manuel boyFrank]. April 8, 1935. bF. Box 8, folder 9.

———. Form letter to Dear Friend [Manuel boyFrank]. April 8, 1935. bF. Box 8, folder 9.

———. "Hitler and Homosexuality." *Chanticleer*, September 1934, 1–2.

———. "Homosexuals." Letter to the editor. *American Mercury*, June 1947, 123–124.

———. [Parisex, pseud.]. "In Defense of Homosexuality." In *We Are Everywhere: A Historical Sourcebook of Gay and Lesbian Politics*, edited by Mark Blasius and Shane Phelan, 220–227. New York: Routledge, 1997.

———. Information sheet for Contacts. N.d. bF. Box 8, folder 9.

———. Letter to Dorr Legg, May 11, 1965. OIR. Box 25, folder 113.

———. Letter to Dorr Legg, August 19, 1965. OIR. Box 25, folder 113.

———. Letter to Frank McCourt, April 25, 1944. bF. Box 1, folder 13.

———. Letter to Frank McCourt, June 20, 1945. bF. Box 1, folder 15.

———. Letter to Manuel boyFrank, January 22, 1940. bF Box 4, folder 29.

———. Letter to Manual boyFrank, January 27, 1940. bF. Box 1, folder 13.

———. Letter to Manuel boyFrank, February 2, 1940. bF. Box 1, folder 13.

———. Letter to Manuel boyFrank, February 19, 1940. bF. Box 1, folder 13.

———. Letter to Manuel boyFrank, March 27, 1941. bF. Box 4, folder 29.

———. Letter to Manuel boyFrank, January 4, 1944. bF. Box 1, folder 15.

———. Letter to Manuel boyFrank, February 20, 1944. bF. Box 1, folder 13.

———. Letter to Manuel boyFrank, March 12, 1944. bF. Box 1, folder 13.

———. Letter to Manuel boyFrank, April 12, 1944. bF. Box 1, folder 19.

———. Letter to Manuel boyFrank, March 19, 1944. bF. Box 1, folder 13.

———. Letter to Manuel boyFrank, March 28, 1944. bF. Box 1, folder 13.

———. Letter to Manuel boyFrank, April 14, 1944. bF. Box 1, folder 19.

———. Letter to Manuel boyFrank, April 20, 1944. bF. Box 1, folder 19.

———. Letter to Manuel boyFrank, April 25, 1944. bF. Box 1, folder 13.

————. Letter to Manuel boyFrank, May 25, 1944. bF. Box 1, folder 14.

————. Letter to Manuel boyFrank, August 5, 1944: bF. Box 1, folder 14.

————. Letter to Manuel boyFrank, August 9, 1944. bF. Box 1, folder 19.

————. Letter to Manuel boyFrank, September 25, 1944. bF. Box 1, folder 14.

————. Letter to Manuel boyFrank, December 3, 1944. bF. Box 1, folder 13.

————. Letter to Manuel boyFrank, January 4, 1945. GS. Box 25, folder 3.

————. Letter to Manuel boyFrank, February 8, 1945. bF. Box 1, folder 15.

————. Letter to Manuel boyFrank, March 6, 1945. bF. Box 1, folder 15.

————. Letter to Manuel boyFrank, April 16, 1945. bF. Box 1, folder 15.

————. Letter to Manuel boyFrank, June 20, 1945. bF. Box 1, folder 15.

————. Letter to Manuel boyFrank, June 22, 1945. bF. Box 1, folder 16.

————. Letter to Manuel boyFrank, July 5, 1945. bF. Box 1, folder 15.

————. Letter to Manuel boyFrank, October 23, 1945. bF. Box 1, folder 15.

————. Letter to Manuel boyFrank, February 18, 1946. bF. Box 1, folder 16.

————. Letter to Manuel boyFrank, March 26, 1946. bF. Box 1, folder 16.

————. Letter to Manuel boyFrank, June 22, 1946. bF. Box 1, folder 16.

————. Letter to Manuel boyFrank, July 9, 1946. bF. Box 1, folder 22.

————. Letter to Manuel boyFrank, September 6, 1946. bF. Box 1, folder 17.

————. Letter to Manuel boyFrank, December 7, 1946. bF. Box 1, folder 16.

————. Letter to Manuel boyFrank, August 9, 1947. bF. Box 1, folder 17.

————. Letter to Manuel boyFrank, September 6, 1947. bF. Box 1, folder 17.

————. Letter to Manuel boyFrank, September 15, 1947. bF. Box 1, folder 17.

————. Letter to Manuel boyFrank, December 25, 1947. bF. Box 1, folder 17.

————. Letter to Manuel boyFrank, September 27, 1948. bF. Box 1, folder 18.

————. Letter to Manuel boyFrank, June 18, 1957. bF. Box 1, folder 18.

————. Letter to Manuel boyFrank, August 31, 1957. bF. Box 1, folder 18.

————. Letter to Manuel boyFrank, n.d. ["Thanks for your interesting letter."] bF. Box 4, folder 29.

————. Letter to ONE Inc., August 12, 1954. OIR. Box 25, folder 113.

————. Letter to ONE Inc., May 27, 1965. OIR. Box 25, folder 113.

————. Letter to ONE Inc., October 29, 1965. OIR. Box 25, folder 113.

————. Letter to ONE Inc., January 17, 1966. OIR. Box 25, folder 113.

————. Letter to [J.D. Nobel], n.d. PR. Box 6, folder 12.

————. Letter to superintendent of mails. April 1, 1924. GS. Box 25, folder 4.

————. [Voluntary Nonparent, pseud.]. Letter to the editor. *American Mercury*, April 9, 1944. bF. Box 1, folder 23.

————. [H.G., pseud.]. Letter to the editor. *Mattachine Review*, April 1956, 39.

——. [H.G., pseud.]. Letter to the editor. *National Defense*, September 15, 1947. bF. Box 1, folder 20.

——. [G.S., pseud.]. Letter to the editor. *ONE* magazine, July 1953, 22. OIMC. Box 2, folder 24.

——. [Pro Domo, pseud.]. Letter to the editor. *Time*, April 5, 1944. bF. Box 1, folder 20.

——. [Tolerant, pseud.]. Letter to the editor. *Times-Herald*, September 4, 1947. bF. Box 1, folder 20.

——. "Love of Solitude Is a Precious Gift." Ad for Contacts. *Saturday Review of Literature*, August 4, 1939, 39.

——. Membership acceptance to 1366 [Manuel boyFrank], April 8, 1935. bF. Box 8, folder 9.

——. "Moral Warfare." *Chanticleer*, October 1934, 6–8.

——. "More Fun than the Theatre." Ad for Contacts. *Saturday Review of Literature*, November 3, 1934, 267.

——. "More Nonsense About Homosexuals." *Chanticleer*, December 1934, 1–3.

——. "A New Deal for Sex." *Chanticleer*, June 1934, 4–6.

——. "Not a Brain Cell in a Carload of Skulls." Ad for Contacts. *Saturday Review of Literature*, March 9, 1935, 543.

——. "On the March, He Says." Letter to the Editor. *Writer's Digest*, July 1954, 11.

——. (Psychoanalyst, pseud.). "A Plea for Sex Sanity." *Washington Post*, n.d. bF. Box 1, folder 20.

——. "Rationalism or Dogma?" *Chanticleer*, November 1934, 7–8.

——. "Recent Homosexual Literature." *Chanticleer*, February 1934, 4–5.

——, trans. "The Role of Homosexual Men and Women in Society." *ONE Institute Quarterly*, Winter/Spring 1963, 22–30.

——. "Sample Descriptions." 1935. ONE. Box 8, folder 9. bF.

——. Self-description for Contacts. N.d. bF. Box 1, folder 22.

——. "The Society for Human Rights: 1925."*ONE*, September 1962, 5–11.

——. "Society Scouting Sex Superstition." March 19, 1944. bF. Box 1, folder 22.

——. "Sodom Rebuilt." [1944–1946.] ONE. Box 1, folder 2. bF.

——. "Sterilization." *Chanticleer*, April 1934, 1–2.

——. "A Study of Pessimism." *Chanticleer*, July 1934, 5–6.

——. "Surrounded by Millions of Cracked Brains." Ad for Contacts. *Saturday Review of Literature*, May 26, 1934, 718.

——. "Die Strafbestimmungen in den 48 Staaten Amerikas und den amerikanischen Territorien für gewisse Geschlechtsakte." *Blätter für Menschenrecht*, August 1929, 5–11.

——. "Tannhaeuser." *Chanticleer*, August 1934, 6–8.

——. "Theism and Atheism Reconciled." *Chanticleer*, January 1934, 3–4.

———. "What Is Atheism?" *Chanticleer*, March 1934, 5–6.

———. "Zwei Dollars oder fünfzehn Jahre Zuchthaus." *Das Freundschaftsblatt* 8 (October 9, 1930): 4.

Gergen, John L. *MFS Bulletin*, January 11, 1943.

G-G Archives. "Camp Grant, World War I Cantonment, A.E.F. Training Center, Illinois," 2019. https://www.gjenvick.com.

Ghosts of D.C. "Murder Victim Admitted His Interest in Men." February 17, 2012. https://ghostsofdc.org/2012/02/17/murder-victim-admitted-his-interest-in-men.

Goldfarb, Kara. "The Lavender Scare: The U.S. Government's Anti-gay Purge." *All That's Interesting*, June 18, 2018. https://allthatsinteresting.com/lavender-scare.

Gonzalez, Donald J. "Police Seek Ex-G.I. in Strange Slaying of Piano Repairman." *Dunkirk (NY) Evening Observer*, June 4, 1946.

Gordon, Mel. *Voluptuous Panic: The Erotic World of Weimar Berlin*. Expanded ed. Venice, CA: Feral House, 2008.

GraduateWay. "Contact Without Friction." July 13, 2017. https://graduateway.com/contact-without-friction.

Graham, Rebecca, and Kisa Hooks. *Historic Context Statement for Washington's LGBTQ Resources*. Washington, DC: District of Columbia, Office of Planning, Historic Preservation Office, 2019.

Grey, Anthony. "To the City by the Lake." *ONE Confidential*, December 1967, 1–5.

Grogan, Stanley J. "Army Publicity and the People: The Chief of the Army Information Service Explains the Function of His Department." *Recruiting News*, December 15, 1931, 13–14.

Habib, Douglas F. "Chastity, Masculinity, and Military Efficiency: The United States Army in Germany, 1918–1923." *International History Review* 28 (December 2006): 643–944.

Hagin, S. Christopher. Letter to Gregory Sprague, December 16, 1982. GS. Box 25, folder 4.

Haller, Stephen A. *Letterman Hospital: A Summary of Its Significance and Integrity*. Washington, DC: Department of the Interior, National Park Service, 1994.

Hamdan, Lara. "Delving Into the History of the Jefferson Barracks Military Post." St. Louis Public Radio, November 12, 2018. https://news.stlpublicradio.org/post/delving-history-jefferson-barracks-military-post#stream/0.

Hamilton, William. "Homosexuality Again." Letter to the editor. *American Mercury*, October 1947, 507.

Harzig, Christiane, "Germans." Encyclopedia of Chicago. Accessed October 4, 2019. http://www.encyclopedia.chicagohistory.org/pages/512.html.

Hatheway, Jay. *Gilded Age Construction of Modern American Homophobia*. New York: Palgrave, 2003.

Hauser, Jacob. "Dedication." *Chanticleer*, January 1934, 1.

Heap, Chad. *Slumming: Sexual and Racial Encounters in American Nightlife, 1885–1940.* Chicago: University of Chicago Press, 2009.

Heatley, Holly S. "'Commies and Queers': Narratives That Supported the Lavender Scare." Master's thesis, Department of History, University of Texas at Arlington, August 2007.

Historic Archives: Nude Male Swimming. "Public Schools, Municipal Pools and YMCA: History of Mandated Nude Swimming." Accessed April 4, 2022. https://sites.google .com/site/historicarchives4maleswimming/home/ii-archives-early-20th-century -after/c-public-schools-municipal-pools-and-ymca-history-of-mandated-nude -swimming.

History.com. "Ellis Island." March 13, 2019. https://www.history.com/topics/immigration /ellis-island.

———. "Prohibition." Accessed April 12, 2014. https://www.history.com/topics/prohibition.

———. "The United States Officially Enters World War I." July 28, 2019. https://www .history.com/this-day-in-history/america-enters-world-war-i.

Hitchcock, Tim, et al. *Proceedings of the Old Bailey: London's Central Criminal Court, 1674–1913*, March 24, 2018. https://www.oldbaileyonline.org.

Hogan, S. Christopher. "File Memorandum, Re: Henry Gerber Arrest (12 July 1925—Chicago)." December 12, 1982. Box 25, folder 4. GS.

Hoover, J. Edgar. "War on the Sex Criminal." *Evening Star*, September 26, 1937.

Horvath, Barton. Ad for *Art in Photography*. bF. Box 1, folder 26.

———. Ad for photographs. *Your Physique*, August 1940, 22.

———. "Catalog G." bF. Box 1, folder 26.

———. Letter to Manuel boyFrank, March 31, 1944. bF. Box 1, folder 26.

Howard, Robert E. Letter to Merlin Wand, May 26, 1928. In *The Collected Letters*, edited by Bobby Derie, 5–7. Robert E. Howard Foundation Press, 2015.

Huggins, Buell Dwight. Letter to Henry Gerber, November 8, 1956. Homophile organizations, Mattachine Society correspondence, January 10, 1955–January 11, 1957. Gay, Lesbian, Bisexual, and Transgender Historical Society, Archives of Sexuality and Gender.

———. Letter to Ken Burns, June 28, 1956. Homophile organizations, Mattachine Society correspondence, January 10, 1955–January 11, 1957. Gay, Lesbian, Bisexual, and Transgender Historical Society, Archives of Sexuality and Gender. Accessed February 23, 2021.

———. Letter to Samuel D. Morford, November 6, 1956. Enclosure. Mattachine Society, Washington, DC, chapter by-laws. Homophile organizations, Mattachine Society Correspondence, January 10, 1955–January 11, 1957. Gay, Lesbian, Bisexual, and Transgender Historical Society, Archives of Sexuality and Gender.

Hughes, Edward J. Memo to Otto Kerner, November 16, 1936. Dissolved Domestic Corporation Charters, May 1, 1849–March 7, 1980. SHR. Record series 103.112, Corporations, box 1783, no. 125058.

Humphries, Roy. Did You Know That—. *U.S. Army Recruiting News*, June 1, 1931, 15.

Investigations Subcommittee, Committee on Expenditures in the Executive Departments. *Report of the Proceedings, 14 July 1950.* Washington, DC: Ward and Paul, 1950. https://www.docsteach.org/documents/document/statement-hoey-committee.

Jackson, Gregory. "Cons Stiff Screws!" *Brevities*, February 12, 1934, 1, 12.

Jenkins, Philip. *Moral Panic: Changing Concepts of the Child Molester in Modern America.* New Haven, CT: Yale University Press, 1998.

Jersey Journal. "Accused of Mailing Obscene Pictures." November 2, 1944.

Johnson, David K. *The Lavender Scare: The Cold War Persecution of Gays and Lesbians in the Federal Government.* Chicago: University of Chicago Press, 2004.

———. "Physique Pioneers: The Politics of 1960s Gay Consumer Culture." *Journal of Social History* 43 (Summer 2010): 867–892.

Justus, Jeremy C. "Personals." Encyclopedia.com. Accessed April 18, 2020. https://www.encyclopedia.com/social-sciences/encyclopedias-almanacs-transcripts-and-maps/personals.

Katz, Jonathan Ned. *Gay American History: Lesbians and Gay Men in the U.S.A., a Documentary History.* Rev. ed. New York: Meridian, 1992.

Kaye, Kerwin. "Male Prostitution in the Twentieth Century." *Journal of Homosexuality* 46, nos. 1/2 (2003): 1–77.

Kellogg, Walter Guest. *The Conscientious Objector.* New York: Boni & Liveright, 1919.

Kennedy, Hubert. *The Ideal Gay Man: The Story of "Der Kreis."* New York: Routledge, 1999.

Kepner, Jim. "A Brief Chronology of Gay/Lesbian History." Part 12: The Movement Redefined. JK. Box 22, folder 2.

———. "A Brief Gay and Lesbian Who's Who and Who Was Who," F–G, circa 1993–1994. JK. Box 15, folder 11.

———. "Goals, Progress & Shortcomings of America's Gay Movement." 1993. JK. Box 24, folder 30.

———. "Henry Gerber, Forerunner of America's Homophile Movement from 1925–1972." Program for ONE's 1978 Midwinter Institute: A Search for Our Roots: Gay Life and Liberation, 1860–1960. *ONEletter*, January 1978, 3–4.

———. "Henry Gerber: Grandfather of America's Gay Movement." N.d. JK. Box 16, folder 1.

———. Letter to Jonathan Ned Katz, January 21, 1974. JK. Box 49, folder 11.

———. Letter to Jonathan Ned Katz, January 31, 1974. JK. Box 49, folder 11.

———. Letter to Jonathan Ned Katz, March 4, 1974. JK. Box 49, folder 11.

———. Letter to Jonathan Ned Katz, March 11, 1974. JK. Box 49, folder 11.

——. Letter to Jonathan Ned Katz, March 19, 1974. JK. Box 49, folder 11.

——. Letter to Jonathan Ned Katz, May 9, 1974. JK. Box 49, folder 11.

——. "Monwell boyFrank: 1899–1982." 1982: 3. JK. Box 15, folder 19.

——. "My First 66 Years of Gay Liberation: 1923–1932." N.d. JK. Box 5, folder 1.

——. "*ONE Magazine*, Started in January 1953." N.d. JK. Box 9, folder 17.

——. "Partial Inventory of Gerber-boyFrank Correspondence, Excluding Some Before 1940 and Some After 1948, Not Yet Checked." N.d. bF. Box 1, folder 31.

——. "Those Who Forget History . . . .," April 21, 1974. JK. Box 26, folder 25.

——. "Who Founded America's Gay Movement?" *Entertainment West*, Summer 1974, 3, 9–10.

Kepner, Jim, and Stephen O. Murray. "Henry Gerber (1895–1972): Grandfather of the American Gay Movement." In *Before Stonewall: Activists for Gay and Lesbian Rights in Historical Context*, edited by Vernon Bullough, 24–34. New York: Haworth, 2002.

Keyes, Jonathan J. "Lexington Hotel." Encyclopedia of Chicago, 2004. http://www.encyclopedia.chicagohistory.org/pages/738.html.

King, Gilbert. "The 'Latin Lover' and His Enemies." *Smithsonian*, June 13, 2012. https://www.smithsonianmag.com/history/the-latin-lover-and-his-enemies-119968944.

Kinsey Institute. "Dr. Alfred C. Kinsey." Accessed February 26, 2021. https://kinseyinstitute.org/about/history/alfred-kinsey.php.

Kosar, Andy, and Jan Todd. "*Physical Fitness* Magazine: Why Did It Fail?" *Iron Game History*, December 1998, 8–11.

Krajicek, David J. "Summer of Pervert Hysteria: 1937." *New York Daily News*, July 18, 2009. https://www.nydailynews.com/news/crime/summer-pervert-hysteria-1937-article-1.396521.

Kroupa, Joseph J. Affidavit, July 18, 1956. Dissolved domestic corporation charters, May 1, 1849–March 7, 1980. SHR. Record series 103.112, Corporations, box 1783, no. 125058.

Lait, Jack, and Lee Mortimer. *Washington Confidential*. New York: Crown, 1951.

Landmarks Preservation Commission. "Designation Report: [Bryant Park]." November 12, 1974. LP-0979. http://neighborhoodpreservationcenter.org/db/bb_files/BRYANT-PARK.pdf.

Lane, John D. "Homosexuality Again." Letter to the editor. *American Mercury*, October 1947, 506–507.

Lee, Cynthia. "The Gay Panic Defense." *University of California—Davis Law Review* 42 (2008): 471–566.

Legg, Dorr. Editorial. *ONE Institute Quarterly, Homophile Studies*, Spring/Summer/Fall 1962, 40.

——. Letter to Henry Gerber, May 19, 1965. OIR. Box 25, folder 113.

——. Letter to Henry Gerber, January 20, 1966. OIR. Box 25, folder 113.

Leider, Emily Wortis. *Dark Lover: The Life and Death of Rudolph Valentino*. New York: Faber, 2003.

Library and Archives, Hoover Institution, Stanford University. Accessed November 17, 2020. https://digitalcollections.hoover.org/objects/35137/become-a-paratrooper -jump-into-the-fight-soldiers-between.

Lim, Kay M., and Julie Kracov, producers. "The Lavender Scare: How the Federal Government Purged Gay Employees." CBS News, June 9, 2019. https://www .cbsnews.com/news/the-lavender-scare-how-the-federal-government-purged-gay -employees.

Lindenauer, Leslie J. "Kinsey Report." Encyclopedia.com, February 26, 2021. https:// www.encyclopedia.com/history/dictionaries-thesauruses-pictures-and-press-releases /kinsey-report.

Literature Network. "Bertha Klausner, Literary Agent." Accessed August 19, 2020. http:// www.online-literature.com/article/upton_sinclair/19608.

Lorenz, Francis S. Memo to Charles F. Carpentier, December 4, 1957. "Dissolved Domestic Corporation Charters, May 1, 1849–March 7, 1980." SHR. Record series 103.112, Corporations, box 1783, no. 125058.

Loughery, John. *The Other Side of Silence: Men's Lives and Gay Identities; A Twentieth-Century History*. New York: Holt, 1998.

Lurie, Jonathan. "'Heaven, Hell, or Hoboken': Anti-German Sentiment in Hoboken, 1917–1918, Some Examples." *NJS: An Interdisciplinary Journal*, Winter 2018, 12–23.

Lvovsky, Anna. "Queer Expertise: Urban Policing and the Construction of Public Knowledge About Homosexuality, 1920–1970." PhD diss., Graduate School of Arts and Sciences, Harvard University, 2015.

Magnus-Hirschfeld-Gesellschaft e.V. "The First Institute for Sexual Science (1919–1933)." Accessed December 9, 2019. https://magnus-hirschfeld.de/ausstellungen /institute.

Marhoefer, Laurie. *Sex and the Weimar Republic: German Homosexual Emancipation and the Rise of the Nazis*. Toronto, ON: University of Toronto Press, 2015.

Martin, John Swallow. "Third Sex Plague Spreads Anew!" *New Broadway Brevities*, November 2, 1931, 1, 12.

Masters, Nathan. "Culver City: From Barley Fields to the Heart of Screenland." *Lost L.A.*, June 6, 2012. https://www.kcet.org/shows/lost-la/culver-city-from-barley-fields-to -the-heart-of-screenland.

Mattachine Review. Letter from the editor to H.G. [Henry Gerber], April 1956, 39.

Mattachine Society of Washington, DC. "Executive Order 10450." Deviant's Trove. Accessed February 27, 2021. https://mattachinesocietywashingtondc.files .wordpress.com/2016/04/exhibit-01-executive-order-number-10450.pdf.

McConville, Capt. Joseph J. Memo to Capt. W. H. Sadler, February 12, 1923. Headquarters, American Forces in Germany, Office of the Port Officer.

McCourt, Frank. Ad for Rocketeers. *Weird Tales*, July 1942, 127.

———. Letter to Al, March 1. bF. Box 1, folder 36.

———. Letter to Henry Gerber, April 22 1944. bF. Box 1, folder 36.

———. Letter to Manuel boyFrank, January 30, 1940. bF. Box 1, folder 33.

———. Letter to Manuel boyFrank, February 1, 1940. bF. Box 1, folder 33.

———. Letter to Manuel boyFrank, February 7, 1940. bF. Box 1, folder 33.

———. Letter to Manuel boyFrank, February 11, 1940. bF. Box 1, folder 33.

———. Letter to Manuel boyFrank, February 20, 1940. bF. Box 1, folder 33.

———. Letter to Manuel boyFrank, March 3, 1940. bF. Box 1, folder 33.

———. Letter to Manuel boyFrank, July 19, 1940. bF. Box 1, folder 33.

———. Letter to Manuel boyFrank, September 21, 1940. bF. Box 1, folder 33.

———. Letter to Manuel boyFrank, October 8, 1940. bF. Box 1, folder 33.

———. Letter to Manuel boyFrank, March 16, 1941. bF. Box 1, folder 33.

———. Letter to Manuel boyFrank, January 24, 1942. bF. Box 1, folder 33.

———. Letter to Manuel boyFrank, July 17, 1942. bF. Box 1, folder 33.

———. Letter to Manuel boyFrank, June 4, 1943. bF. Box 1, folder 35.

———. Letter to Manuel boyFrank, August 15, 1943. bF. Box 1, folder 34.

———. Letter to Manuel boyFrank, October 7, 1944. bF. Box 1, folder 34.

———. Letter to Manuel boyFrank, January 5, 1945. bF. Box 1, folder 34.

———. Letter to Manuel boyFrank, January 26, 1945, 2. BF. Box 1, folder 34.

———. Letter to Manuel boyFrank, January 29, 1945. bF. Box 1, folder 34.

———. Letter to Manuel boyFrank, June 4, 1947. bF. Box 1, folder 35.

———. Letter to Manuel boyFrank, n.d. ["Had the heat turned on yesterday"]. bF. Box 1, folder 34.

———. Letter to Manuel boyFrank, n.d. ["Midway in a reply to Walter S's. latest"]. bF. Box 1, folder 34.

———. Letter to Manuel to boyFrank, n.d. ["So far unable to do more than sample"]. bF. Box 1, folder 34.

———. "Rocketeers: Members of the United States Rocket Society." N.d. bF. Box 5, folder 15.

———. Self-description for Contacts. N.d. bF. Box 1, folder 32.

———. "Supplement to the October Address List." N.d. bF. Box 5, folder 15.

McDonald, Alva L. "Dan, the Old Timer." *Recruiting News*, October 1, 1923, 11.

McDonough, Joseph J. Memo to Charles F. Carpentier. November 12, 1964. "Dissolved Domestic Corporation Charters, May 1, 1849–March 7, 1980." SHR. Record series 103.112, Corporations, Box 1783, no. 125058.

Milne, Andrew. "How the Hays Code Censored Hollywood but Led to the Golden Age of Film." July 17, 2019. *All That's Interesting.* https://allthatsinteresting.com/hays-code.

Morgan, Kyle. "Timeline of Events." In *Finding Aid of the ONE, Incorporated Records, 1907–2001, Bulk 1952–1994.* Accessed February 23, 2021. https://oac.cdlib.org/findaid/ark:/13030/kt7290389h/entire_text.

Morris, Charles E., III. "Pink Herring & the Fourth Persona: J. Edgar Hoover's Sex Crime Panic." *Quarterly Journal of Speech* 88 (May 2002): 228–244.

Mullins, Greg. "Nudes, Prudes, and Pigmies: The Desirability of Disavowal in 'Physical Culture.'" *Discourse* 15 (Fall 1992): 27–48.

Myers, Quinn. "Chicago's Dill Pickle Club: Where Anarchists Mixed with Doctors and Poets." *Curious City.* Podcast audio and transcript, February 2, 2019. https://www.wbez.org/shows/curious-city/chicagos-dill-pickle-club-where-anarchists-mixed-with-doctors-and-poets/bb4c1400-197c-4746-9130-c4ea91f79a0d.

National Archives at College Park, MD. "List of United States Citizens (for the Immigration Authorities)," February 21, 1923. Records of the Office of the Quartermaster General, 1774–1985. Record group no. 92. Roll or box no. 107.

———. "Passenger List: Overseas Casual Detachment #47." *Records of the Office of the Quartermaster General, 1774–1985.* Record group no. 92. Roll or box no. 67.

———. "Passenger List of Organizations and Casuals Returning to the United States," February 21, 1923. *Records of the Office of the Quartermaster General, 1774–1985.* Record group no. 92. Roll or box no. 107.

———. "Special Orders, No. 22: Extract." February 5, 1923. *Records of the Office of the Quartermaster General, 1774–1985*; Record group no. 92. Roll or box no. 67.

———. "Special Orders, No. 22: Extract." February 5, 1923. *Records of the Office of the Quartermaster General, 1774–1985.* Record group no. 92. Roll or box no. 107.

National Park Service. "Prisoners on Governors Island." Governors Island, National Monument, New York, February 26, 2015. https://www.nps.gov/gois/learn/historyculture/prisoners.htm.

Neff, Edwin. "2 Doctors Urge Long Sentences for Sex Perverts." *Times-Herald* (Washington, DC), July 4, 1946. Clipping in Henry Gerber to Manuel boyFrank, July 9, 1946. bF. Box 1, folder 22.

New, Zachary R. "Ending Citizenship for Service in the Forever Wars." *Yale Law Journal* 129 (February 11, 2020): 552–566. https://www.yalelawjournal.org/forum/ending-citizenship-for-service-in-the-forever-wars.

New Masses. "Contact Without Friction." December 1927, 29.

New York City Landmarks Preservation Commission. *Governors Island Historic District Designation Report.* June 18, 1996.

Newberry. "The Old Man's Draft." July 21, 2012. https://www.newberry.org/old-mans-draft.

Newsweek. "Queer People." October 10, 1949, 52.

Newton, Michael. "Tucker, Ray." In *The FBI Encyclopedia*, 342. Jefferson, NC: McFarland, 2003.

Niagara Falls Gazette. "Falls Policeman's Memory Brings About Capture of Washington Murder Suspect." June 14, 1946, 1–2.

Nobel, J. D. Letter to Henry Gerber. March 16, 1936. PR. Box 6, folder 12.

NYC LGBT Historic Sites Project. *Historic Context Statement for LGBT History in New York City.* Edited by Kathleen Howe and Kathleen LaFrank. New York: National Park Service and New York State Office of Parks, Recreation, and Historic Preservation, 2018.

Nye, Logan. "Here's How Much U.S. Troops Were Paid in Every American War." *Business Insider*, March 7, 2018. https://www.businessinsider.com/how-much-us-troops-were-paid-in-every-american-war-2018-3.

O'Brien, Booker, and John D. Fair. "'As the Twig Is Bent': Bob Hoffman and Youth Training in the Pre-Stonewall Era." *Iron Game History*, August 2012, 28–51.

Official Gazette of the United States Patent Office. July 5, 1932.

———. May 11, 1937.

Olszewski, George J. *Lafayette Park, Washington, D.C.* Washington, DC: US National Park Service, Department of the Interior, 1964.

ONE Archives at the USC Libraries. "*Mattachine Review.*" Accessed March 3, 2021. https://one.usc.edu/archive-location/one-magazine.

———. "*ONE* Magazine." 2018. https://one.usc.edu/archive-location/one-magazine.

ONE Calendar. "A Bold Pioneer of Gay Liberation." March 1987. OIR. Box 16, folder 22.

ONE Confidential. "To the Friends of ONE." October 1967, 1–2.

ONE 30 Year Celebration. "In Memoriam." Los Angeles: ONE Inc., 1982. LM. Box 20, folder 25.

ONEletter. "Baker Memorial Library." November 1983, 5–6.

———. Program for "ONE's 1978 Midwinter Institute: A Search for Our Roots, Gay Life and Liberation, 1860–1960." January 1978, 1–5.

O'Toole, James J. Notary Public Form, December 8, 1924. "Dissolved Domestic Corporation Charters, May 1, 1849–March 7, 1980." SHR. Record series 103.112, Corporations, box 1783, no. 125058.

Oxford English Dictionary: The Definitive Record of the English Language. 3rd ed. Oxford: Oxford University Press, 2020. https://www.oed.com.

Padden, Frank M. Order. July 20, 1956. "Dissolved Domestic Corporation Charters, May 1, 1849–March 7, 1980." SHR. Record series 103.112, Corporations, box 1783, no. 125058.

Painter, George. "District of Columbia." The Sensibilities of Our Forefathers: The History of Sodomy Laws in the United States, last updated January 31, 2005. https://www.glapn.org/sodomylaws/sensibilities/districtofcolumbia.htm.

———. "Illinois," The Sensibilities of Our Forefathers: Sodomy Laws in the United States, last updated August 10, 2004. https://www.glapn.org/sodomylaws/sensibilities/illinois.htm.

———. "New York." The Sensibilities of Our Forefathers: The History of Sodomy Laws in the United States, last updated August 10, 2004. https://www.glapn.org/sodomylaws/sensibilities/new_york.htm.

Paschall, Harry B. "'Let Me Tell You a Fairy Tale.'" Strength and Health, October 1957, 61. http://musclememory.com/articles/fairyTale.html.

Paterson, Tony. "Revealed: The Forgotten Secrets of Stalingrad." Independent, November 5, 2012. https://www.independent.co.uk/news/world/world-history/revealed-forgottensecrets-stalingrad-8282751.html.

Pawtucket Times. "Head of Anti-vice Squad Tells About His Orders to 'Clean Up Newport.'" April 7, 1920.

Plater, J. W. Physician's certificate. April 19, 1924. GS. Box 25, folder 4.

Pleck, Elizabeth. Domestic Tyranny: The Making of American Social Policy Against Family Violence from Colonial Times to the Present. Chicago: University of Illinois Press, 2004.

Polchin, James. Indecent Advances: A Hidden History of True Crime and Prejudice Before Stonewall. Berkeley, CA: Counterpoint, 2019.

Pollack, Benjamin, and Janice Todd. "Before Charles Atlas: Earle Liederman, the 1920s King of Mail-Order Muscle." Journal of Sport History 44 (Fall 2017): 399–420.

Popular Science. Ad for US Rocket Society. March 1945, 41.

Qu, Anna. Queer Expertise: Urban Policing and the Construction of Public Knowledge About Homosexuality, 1920–1970. PhD diss., Graduate School of Arts and Sciences, Harvard University, 2015.

Raven-Hart, Roland. Down the Mississippi. Boston: Houghton-Mifflin, 1938.

Reay, Barry. New York Hustlers: Masculinity and Sex in Modern America. New York: Manchester University Press, 2010.

Reckless, Walter. "Natural History of Vice Areas in Chicago." PhD diss., University of Chicago, 1925.

Recruiting News. "Some of the Advantages of Being a Soldier." November 15, 1923.

Reed, Alfred C. "Going Through Ellis Island." Popular Science Monthly, January 1913. https://www.gjenvick.com/Immigration/EllisIsland/1913-01-ImmigrantsGoing ThroughEllisIsland.html.

Richeson, Voorheis. "The United States Soldiers' Home." *Army Recruitment News*, January 1, 1937, 6–7, 18.

Rogan, Clare I. "'Good Nude Photographs:' Images for Desire in Weimar Germany's Lesbian Journals." In *Tribades, Tommies and Transgressives; Hisotries of Sexualities*, edited by Mary McAuliffe and Sonja Tiernan, 145–161. Vol. 1. Newcastle, UK: Cambridge Scholars, 2008.

Roloff, Bernard C. Letter to Chicago Post Office. April 26, 1924. GS. Box 25, folder 4.

Ryan, Hugh. "Inventing, and Policing, the Homosexual in Early 20th C. NYC." *Gotham Center for New York City History* (blog), April 4, 2017. https://www.gothamcenter.org /blog/inventing-and-policing-the-homosexual-in-early-20th-c-nyc.

———. *When Brooklyn Was Queer*. New York: St. Martin's, 2019.

Ryan, John A. Letter to the editor. *American Mercury*, April 1944, 504–505.

Sangaramoorthy, Thurka. "'The Hilton of Migrant Camps'—Westover Labor Camp, Somerset County, MD." August 15, 2014. https://www.thurkasangaramoorthy .com/2014814westover-migrant-camp-somerset-county-md.

Schafer, Walter. Letter to Frank McCourt, February 26, 1945. bF. Box 1, folder 34.

———. Letter to Frank McCourt, n.d. ["This letter is for yourself"]. bF. Box 1, folder 34.

Schlaeger, Victor L. Memo to Edward J. Hughes, June 7, 1937. "Dissolved Domestic Corporation Charters, May 1, 1849–March 7, 1980." SHR. Record series 103.112, Corporations, box 1783, no. 125058.

Schulz, Dana. "Kleindeutschland: The History of the East Village's Little Germany." 6sqft (website), October 2, 2014. https://www.6sqft.com/kleindeutschland-the-history-of -the-east-villages-little-germany.

Schultz, Fred. "Fags Ram Heinies!" *Brevities*, September 19, 1932, 1–12.

Sears, James T. *Behind the Mask of the Mattachine: The Hal Call Chronicles and the Early Movement for Homosexual Emancipation*. Kindle ed. Binghamton, NY: Haworth, 2006.

Segura, Gonzalo. Letter to Dale Olson, August 14, 1956. New York Area Correspondence, Mattachine Society, Call Papers.

Shank, Patrick. "Dougherty's Movie Boycott." Catholic Historical Research Center of the Archdiocese of Philadelphia, February 6, 2019. https://chrc-phila.org/doughertys -movie-boycott.

Shibuyama, Loni. "*Mattachine Review*." *Finding Aid of the Mattachine Society Project Collection*. ONE: National Gay and Lesbian Archives, 2015. https://oac.cdlib .org/findaid/ark:/13030/kt7w1035mz/dsc/?query=Mattachine%20Review;dsc .position=1#hitNum7.

Shilts, Randy. *Conduct Unbecoming: Gays and Lesbians in the U.S. Military*. New York: St. Martin's Griffin, 1994.

Shockley, Jay, Amanda Davis, Ken Lustbader, and Andrw Dolkart. "Historic Context Statement for LGBT History in New York City." NYC LGBT Historic Sites Project, May 2018. http://www.nyclgbtsites.org/wp-content/uploads/2018/11/NYC_LGBT _Sites_Context_Statement_102618_web-compressed1.pdf.

Smith, Alson J. *Chicago's Left Bank*. Chicago: Henry Regnery, 1953.

Somerville, Siobhan. "Scientific Racism and the Emergence of the Homosexual Body." *Journal of the History of Sexuality* 5 (October 1994): 243–266.

Sprague, "On the 'Gay Side' of Town." 1983. GS. Box 5, folder 12.

———. "60th Anniversary of the First U.S. Gay Rights Organization." [1984.] GS. Box 25, folder 2.

Stanley, Jay. "Fags Tickle Nudes." *Brevities*, November 23, 1933, 1, 12.

Stein, Marc. *City of Sisterly and Brotherly Loves: Lesbian and Gay Philadelphia, 1945–1972*. Philadelphia: Temple University Press 2004.

Stibbe, Matthew. "Enemy Aliens and Internment." International Encyclopedia of the First World War, October 8, 2014. https://encyclopedia.1914-1918-online.net /article/enemy_aliens_and_internment.

Straw, Will. "Remembering the Creator of Modern Gossip Journalism." HuffPost Canada, updated February 8, 2017. https://www.huffingtonpost.ca/will-straw-phd/gossip -king-stephen-g-clow_b_9169414.html.

———. "Traffic in Scandal: The Story of *Broadway Brevities*." *University of Toronto Quarterly* 73 (Fall 2004): 947–971.

Strength and Health. "Iron Grapevine." October 1957, 61.

———. "Physique Poses." August 1939, 44.

———. "*S & H* Leaguers' Page." Multiple Classified Advertisements. Archives of Sexuality and Gender. Gale Primary Sources, 2020.

Strub, Whitney. "In Hispanic Heritage Month, Let's Remember Gay Rights Pioneer Tony Segura." *Slate*, October 10, 2016. https://slate.com/human-interest/2016/10 /tony-segura-may-have-been-the-most-important-early-gay-rights-organizer.html.

Suffolk News-Herald. "D.C. Student Hangs Self." July 2, 1946.

Sutherland, Edwin H. "The Diffusion of Sexual Psychopath Laws." *American Journal of Sociology* 56 (September 1950): 142–147.

T. [pseud.]. Letter to the editor. *ONE*, December 1962, 32.

Tadic, Nenad. "A Look Back at Al Capone's Former HQ, the Lexington Hotel." Curbed Chicago. March 26, 2014. https://chicago.curbed.com/2014/3/26/10125808/a-look -back-at-al-capones-former-hq-the-lexington-hotel.

Tamagne, Florence. *A History of Homosexuality in Europe*. Vol. 1, *Berlin, London, Paris, 1919–1939*. New York: Algora, 2004.

Tatchell, Peter. "This Week in History: Sex Scientist Magnus Hirschfeld." *People's World*, May 14, 2018. https://www.peoplesworld.org/article/this-week-in-history -sex-scientist-magnus-hirschfeld.

Taylor, Michael Thomas. "Magnus Hirschfeld's Institute for Sexual Science as Archive, Museum, and Exhibition." In *Not Straight from Germany: Sexual Publics and Sexual Citizenship Since Magnus Hirschfeld*, edited by Michael Thomas Taylor, Annette F. Timm, and Rainer Herrn, 12–36. Ann Arbor: University of Michigan Press, 2017.

Terry, Jennifer. *An American Obsession: Science, Medicine, and Homosexuality in Modern Society*. Chicago: University Chicago Press, 1999.

Theoharis, Athan, ed. *From the Secret Files of J. Edgar Hoover*. Chicago: Ivan R. Dee, 1993.

———. *J. Edgar Hoover, Sex, and Crime: An Historical Antidote*. Chicago, Ivan R. Dee, 1995.

Thomas, Gwyn, and Jack Batten. "Wife Killer—or Fall Guy?" *Maclean's*, July 3, 1965, 20, 38–39.

Thompson, Frank. "The Perfect Man: The Adonis Without Steroids." *All Things Wildly Considered* (blog), July 15, 2014. https://allthingswildlyconsidered.blogspot .com/2014/07/the-perfect-man-adonis-without-steroids.html.

Time. "The Lonergan Case. April 3, 1944, 68–70.

Tobin, Robert. "On Research Trip, Professor Explores Rich History of LGBTQ Life in Berlin." *Clark Now*, August 11, 2016. https://clarknow.clarku.edu/2016/08/11 /on-research-trip-professor-explores-rich-history-of-lgbtq-life-in-berlin.

Toledo, Charlotte N. "She Would Not Be Silenced: Mae West's Struggle Against Censorship." *Downtown Review* 3, no. 2 (December 2016): 1–8. https://engagedscholarship .csuohio.edu/cgi/viewcontent.cgi?article=1050&context=tdr.

Trenton Evening Times. Weather forecast, July 12, 1920.

Tucker, Ray. "Hist! Who's That?" *Collier's*, August 19, 1933, 15, 49

United States Transport. "Detachment 1st Infantry Unassigned: SS *Thomas*," March 12, 1914. Records of the Office of the Quartermaster General, 1774–1985. Record group no. 92. Roll or box no. 591. National Archives at College Park, MD.

———. "Enlisted Men Sick in Hospital: SS *Logan*." February 5, 1915. Records of the Office of the Quartermaster General, 1774–1985. Record group no. 92. Roll or box no. 478. National Archives at College Park, MD.

University of Michigan. *Henry Gerber House*. Public History Initiative. Ann Arbor, MI: National Historic Landmark Program, December 12, 2014.

University of Michigan Health. "Stages of Syphilis. September 11, 2018. https://www .uofmhealth.org/health-library/tm6404.

Upham, J. H. J. "Catholics and Birth Control." *American Mercury*, February 1944, 157–164.

US Army Recruiting Publicity Bureau. "U.S. Army Recruiting Stations." New York: Recruiting Publicity Bureau, n.d.

US Bureau of Labor Statistics. CPI Inflation Calculator. https://www.bls.gov/data/inflation_calculator.htm.

US Capitol Visitor Center. *Nurses Are Needed Now!* poster. May 20, 1944. https://www.visitthecapitol.gov/exhibitions/artifact/army-recruiting-poster-nurses-are-needed-now-stu-l-savage-1944.

US Department of the Interior, National Park Service. "Army and Navy YMCA." National Register of Historic Places Registration Form [1988]. Accessed December 17, 2019. http://www.preservation.ri.gov/pdfs_zips_downloads/national_pdfs/newport/newp_washington-square-50_army-and-navy-ymca.pdf.

———. *Historic American Buildings Survey: Governor's Island, Infantry Regimental Barracks.* Washington, DC: National Park Service, October 1984. http://lcweb2.loc.gov/master/pnp/habshaer/ny/ny1500/ny1504/data/ny1504data.pdf.

———. "LGBT History on Governors Island." Governors Island. 26 F. 2015. Accessed April 15, 2020. https://www.nps.gov/gois/learn/historyculture/henry-gerber.htm.

———. National Register of Historic Places Inventory: Nomination Form for Federal Properties. Accessed April 19, 2020. https://www.gvshp.org/_gvshp/resources/doc/SNR_CSPO.pdf.

US House of Representatives Committee on the District of Columbia. "Table 9: Tabulation of Subjects in the Sex Perversion Elimination Program for the Period of October 1, 1947 to December 31, 1948." In *Home Rule and Reorganization in the District of Columbia: Hearings.* Washington, DC: Government Printing Office, 1949.

US Post Office, Chicago, IL, Lake View Station. "Record of Employe." August 23, 1923. GS. Box 25, folder 4.

———. "Statement of Employe's Record." October 1, 1924. GS. Box 25, folder 4.

———. "Statement of Employe's Record." April 15, 1925. GS. Box 25, folder 4.

———. ["Salary History."] https://twitter.com/StLouisArchives/status/875077875476692992.

———. "Oath of Post Office Employee." August 23, 1923. GS. Box 25, folder 4.

———. "Statement of Employe's Record." October 1, 1924. GS. Box 25, folder 4.

———. "Statement of Employe's Record." April 15, 1925. GS. Box 25, folder 4.

US Senate. *Policy Concerning Homosexuality in the Armed Forces.* Washington, DC: Committee on Armed Services, 1994, 14.

US Senate Committee on Expenditures in the Executive Departments. *Employment of Homosexuals and Other Sex Perverts in Government.* Washington, DC: Government Printing Office, 1950.

US Senate Committee on Naval Affairs. Report. *Alleged Immoral Conditions at Newport (R.I.) Naval Training Station. Sixty-Seventh Congress, First Session.* Washington, DC: Government Printing Office, 1921.

US Selective Service System. "Conscientious Objection and Alternative Service." Selective Service System, 2019. https://www.sss.gov/consobj.

US Statutes at Large. Vol. 55, pt. 1. Washington, DC: Government Printing Office, 1942. https://tile.loc.gov/storage-services/service/ll/llsl//llsl-c77s1/llsl-c77s1.pdf.

US Surgeon-General's Office. Medicine in the Americas, 1610–1920. Vol. 7, The Medical Department of the United States Army in the World War. Washington, DC: Government Printing Office, 1925.

US War Department. Regulations for the Army of the United States, 1913. Washington, DC: Government Printing Office, 1918. https://play.google.com/books/reader?id=zwgSAAAAYAAJ.

Vendeville, Geoffrey. "U of T's Fisher Library Acquires Copies of Der Eigene, the World's First Gay Magazine." U of T News, July 16, 2019. https://www.utoronto.ca/news/u-t-s-fisher-library-acquires-copies-der-eigene-world-s-first-gay-magazine.

"Visitors at the Subway Bar." N.d. EWB. Box 98, folder 11.

"Vote 'Yes' on Proposition ONE." 1964. OIR. Box 25, folder 113.

Waldrop, Frank C. "Murder as a Sex Practice." American Mercury, February 1948, 144–149.

Walsh, Ed. "Florida's Anything-Goes Gay Getaway." Bay Area Reporter, November 21, 2006. https://www.ebar.com/news///237479.

Wand, Merlin. Ad for Contacts. New Masses, December 1927, 29.

Wannall, Ray. The Real J. Edgar Hoover for the Record. Padukah, KY: Turner, 2000.

Washington Newsletter. "Aims and Principles." July 16, 1956.

———. "First Organization and Magazine for Inverts." July 16, 1956.

———. "Forward and Foreward." July 16, 1956.

———. "What Is the Mattachine Society?" July 16, 1956.

Washington Post. "City's Pervert Fringe Blamed by Police for Suicide of Boy, 16." July 3, 1946.

———. "Park Police to Act Against Sex Offenders." December 19, 1946.

Waugh, Thomas. Hard to Imagine: Gay Male Eroticism in Photography and Film from Their Beginnings to Stonewall. New York: Columbia University Press, 1996.

———. "Homosociality in the Classical American Stag Film: Off-Screen, On-Screen." Sexualities 4, no. 3 (August 2001): 275–291.

———. "Strength and Stealth: Watching (and Wanting) Turn of the Century Strongmen." Revue Canadienne d'Études cinématographiques/Canadian Journal of Film Studies 2, no. 1 (Spring 1992): 1–20.

Wertz, Frederick. "A New Look at the Demographics of a 19th Century Lower East Side Neighborhood." New York Genealogical and Biographical Society. August 21, 2017. https://www.newyorkfamilyhistory.org/blog/new-look-demographics-19th-century-lower-east-side-neighborhood.

Wheeler, William. "From Havana to Quito: A Refugee's Fight for LGBT Rights in Cuba." MinnPost.com, December 13, 2013. https://www.minnpost.com/global -post/2013/12/havana-quito-refugees-fight-lgbt-rights-cuba.

Whisnant, Clayton J. *Queer Identities and Politics in Germany: A History, 1880–1945.* New York: Harrington Park, 2016.

Whitman, Howard. "Terror in Washington," *Collier's*, June 24, 1950, 20–21, 52–53.

Williams, Tennessee. *Notebooks.* Edited by Margaret Bradham Thornton. New Haven: Yale University Press, 2006.

Woycke, James. *Espirit de Corps: A History of North American Bodybuilding.* History eBook Collection, 2016. https://ir.lib.uwo.ca/historybooks/2.

Yoder, Anne M. "Brief History of Conscientious Objection." Conscientious Objection in America: Primary Sources for Research, November 2007. https://www.swarthmore .edu/Library/peace/conscientiousobjection/co%20website/pages/HistoryNew.htm.

Zegler-McPherson, Christina. "German Immigrants in New York City, 1840–1920." Conference paper. August 2, 2016.

Zorbaugh, Ernest. *The Gold Coast and the Slum.* Chicago: University of Chicago Press, 1929.

INDEX